HOW TO READ
AND WHY

HAROLD BLOOM

SCRIBNER

New York   London   Toronto   Sydney   Singapore

SCRIBNER
1230 Avenue of the Americas
New York, NY 10020

SCRIBNER and design are trademarks of Macmillan Library Reference, USA,
Inc., used under license by Simon & Schuster, the publisher of this work.

DESIGNED BY ERICH HOBBING

Set in Adobe Garamond

Manufactured in the United States of America

1   3   5   7   9   10   8   6   4   2

Library of Congress Cataloging-in-Publication Data is available.

ISBN 0-684-85906-8

For Miriam Bratu Hansen

ACKNOWLEDGMENTS

My principal debt is to my gifted and devoted editor, Gillian Blake, who helped reshape this book for me.

I owe much also to my literary agents, Glen Hartley and Lynn Chu.

Mirjana Kalezic, my research assistant, was endlessly helpful in the composition of this book.

I thank also my assistants at Yale: Eric Boles, Trevor Eppeheimer, Scott Kershner, Octavio DiLeo, and as always, the libraries and librarians of Yale University.

Harold Bloom
Timothy Dwight College
Yale University
October 15, 1999

CONTENTS

Contents

CONTENTS

Contents

The reader became the book; and summer night
Was like the conscious being of the book.

—WALLACE STEVENS

HOW TO READ
AND WHY

PREFACE

There is no single way to read well, though there is a prime reason why we should read. Information is endlessly available to us; where shall wisdom be found? If you are fortunate, you encounter a particular teacher who can help, yet finally you are alone, going on without further mediation. Reading well is one of the great pleasures that solitude can afford you, because it is, at least in my experience, the most healing of pleasures. It returns you to otherness, whether in yourself or in friends, or in those who may become friends. Imaginative literature is otherness, and as such alleviates loneliness. We read not only because we cannot know enough people, but because friendship is so vulnerable, so likely to diminish or disappear, overcome by space, time, imperfect sympathies, and all the sorrows of familial and passional life.

This book teaches how to read and why, proceeding by a multitude of examples and instances: poems short and long; stories and novels and plays. The selections should not be interpreted as an exclusive list of what to read, but rather as a sampling of works that best illustrate why to read. Reading well is best pursued as an implicit discipline; finally there is no method but yourself, when your self has been fully molded. Literary criticism, as I have learned to understand it, ought to be experiential and pragmatic, rather than theoretical. The critics who are my masters—Dr. Samuel Johnson and William Hazlitt in particular—practice their art in order to make what is implicit in a book finely explicit. In what follows, whether I deal with a lyric by A. E. Housman or a play by Oscar Wilde, with a story by Jorge Luis Borges or a novel by Marcel Proust, my principal concern will be with ways of noticing and realizing what can and should be made explicit. Because, for me, the question of how to read always leads on to the motives and uses of reading, I shall never separate the "how" and the "why" of this book's subject. Virginia Woolf, in "How Should One Read a Book?"—the final brief essay in her *Second Common Reader*—charmingly warns: "The only advice, indeed, that one person can give another about reading is to take no advice." But she then adds many codicils to the reader's enjoyment of freedom, culminating in the grand question "Where are we to begin?" To get the deepest and widest pleasures of reading, "we must not squander our powers, helplessly and ignorantly." So it seems that, until we become wholly ourselves, some advice about reading may be helpful, even perhaps essential.

Woolf herself had found that advice in Walter Pater (whose sister had tutored her), and also in Dr. Johnson and in the Romantic critics Thomas De Quincey and William Hazlitt, of whom she wonderfully remarked: "He is one of those rare critics who have thought so much that they can dispense with reading." Woolf thought incessantly, and never would stop reading. She herself had a good deal of advice to give to other readers, and I have happily taken it throughout this book. Her best advice is to remind us that "there is always a demon in us who whispers, 'I hate, I love,' and we cannot silence him." I cannot silence my demon, but in this book anyway I will listen to him only when he whispers, "I love," as I intend no polemics here, but only to teach reading.

WHY READ?

It matters, if individuals are to retain any capacity to form their own judgments and opinions, that they continue to read for themselves. How they read, well or badly, and what they read, cannot depend wholly upon themselves, but why they read must be for and in their own interest. You can read merely to pass the time, or you can read with an overt urgency, but eventually you will read against the clock. Bible readers, those who search the Bible for themselves, perhaps exemplify the urgency more plainly than readers of Shakespeare, yet the quest is the same. One of the uses of reading is to prepare ourselves for change, and the final change alas is universal.

I turn to reading as a solitary praxis, rather than as an educational enterprise. The way we read now, when we are alone with ourselves, retains considerable continuity with the past, however it is performed in the academies. My ideal reader (and lifelong hero) is Dr. Samuel Johnson, who knew and expressed both the power and the limitation of incessant reading. Like every other activity of the mind, it must satisfy Johnson's prime concern, which is with "what comes near to ourself, what we can put to use." Sir Francis Bacon, who provided some of the ideas that Johnson put to use, famously gave the advice: "Read not to contradict and confute, nor to believe and take for granted, nor to find talk and discourse, but to weigh and consider." I add to Bacon and Johnson a third sage of reading,

Emerson, fierce enemy of history and of all historicisms, who remarked that the best books "impress us with the conviction, that one nature wrote and the same reads." Let me fuse Bacon, Johnson, and Emerson into a formula of how to read: find what comes near to you that can be put to the use of weighing and considering, and that addresses you as though you share the one nature, free of time's tyranny. Pragmatically that means, first find Shakespeare, and let him find you. If *King Lear* is fully to find you, then weigh and consider the nature it shares with you; its closeness to yourself. I do not intend this as an idealism, but as a pragmatism. Putting the tragedy to use as a complaint against patriarchy is to forsake your own prime interests, particularly as a young woman, which sounds rather more ironical than it is. Shakespeare, more than Sophocles, is the inescapable authority upon intergenerational conflict, and more than anyone else, upon the differences between women and men. Be open to a full reading of *King Lear,* and you will understand better the origins of what you judge to be patriarchy.

Ultimately we read—as Bacon, Johnson, and Emerson agree—in order to strengthen the self, and to learn its authentic interests. We experience such augmentations as pleasure, which may be why aesthetic values have always been deprecated by social moralists, from Plato through our current campus Puritans. The pleasures of reading indeed are selfish rather than social. You cannot directly improve anyone else's life by reading better or more deeply. I remain skeptical of the traditional social hope that care for others may be stimulated by the growth of individual imagination, and I am wary of any arguments whatsoever that connect the pleasures of solitary reading to the public good.

The sorrow of professional reading is that you recapture only rarely the pleasure of reading you knew in youth, when books were a Hazlittian gusto. The way we read now partly depends upon our distance, inner or outer, from the universities, where reading is scarcely taught as a pleasure, in any of the deeper senses of the aesthetics of pleasure. Opening yourself to a direct confrontation with Shakespeare at his strongest, as in *King Lear,* is never an easy pleasure, whether in youth or in age, and yet not to read *King Lear* fully (which means without ideological expectations) is to be cognitively as well as aesthetically defrauded. A childhood largely spent watching television yields to an adolescence with a computer, and the university receives a student unlikely to welcome the suggestion that we must endure our going hence even as our going hither: ripeness is all. Reading falls apart, and much of the self scatters with it. All this is past lamenting, and will not be remedied by any vows or programs. What is to be done can only be performed by some version of elitism, and that is now unacceptable, for reasons both good and bad. There are still solitary readers, young and old, everywhere, even in the universities. If there is a function of criticism at the present time, it must be to address itself to the solitary reader, who reads for herself, and not for the interests that supposedly transcend the self.

Value, in literature as in life, has much to do with the idiosyncratic, with the excess by which meaning gets started. It is not accidental that historicists—critics who believe all of us to be overdetermined by societal history—should also regard literary characters as marks upon a page, and nothing more. Hamlet is not even a case history if our thoughts are not at all our own. I come then to the first principle if we are to restore the way we read now, a principle I appropriate from Dr. Johnson: *Clear your mind of cant.* Your dictionary will tell you that *cant* in this sense is speech overflowing with pious platitudes, the peculiar vocabulary of a sect or coven. Since the universities have empowered such covens as "gender and sexuality" and "multiculturalism," Johnson's admonition thus becomes "Clear your mind of academic cant." A university culture where the appreciation of Victorian women's underwear replaces the appreciation of Charles Dickens and Robert Browning sounds like the outrageousness of a new Nathanael West, but is merely the norm. A side product of such "cultural poetics" is that there can be no new Nathanael West, for how could such an academic culture sustain parody? The poems of our climate have been replaced by the body stockings of our culture. Our new Materialists tell us that they have recovered the body for historicism, and assert that they work in the name of the Reality Principle. The life of the mind must yield to the death of the body, yet that hardly requires the cheerleading of an academic sect.

Clear your mind of cant leads on to the second principle of restoring reading: *Do not attempt to improve your neighbor or your neighborhood by what or how you read.* Self-improvement is a large enough project for your mind and spirit: there are no ethics of reading. The mind should be kept at home until its primal ignorance has been purged; premature excursions into activism have their charm, but are time-consuming, and for reading there will never be enough time. Historicizing, whether of past or present, is a kind of idolatry, an obsessive worship of things in time. Read therefore by the inner light that John Milton celebrated and that Emerson took as a principle of reading, which can be our third: *A scholar is a candle which the love and desire of all men will light.* Wallace Stevens, perhaps forgetting his source, wrote marvelous variations upon that metaphor, but the original Emersonian phrasing makes for a clearer statement of the third principle of reading. You need not fear that the freedom of your development as a reader is selfish, because if you become an authentic reader, then the response to your labors will confirm you as an illumination to others. I ponder the letters that I receive from strangers these last seven or eight years, and generally I am too moved to reply. Their pathos, for me, is that all too often they testify to a yearning for canonical literary study that universities disdain to fulfill. Emerson said that society cannot do without cultivated men and women, and prophetically he added: "The people, and not the college, is the writer's home." He meant strong writers, representative men and women, who represented themselves, and not constituencies, since his politics were those of the spirit.

The largely forgotten function of a university education is caught forever in Emerson's address "The American Scholar," when he says of the scholar's duties: "They may all be comprised in self-trust." I take from Emerson also my fourth principle of reading: *One must be an inventor to read well.* "Creative reading" in Emerson's sense I once named as "misreading," a word that persuaded opponents that I suffered from a voluntary dyslexia. The ruin or blank that they see when they look at a poem is in their own eye. Self-trust is not an endowment, but is the Second Birth of the mind, which cannot come without years of deep reading. There are no absolute standards for the aesthetic. If you wish to maintain that Shakespeare's ascendancy was a product of colonialism, then who will bother to confute you? Shakespeare after four centuries is more pervasive than ever he was before; they will perform him in outer space, and on other worlds, if those worlds are reached. He is not a conspiracy of Western culture; he *contains* every principle of reading, and he is my touchstone throughout this book. Borges attributed this universalism to Shakespeare's apparent selflessness, but that quality is a large metaphor for Shakespeare's difference, which finally is cognitive power as such. We read, frequently if unknowingly, in quest of a mind more original than our own.

Since ideology, particularly in its shallower versions, is peculiarly destructive of the capacity to apprehend and appreciate irony, I suggest that the *recovery of the ironic* might be our fifth principle for the restoration of reading. Think of the endless irony of Hamlet, who when he says one thing almost invariably means another, frequently indeed the opposite of what he says. But with this principle, I am close to despair, since you can no more teach someone to be ironic than you can instruct them to become solitary. And yet the loss of irony is the death of reading, and of what had been civilized in our natures.

I stepped from Plank to Plank
A slow and cautious way
The Stars about my Head I felt
About my Feet the Sea.

I knew not but the next
Would be my final inch—
This gave me that precarious Gait
Some call Experience.

Women and men can walk differently, but unless we are regimented we all tend to walk somewhat individually. Dickinson, master of the precarious Sublime, can hardly be apprehended if we are dead to her ironies. She is walking the only path available, "from Plank to Plank," but her slow caution ironically juxtaposes with a titanism in which she feels "The Stars about my Head," though her feet very nearly are in the sea. Not knowing whether the next step will be her "final inch" gives her "that precarious Gait" she will not name, except to tell us that "some" call it Experience. She had read Emerson's essay "Experience," a culmination much in the way "Of Experience" was for his master Montaigne, and her irony is an amiable response to Emerson's opening: "Where do we find ourselves? In a series of which we do not know the extremes, and believe that it has none." The extreme, for Dickinson, is the not knowing whether the next step is the final inch. "If any of us knew what we were doing, or where we are going, then when we think we best know!" Emerson's further reverie differs from Dickinson's in temperament, or as she words it, in gait. "All things swim and glitter," in Emerson's realm of experience, and his genial irony is very different from her irony of precariousness. Yet neither is an ideologue, and they live still in the rival power of their ironies.

At the end of the path of lost irony is a final inch, beyond which literary value will be irrecoverable. Irony is only a metaphor, and the irony of one literary age can rarely be the irony of another, yet without the renaissance of an ironic sense more than what we once called imaginative literature will be lost. Thomas Mann, most ironic of this century's great writers, seems to be lost already. New biographies of him appear, and are reviewed almost always on the basis of his homoeroticism, as though he can be saved for our interest only if he can be certified as gay, and so gain a place in our curriculum. That is akin to studying Shakespeare mostly for his apparent bisexuality, but the vagaries of our current counter-Puritanism seem limitless. Shakespeare's ironies, as we would expect, are the most comprehensive and dialectical in all of Western literature, and yet they do not always mediate his characters' passions for us, so vast and intense is their emotional range. Shakespeare therefore will survive our era; we will lose his ironies, and hold on to the rest of him. But in Thomas Mann every emotion, narrative or dramatic, is mediated by an ironic aestheticism; to teach *Death in Venice* or *Disorder and Early Sorrow* to most current undergraduates, even the gifted, is nearly impossible. When authors are destroyed by history, we rightly call their work period pieces, but when they are made unavailable through historicized ideology, I think that we encounter a different phenomenon.

Irony demands a certain attention span, and the ability to sustain antithetical ideas, even when they collide with one another. Strip irony away from reading, and it loses at once all discipline and all surprise. Find now what comes near to you, that can be used for weighing and considering, and it very likely will be irony, even if many of your teachers will not know what it is, or where it is to be found. Irony will clear your mind of the cant of the ideologues, and help you to blaze forth as the scholar of one candle.

Going on seventy, one doesn't want to read badly any more than live badly, since time will not relent. I don't know that we owe God or nature a death, but nature will collect anyway, and we certainly owe mediocrity nothing, whatever collectivity it purports to advance or at least represent.

Because my ideal reader, for half a century, has been Dr. Samuel Johnson, I turn next to my favorite passage in his *Preface to Shakespeare:*

> This, therefore, is the praise of Shakespeare, that his drama is the mirror of life; that he who has mazed his imagination in following the phantoms which other writers raise up before him may here be cured of his delirious ecstasies by reading human sentiments in human language, by scenes from which a hermit may estimate the transactions of the world and a confessor predict the progress of the passions.

To read human sentiments in human language you must be able to read humanly, with all of you. You are more than an ideology, whatever your convictions, and Shakespeare speaks to as much of you as you can bring to him. That is to say: Shakespeare reads you more fully than you can read him, even after you have cleared your mind of cant. No writer before or since Shakespeare has had anything like his control of perspectivism, which outleaps any contextualizations we impose upon the plays. Johnson, admirably perceiving this, urges us to allow Shakespeare to cure us of our "delirious ecstasies." Let me extend Johnson by also urging us to recognize the phantoms that the deep reading of Shakespeare will exorcise. One such phantom is the Death of the Author; another is the assertion that the self is a fiction; yet another is the opinion that literary and dramatic characters are so many marks upon a page. A fourth phantom, and the most pernicious, is that language does the thinking for us.

Still, my love for Johnson, and for reading, turns me at last away from polemic, and towards a celebration of the many solitary readers I keep encountering, whether in the classroom or in messages I receive. We read Shakespeare, Dante, Chaucer, Cervantes, Dickens, Proust, and all their peers because they more than enlarge life. Pragmatically, they have become the Blessing, in its true Yahwistic sense of "more life into a time without boundaries." We read deeply for varied reasons, most of them familiar: that we cannot know enough people profoundly enough; that we need to know ourselves better; that we require knowledge, not just of self and others, but of the way things are. Yet the strongest, most authentic motive for deep reading of the now much-abused traditional canon is the search for a difficult pleasure. I am not exactly an erotics-of-reading purveyor, and a pleasurable difficulty seems to me a plausible definition of the Sublime, but a higher pleasure remains the reader's quest. There is a reader's Sublime, and it seems the only secular transcendence we can ever attain, except for the even more precarious transcendence we call "falling in love." I urge you to find what truly comes near to you, that can be used for weighing and for considering. Read deeply, not to believe, not to accept, not to contradict, but to learn to share in that one nature that writes and reads.

I

SHORT STORIES

Introduction

The Irish writer Frank O'Connor celebrated the short story in his *Lonely Voice,* believing that it dealt best with isolated individuals, particularly those upon society's fringes. If this were wholly true, the short story would have developed almost into the opposite of one of its likeliest origins, the folktale. Then the short story, unlike the lyrical poem, would wound once and once only, and also unlike novels, which can afflict us with many sensations, with multiple sorrows and joys. But so indeed can the stories of Chekhov and his few peers.

Short stories are not parables or wise sayings, and so cannot be fragments; we ask them for the pleasures of closure. Kafka's magnificent fragment, "The Hunter Gracchus," ends when the undead hunter, a kind of Wandering Jew or Ancient Mariner, is asked by a sea town's mayor how long he intends to prolong his visit. "I cannot tell, Burgomeister," Gracchus replies: ". . . My ship has no rudder and is driven by a wind that rises from the icy regions of death." That is not closure, but what could Kafka have added? Gracchus's final sentence is more memorable than all but a few deliberate endings of stories.

How does one read a short story? Edgar Allan Poe would have said: at one sitting. Poe's stories, despite their permanent, world-wide popularity, are atrociously written (as are his poems) and benefit by translation, even into English. But Poe is hardly one of the authentic ancestors of the modern short story. These include Pushkin and Balzac, Gogol and Turgenev, Maupassant and Chekhov and Henry James. The modern masters of the form are James Joyce and D. H. Lawrence, Isaak Babel and Ernest Hemingway, and a varied group including Borges, Nabokov, Thomas Mann, Eudora Welty, Flannery O'Connor, Tommaso Landolfi, and Italo Calvino. I will center here upon stories by Turgenev and by Chekhov, by Maupassant and by Hemingway, by Flannery O'Connor and by Vladimir Nabokov, Jorge Luis Borges, Tommaso Landolfi and by Italo Calvino, because all of them achieved something like perfection in their art.

Ivan Turgenev

Frank O'Connor set Turgenev's *Sketches from a Hunter's Album* (1852) over any other single volume of short stories. A century and a half after its composition, *Sketches* remains astonishingly fresh, though its topicality, the need to emancipate the serfs, has yielded to all the disasters of Russian history. Turgenev's stories are uncannily beautiful; taken together, they are as magnificent an answer to the question "Why read?" as I know (always excepting Shakespeare). Turgenev, who loved Shakespeare and Cervantes, divided up all mankind (of the questing sort) into either Hamlets or Don Quixotes. He might have added Falstaffs or Sancho Panzas, since with Hamlet and the Don, they form a fourfold paradigm for so many other fictive beings.

It is difficult to single out particular stories from the twenty-five in *Sketches,* but I join several other critics in a special fondness for "Bezhin Lea" (or "meadow") and "Kasyan from the Beautiful Lands." "Bezhin Lea" begins on a beautiful July morning, with

Turgenev out grouse-shooting. The hunter loses his way and comes at night to a meadowland where a group of five peasant boys sit around two fires. Joining them, Turgenev introduces us to them. They range in age from seven to fourteen, and all of them believe in "goblins," "the little people," who share their world. Turgenev's art wisely allows the boys to talk to one another, while he listens and does not intrude. Their life of hard work (they and their parents are serfs), superstition, village legend, is revealed to us, complete with Trishka, the Antichrist to come, enticing mermaids who catch souls, the walking dead, and those marked to die. One boy, Pavlusha, stands out from the rest as the most intelligent and likable. He demonstrates his courage when he rushes forth bare-handed to drive away what could be wolves, who threaten the grazing horses that the boys guard in the night.

After some hours, Turgenev falls asleep, to wake up just before dawn. The boys sleep on, though Pavlusha raises himself up for a last, intense glance at the hunter. Turgenev starts home, describing the beautiful morning, and then ends the sketch by adding that, later that year, Pavlusha died in a fall from a horse. We feel the pity of the loss, with Turgenev, who remarks that Pavlusha was a fine boy, but the pathos of the death is not rendered as such. A continuum engages us: the beauty of the meadow and of the dawn; the vividness of the boys' preternatural beliefs; the fate, not to be evaded, that takes away Pavlusha. And the rest? That is the pragmatic yet somehow still quixotic Turgenev, shooting his grouse and sketching the boys and the landscape in his album.

Why read "Bezhin Lea"? At the least, to know better our own reality, our vulnerability to fate, while learning also to appreciate aesthetically Turgenev's tact and only apparent detachment as a storyteller. If there is any irony in this sketch, it belongs to fate itself, a fate just about as innocent as the landscape, the boys, the hunter. Turgenev is one of the most Shakespearean of writers in that he too refrains from moral judgments; he also knows that a favorite, like Pavlusha, will vanish by a sudden accident. There is no single interpretative point to carry away from the Bezhin meadow. The narrative voice is not to be distinguished from Turgenev's own self, which is wisely passive, loving, meticulously observant. That self, like Pavlusha's, is part of the story's value. Something in most of us is where it wants to be, with the boys, the horses, the compassionate hunter-writer, the talk of goblins and river temptresses, in perfect weather, in Bezhin Lea.

To achieve Turgenev's apparent simplicity as a writer of sketches you need the highest gifts, something very like Shakespeare's genius for rediscovering the human. Turgenev too shows us something that perhaps is always there, but that we could not see without him. Dostoevsky learned from Shakespeare how to create the supreme nihilists Svidrigailov and Stavrogin by observing Iago, satanic majesty of all nihilists. Turgenev, like Henry James, learned something subtler from Shakespeare: the mystery of the seemingly commonplace, the rendering of a reality that is perpetually augmenting.

Directly after "Bezhin Lea" comes "Kasyan from the Beautiful Lands," where Turgenev gives us a fully miraculous character, the dwarf Kasyan, a mystical serf and faith healer, perhaps a sect of one. Returning from a hunting trip, the author's horse-drawn cart suffers a broken axle. In a nearby town that is no town, Turgenev and his surly driver encounter

> a dwarf of about fifty years old, with a small, swarthy, wrinkled face, a little painted nose, barely discernible little brown eyes and abundant curly black hair which sat upon his tiny head just as broadly as the cap sits on the stalk of a mushroom. His entire body was extraordinarily frail and thin . . .
>
> (Translated by Richard Freeborn)

We are constantly reminded how uncanny, how unexpected Kasyan truly is. Though his voice invariably is gentle and sweet, he severely condemns hunting as ungodly, and he maintains throughout a strong dignity, as well as the sorrow of an exile, resettled by the authorities and so deprived of "the beautiful lands" of the Don region. Everything about little Kasyan is paradoxical; Turgenev's driver explains that the dwarf is a holy man known as The Flea.

Hunter and healer go off together for a walk in the woods while the axle is being mended. Gathering herbs, jumping as he goes, muttering to himself, Kasyan speaks to the birds in their own language, but says not a word to Turgenev. Driven by the heat to find shelter together in the bushes, hunter and holy dwarf enjoy their silent reveries until Kasyan demands justification for the shooting of birds. When Turgenev asks the dwarf's occupation, Kasyan replies that he catches nightingales to give them away to others, that he is literate, and admits his healing powers. And though he says he has no family, his secret is revealed when his small, teenage natural daughter, Annushka, suddenly appears in the woods. The child is beautiful and shy, and has been out gathering mushrooms. Though Kasyan denies his parentage, neither we nor Turgenev are persuaded, and after the child departs, Kasyan scarcely speaks for the remainder of the story.

We are left with enigmas, as his driver can scarcely enlighten Turgenev when they depart; to him Kasyan is nothing but contradictions: "untellable." Nothing more is told, and Turgenev returns home. His thoughts on Kasyan remain unexpressed, but do we need them? The peasant healer lives in his own world, not the Russia of the serfs but a Russian vision of the biblical world, albeit totally unlike the rival biblical visions of Tolstoy and Dostoevsky. Kasyan, though he shies away from rebellion, has rejected Russian society and returned to the arts and ways of the folk. He will not let his daughter abide a moment in the presence of the benign Turgenev, who admires the child's beauty. One need not idealize Kasyan; his peasant shrewdness and perceptions exclude a great deal of value, but he incarnates truths of folklore that he himself may scarcely know that he knows.

The dominant atmosphere of Turgenev's sketches is the beauty of the landscape when experienced in ideal weather. Yet there is a large difference between the natural beauty shared by Turgenev and the peasant boys in "Bezhin Lea," and the something less than communion between Kasyan and Turgenev when they shade themselves in the forest. Pavlusha's fate cannot be resisted, only accepted, but Kasyan is, in his own subtle way, as much a magical master of reality as Shakespeare's Prospero was. Kasyan's magical natural world is not akin to Turgenev's aesthetically apprehended nature, even when holy man and hunter-writer rest side by side. Nor will Kasyan admit Turgenev into his secret, or even a momentary exchange with his beautiful elf of a daughter. Finally, we come to see that Kasyan is still "from the beautiful lands," even though he has lost his original home near the Don. "The beautiful lands" belong to closed folk tradition, of which Kasyan is a kind of shaman. We read "Kasyan from the Beautiful Lands" to attain a vision of otherness closed to all but a few of us, and closed to Turgenev as well. The reward for reading Kasyan's story is that we are admitted—very briefly—into an alternate reality, where Turgenev himself entered only briefly, and yet sublimely brought back in his *Sketches*.

Anton Chekhov

It is a long journey from Turgenev's stories to Chekhov's and Hemingway's, even though the Nick Adams stories could have been called *Sketches from a Fisherman's Album*. Still, Turgenev, Chekhov, and Hemingway share a quality that looks like detachment, and turns out to be something else. Their affinity with their landscape and human figures is central in Turgenev, Chekhov, and Hemingway. This is very different from the sense of immersion in social worlds and in geysers of characters in Balzac and in Dickens. The genius of both novelists was lavish at peopling Paris and London with entire social classes as well as grotesquely impressive individuals. Balzac, unlike Dickens, excelled also at the short story, and built many of them into his *Human Comedy*. Yet they lack the resonances of Balzac's novels, and cannot compare to the stories of Turgenev and Chekhov, Maupassant and Hemingway.

Even Chekhov's earliest stories can have the formal delicacy and somber reflectiveness that make him the indispensable artist of the unlived life, and the major influence upon all story-writers after him. I say *all* because Chekhov's formal innovations as a storyteller, though profuse, are less consequential than his Shakespearean inwardness, his carrying over into the stories, longer or shorter, the major newness in Shakespeare's characterizations, a "foregrounding" that I discuss elsewhere in this book, in regard to *Hamlet*. In a sense, Chekhov was more Shakespearean even than Turgenev, who in his novels took care to background the earlier lives of his protagonists. One should write, Chekhov said, so that the reader needs no explanations from the author. The actions, conversations, and meditations of the characters had to be sufficient, a practice followed also in Chekhov's finest plays, *Three Sisters* and *The Cherry Orchard*.

My favorite early Chekhov story is "The Kiss," written when he was twenty-seven. Ryabovich, the "shyest, drabbest, and most retiring officer" in an artillery brigade, accompanies his fellow officers to an evening social at the country manor of a retired general. Wandering about the house, the bored Ryabovich enters a dark room and experiences an adventure. Mistaking him for someone else, a woman kisses him, and recoils. He rushes away, and henceforth is obsessed with the encounter, which initially brings exultation but then becomes a torment. The wretched fellow is in love, albeit with a woman totally unknown and never to be encountered again.

When his brigade next approaches the general's manor, Ryabovich walks upon a little bridge, near the bathhouse, where he reaches out and touches a wet sheet, hanging there to dry. A sensation of cold and roughness assails him, and he glances down at the water, where a red moon is reflected. Staring at the flowing water, Ryabovich experiences a conviction that all of life is an incoherent joke. In the story's close, all the other officers have returned to the general's house, but Ryabovich goes to his solitary bed.

Except for the kiss itself, that touch of the cold, wet sheet—the antikiss, as it were—is the dominant moment of the story. It destroys Ryabovich, but then so does the kiss. Hope and joy, however irrational, are stronger than despair, and ultimately more pernicious. I read "The Kiss" and repeat to myself an observation I once made in writing about Chekhov: you shall know the truth and the truth shall make you despair is Chekhov's gospel, except that this gloomy genius insists upon being cheerful. Ryabovich may think that his fate in life is settled, but it certainly isn't, though we will never know, since that lies beyond the story.

The best observations on Chekhov (and on Tolstoy also) that I've ever read are in Maxim Gorky's *Reminiscences,* where we are told: "It seems to me that in the presence of [Chekhov], everyone felt an unconscious desire to be simpler, more truthful, more himself."

When I reread "The Kiss" or attend a good performance of *Three Sisters,* I am in Chekhov's presence, and while he doesn't make me simpler, more truthful, more myself, I do *wish* I could be better (though I can't be). My wish seems to me an aesthetic rather than a moral phenomenon because Chekhov has a great writer's wisdom, and teaches me implicitly that literature is a form of the good. Shakespeare and Beckett teach me the same, which is why I read. Sometimes I reflect that of all the writers whose inner biographies are known, Chekhov and Beckett were the kindest human beings. Of Shakespeare's inner life we know nothing, but if you read the plays incessantly, then you suspect that this wisest of persons must be a third with Chekhov and Beckett. The creator of Sir John Falstaff, of Hamlet, and of Rosalind (in *As You Like It*) also makes me wish I could be more myself. But that, as I argue throughout this book, is why we should read, and why we should read only the best of what has been written.

"The Kiss" is early work, however marvelous; Chekhov himself thought his best story was the three-page "The Student," composed when he was thirty-three, the age when Jesus died, according to tradition. Like Shakespeare, Chekhov cannot be called either a believer or a skeptic; they are too large for such a categorization. "The Student" is ardently simple, though beautifully arranged. A young clerical student, cold and hungry, comes upon two widows, mother and daughter, on Good Friday. He warms himself at their campfire, and tells them the story of how the Apostle Peter denied Jesus three times, as Jesus had prophesied. Peter, returning to himself, wept bitterly, and so does the widowed mother. The student goes off and broods on the relation between the Apostle's tears and the mother's, which seem linked in an unbroken train. Joy suddenly stirs in the student, because he feels that truth and beauty persist in and by this chain that binds past to present. And that is all; the story ends with the student's transformation of this sudden joy into an expectation of a happiness still to come to his life. "He was only twenty-two," Chekhov dryly remarks, perhaps having an intimation that he himself, at thirty-three, had already lived three-quarters of his life (he died of tuberculosis at forty-four).

The reader can reflect upon the subtle transition in the student's joy, from a past-to-present train of truth and beauty to a twenty-two-year-old's anticipation of a not impossible personal happiness. It is Good Friday, and the tale-within-a-tale is of Jesus and Simon Peter, and yet neither of the rejoicings has any trace of authentic piety or of salvation. Chekhov, the subtlest dramatic psychologist since Shakespeare himself, has written a dark lyric about suffering and change. Jesus is present only as a supreme representation of suffering and change, one that Shakespeare (in his dangerous era) shrewdly and invariably avoided.

Why did Chekhov prefer this short story to scores of what seem to many of his admirers far more consequential and vital tales? I have no clear answer, but regard the question as worthy of pondering. Nothing in "The Student," except what happens in the protagonist's mind, is anything but dreadfully dismal. It is the irrational rise of impersonal joy and personal hope out of cold and misery, and the tears of betrayal, that appears to have moved Chekhov himself.

A late story, "The Lady with the Dog," of 1899, is among my favorites by Chekhov, and is generally regarded as being one of his finest. Gurov, a married man vacationing alone in Yalta, the seaside resort, is moved by encountering a fair young woman always accompanied by her white Pomeranian. An incessant womanizer, Gurov begins an affair with the lady, Anna Sergeyevna, herself unhappily married. She departs, insisting that the farewell must be forever. Experienced amorist as he is, Gurov accepts this with an autumnal relief, and returns to his wife and children in Moscow, only to find himself haunted and suffering. Has he fallen in love, presumably for the first time? He does not know, nor does Chekhov, so we cannot know either. Yet he is certainly obsessed, and therefore travels to Anna Sergeyevna's provincial town, where he seeks her out when she attends the opera. Anguished, she urges him to go immediately, promising that she will visit him in Moscow.

The Moscow meetings, every two or three months, become a tradition, enjoyable enough for Gurov, but hardly for the perpetually weeping Anna Sergeyevna. Until at last, catching sight of himself in a mirror, Gurov sees that his hair is graying, and simultaneously awakens to the incessant dilemma he has entered, which he interprets as his belated falling in love. What is to be done? Gurov at once feels that he and his beloved are on the verge of a beautiful new life, and also that the end of the relationship is far off, and the hardest part of their mutual travail has just begun.

That is all Chekhov gives us, but the reverberations go on long after this conclusion that concludes nothing. Gurov and Anna Sergeyevna are evidently both somewhat changed, but not necessarily for the better. Nothing either can do for the other is redemptive; what then redeems their story from its mundane staleness? How does it differ from the tale of every other hapless adultery?

Not by our interest in Gurov and Anna, as any reader would have to conclude; there is nothing remarkable about them. He is another womanizer, and she another weeping woman. Chekhov's artistry is never more mysterious than here, where it is palpable yet scarcely definable. Clearly Anna is in love, though Gurov is hardly a worthy object. Just how to value the mournful Anna, we cannot know. What passes between the lovers is presented by Chekhov with such detachment that we lack not information but judgment, including our own. For the story is weirdly laconic in its universalism. Does Gurov really believe that at last he has fallen in love? He has no clue, nor does the reader, and if Chekhov knows, he won't tell us. As in Shakespeare, where Hamlet tells us that he loves, and we don't know if we can believe him, we are not tempted to trust Gurov's assertion that this at last is the real right thing. Anna complains bitterly that theirs is a "dark secret love" (to use William Blake's great phrase from his "The Sick Rose"), but Gurov seems to revel in the secret life, which he thinks uncovers his true self. He is a banker, and doubtless many bankers have true selves, but Gurov isn't one of them. The reader can credit Anna's tears, but not Gurov's "How? How? How?" as he clutches his head. Chekhov-in-love parodied himself in *The Seagull*'s Trigorin, and I suggest that Gurov is a more transposed self-parody. We don't much like Gurov, and we want Anna to stop crying, but we cannot cast their story off, because it is our story.

Gorky says of Chekhov that he was "able to reveal in the dim sea of banality its tragic humor." It sounds naïve, and yet Chekhov's greatest power is to give us the impression, as we read, that here at last is the truth about human existence's constant blend of banal misery and tragic joy. Shakespeare was Chekhov's (and our) authority on tragic joy, but the banal does not appear in Shakespeare, even when he writes travesty or farce.

Guy de Maupassant

Chekhov had learned from Maupassant how to represent banality. Maupassant, who had learned everything, including that, from his master, Flaubert, rarely matches the genius of Chekhov, or of Turgenev, as a storyteller. Lev Shestov, a remarkable Russian religious thinker of the earlier twentieth century, expressed this with considerable force:

> Chekhov's wonderful art did not die—his art to kill by a mere touch, a breath, a glance, everything whereby men live and wherein they take their pride. And in the art he was constantly perfecting himself, and he attained to a virtuosity beyond the reach of any of his rivals in European literature. Maupassant often had to strain every effort to overcome his victim. The victim often escaped from Maupassant, though crushed and broken, yet with his life. In Chekhov's hands, nothing escaped death.

That is a very dark view and no reader wants to think of herself as a writer's victim, and yet Shestov accurately weighs Maupassant against Chekhov, rather as one might weigh Christopher Marlowe against Shakespeare. Yet Maupassant is the best of the really "popular" story-writers, vastly superior to O. Henry (who could be quite good) and greatly preferable to the abominable Poe. To be an artist of the popular is itself an extraordinary achievement; we have nothing like it in the United States today.

Chekhov can seem simple, but is always profoundly subtle; many of Maupassant's simplicities are merely what they seem to be, yet they are not shallow. Maupassant had learned from his teacher, Flaubert, that "talent is a prolonged patience" at seeing what others tend not to see. Whether Maupassant can make us see what we could never have seen without him, I very much doubt. That calls for the genius of Shakespeare, or of Chekhov.

There is also the problem that Maupassant, like so many nineteenth- and early-twentieth-century writers of fiction, saw everything through the lens of Arthur Schopenhauer, philosopher of the Will-to-Live. I would just as soon wear Schopenhauerian as Freudian goggles; both enlarge and both distort, almost equally. But I am a literary critic, not a story-writer, and Maupassant would have done better to discard philosophical spectacles when he contemplated the vagaries of the desires of men and of women.

At his best, he is marvelously readable, whether in the humorous pathos of "Madame Tellier's Establishment" or in a horror story like "The Horla," both of which I shall consider here. Frank O'Connor insisted that Maupassant's stories were not satisfactory when compared to those of Chekhov and Turgenev, but then few story-writers rival the two Russian masters. O'Connor's real objection was that he thought "the sexual act itself turns into a form of murder" in Maupassant. A reader who has just enjoyed "Madame Tellier's Establishment" would hardly agree. Flaubert, who did not live to write it, wished to set his final novel in a provincial whorehouse, which his son had already done in this robust story.

Everyone in "Madame Tellier's Establishment" is benign and amiable, which is part of the story's authentic charm. Madame Tellier, a respectable Norman peasant, keeps her establishment as one might run an inn or even a boarding school. Her five sex-workers (as some call them now) are vividly, even lovingly described by Maupassant, who emphasizes the peace kept in the house by Madame's talent for conciliation, and her incessant good humor.

On an evening in May, none of the regular clients are in good humor, because the establishment is festooned with a notice: CLOSED FOR A FIRST COMMUNION. Madame and her staff have gone off for this event, the celebrant being Madame's niece (and god-daughter). The First Communion develops into an extraordinary occasion when the prolonged weeping of the whores, moved to remember their own girlhoods, becomes contagious, and the entire congregation is swept by an ecstasy of tears. The priest proclaims that the Holy Christ has descended, and particularly thanks the visitors, Madame Tellier and her staff.

After a boisterous trip back to their establishment, Madame and her ladies return to their ordinary evening labors, performed however with more than the routine zest and in high good spirits. "It isn't every day we have something to celebrate," Madame Tellier concludes the story by remarking, and only a joyless reader declines to celebrate with her. For once, at least, Schopenhauer's disciple has broken loose from gloomy reflections on the close relations between sex and death.

Exuberance in storytelling is hard to resist, and Maupassant never writes with more gusto than in "Madame Tellier's Establishment." This tale of Normandy has warmth, laughter, surprise, and even a kind of spiritual insight. The Pentecostal ecstasy that burns through the congregation is as authentic as the weeping of the whores that ignites it. Maupassant's irony is markedly kinder (though less subtle) than his master Flaubert's. And the story is bawdy, not prurient, in the Shakespearean spirit; it enlarges life, and diminishes no one.

Maupassant's own life ended badly; by his late twenties, he was syphilitic. At thirty-nine, the disease affected his mind, and he spent his final years locked in an asylum, after a suicide attempt. His most upsetting horror story, "The Horla," has a complex and ambiguous relation to his illness and its consequences. The nameless protagonist of the story is perhaps a syphilitic going mad, though nothing that Maupassant narrates actually tells us to make such an inference. A first-person narration, "The Horla" gives us more clues than we can interpret, because we cannot understand the narrator, and do not know whether we can trust his impressions, of which we receive little or no independent verification.

"The Horla" begins with the narrator—a prosperous young Norman gentleman—persuading us of his happiness on a beautiful May morning. He sees a splendid Brazilian three-master boat flow by his house, and salutes it. This gesture evidently summons the Horla, an invisible being that we later learn has been afflicting Brazil with demonic possession and subsequent madness. Horlas are evidently refined cousins of the vampires; they drink milk and water, and drain vitality from sleepers, without actually drawing blood. Whatever has been happening in Brazil, we are free to doubt precisely what is going on in Normandy. Our narrator eventually sets fire to his own house, to destroy his Horla, but neglects to tell the servants, who are consumed with their home. When the tale-teller apprehends that his Horla is still alive, he concludes by telling us that he will have to kill himself.

Clearly it is indeed *his* Horla, whether or not it made the voyage from Brazil to Normandy. The Horla is the narrator's madness, and not just the cause of madness. Has Maupassant written the story of what it means to be possessed by syphilis? At one point the sufferer glances in the mirror and cannot see his reflection. Then he sees himself in a mist at the back of the mirror. The mist recedes until he sees himself completely, and of the mist or blocking agent he cries out: "I had seen him!"

The narrator says that the Horla's advent means that the reign of man is over. Magnetism, hypnotism, suggestion, are all aspects of the Horla's will. "He has come," the victim cries out, and suddenly the interloper shouts his name in one's ears: "The Horla . . . he has come!" Maupassant invents the name *Horla*; is it an ironic play upon the English word *whore*? That seems very remote, unless indeed Maupassant's venereal disease is the story's hidden center.

The horror story is a large and fascinating genre, in which Maupassant excelled, but never again as powerfully as in "The Horla." I think that it is because, on some level, he knew that he prophesied his own madness and (attempted) suicide. Maupassant is not of the artistic eminence of Turgenev, Chekhov, Henry James, or Hemingway as a short story writer, but his immense popularity is well deserved. Someone who created both "Madame Tellier's

Establishment," with its amiable ecstasies, and "The Horla," with its convincing fright, was a permanent master of the story. Why read Maupassant? At his best, he will hold you as few others do. You receive pretty much what his narrative voice gives you. It is not God's plenty, but it pleases many and serves as an introduction to the more difficult pleasures of storytellers subtler than Maupassant.

Ernest Hemingway

Hemingway's best short stories surpass even *The Sun Also Rises,* his only novel that seems now to be something more than a period piece. Wallace Stevens, the strongest of modern American poets, once termed Hemingway "the most significant of living poets, so far as the subject of extraordinary reality is concerned." By "poet" here, Stevens meant the remarkable stylist of Hemingway's short stories, and by "extraordinary reality" he meant a poetic realm in which "consciousness takes the place of imagination." This high praise is merited by Hemingway's permanent achievements in the short story, some fifteen or so masterpieces, easy to parody (frequently by Hemingway himself) but impossible to forget.

Frank O'Connor, who disliked Hemingway as intensely as he liked Chekhov, remarks in *The Lonely Voice* that Hemingway's stories "illustrate a technique in search of a subject," and therefore become "a minor art." Let us see. Read the famous sketch called "Hills Like White Elephants," five pages that are almost all dialogue, between a young woman and her lover, while they wait for a train at a station in a provincial Spanish town. They are continuing a disagreement as to the abortion he wishes her to undergo when they reach Madrid. The story catches the moment of her defeat, and very likely of the death of their relationship. And that is all. The dialogue makes clear that the woman is vital and decent, while the man is a sensible emptiness, selfish and unloving. The reader is wholly with her when she responds to his "I'd do anything for you" with "Would you please please please please please please please stop talking." Seven *please*s are a lot, but as repetition they are precise and persuasive in "Hills Like White Elephants." The story is beautifully prefigured in that simile of a title. Long and white, the hills across the valley of the Ebro "look like white elephants" to the woman, not to the man. White elephants, proverbial Siamese royal gifts to courtiers who would be ruined by the expense of their upkeep, become a larger metaphor for unwanted babies, and even more for erotic relationships too spiritually costly when a man is inadequate.

Hemingway's personal mystique—his bravura poses as warrior, big-game hunter, bullfighter, and boxer—is as irrelevant to "Hills Like White Elephants" as its male protagonist's insistence that "You know I love you." More relevant is the remark of Hemingway's surrogate, Nick Adams, in "The End of Something," when he terminates a relationship: "It isn't fun any more." I don't know many women readers who like that sentence, but it hardly is an apologia, only a very young man's self-indictment.

The Hemingway story that wounds me most is another five-pager, "God Rest You Merry, Gentlemen," which is almost entirely dialogue, after its opening paragraphs, including an outrageous initial sentence:

> In those days the distances were all very different, the dirt blew off the hills that now have been cut down, and Kansas City was very like Constantinople.

You can parody that by saying: "In those days Bridgeport, Connecticut, was very like Haifa." Still, we are in Kansas City on Christmas Day, and listening to the conversation between two physicians: the incompetent Doctor Wilcox, who relies upon a limp leather, indexed volume, *The Young Doctor's Friend and Guide,* and the mordant Doc Fischer, who begins by quoting his coreligionist Shylock: "What news along the Rialto?" The news is very bad, as we learn soon enough: a boy of about sixteen, obsessed with purity, had come into the hospital to ask for castration. Turned away, he had mutilated himself with a razor, and will probably die from loss of blood.

The interest of the story centers in Doc Fischer's lucid nihilism, prophetic of Nathanael West's Shrike in *Miss Lonelyhearts:*

> "Ride you, Doctor, on the day, the very anniversary, of our Savior's birth?"
>
> "*Our* Savior? Ain't you a Jew?" Doctor Wilcox said.
>
> "So I am. So I am. It always is slipping my mind. I've never given it its proper importance. So good of you to remind me. *Your* Savior. That's right. *Your* Savior, undoubtedly *your* Savior—and the ride for Palm Sunday."

"You, Wilcox, are the donkey upon whom I ride into Jerusalem" is the implication of that last phrase. Rancid and brilliant, Doc Fischer has peeked, as he says, into hell. His Shylockian intensity is a Hemingwayesque tribute to Shakespeare, described by Colonel Cantwell (Hemingway's surrogate) in *Across the River and into the Trees* as "the winner and still the undisputed champion." When he is most ambitious in his stories, Hemingway is most Shakespearean, as in the famous, quasi-autobiographical "The Snows of Kilimanjaro," its author's favorite. Of the story's protagonist, the failed writer Harry, Hemingway observes: "He had loved too much, demanded too much, and he wore it all out." That would be a superb critical remark to make about King Lear, Hemingway's most admired character in all of Shakespeare. More than anywhere else, Hemingway attempts and achieves tragedy in the relatively brief compass of "The Snows of Kilimanjaro."

The meditation of a dying man rather than the description of an action, this baroque story is Hemingway's most intense self-chastisement, and I think that Chekhov himself, much given to that mode, would have been impressed by it. One doesn't think of Hemingway as a visionary writer, but "The Snows of Kilimanjaro" begins with an epigraph telling us that the snow-covered western summit of the mountain is called the House of God, and close to it is the carcass, dried and frozen, of a leopard. There is no explanation as to what a leopard could have been seeking nearly twenty thousand feet above sea level.

Very little is gained by saying that the leopard is a symbol of the dying Harry. Originally, in ancient Greek, a *simbolon* was a token for identification, that could be compared to a counterpart. Commonly, we use *symbol* more loosely, as something that stands for something else, whether by association or resemblance. If you identify the corpse of the leopard with Harry's lost but still residual ambition or aesthetic idealism as a writer, then you plunge Hemingway's story into bathos and grotesquerie. Hemingway himself did that in "The Old Man and the Sea," but not in the masterful "The Snows of Kilimanjaro."

Harry is dying, slowly, of gangrene in an African hunting-camp, surrounded by vultures and hyenas, palpably unpleasant presences that need not be interpreted as symbolic. Neither need the leopard be so interpreted. Like Harry, it is out of place, but the writer's vision of Kilimanjaro does seem another of Hemingway's nostalgic visions of a lost spirituality, qualified as always by a keen sense of nothingness, a Shakespearean nihilism. It seems useful to regard the uncanny presence of the dead leopard as a strong irony, a forerunner of Harry's vain quest to recover his identity as a writer at Kilimanjaro, rather than say at Paris, Madrid, Key West, or Havana. The irony is at Hemingway's own expense, insofar as Harry prophesies the Hemingway who, nineteen days short of his sixty-second birthday, turned a double-barreled shotgun on himself in the mountains of Idaho. Yet the story is not primarily ironical, and need not be read as a personal prophecy. Harry is a failed Hemingway; Hemingway, by being able to compose "The Snows of Kilimanjaro," is precisely not a failure, at least as a writer.

The best moment in the story is hallucinatory, and comes just before the end. It is Harry's dying vision, though the reader cannot know that, until Harry's wife, Helen, realizes she can no longer hear him breathing. As he died, Harry dreamed that the rescue plane had come for him, but could carry only one passenger. On the visionary flight, Harry is taken up to see the square top of Kilimanjaro: "great, high, and unbelievably white in the sun." This apparent image of transcendence is the most illusive moment in the story; it represents death, and not the House of God. A dying man's phantasmagoria is not to be regarded as triumphal, when the entire story conveys Harry's conviction that he has wasted his gifts as a writer.

Yet Hemingway may have remembered King Lear's dying fantasy, in which the old, mad king is persuaded that his beloved daughter Cordelia breathes again, despite her murder. If you love too much, and demand too much, then you, like Lear and Harry (and, at last, Hemingway), will wear it all out. Fantasy, for Harry, takes the place of art.

Hemingway was so wonderful and unexpected a story-writer that I choose to end my account of him here with one of his unknown masterpieces, the splendidly ironic "A Sea Change," which prefigures his posthumously published novel *The Garden of Eden*, with its portrayal of ambiguous sexualities. In "A Sea Change" we are in a Parisian bar, where an archetypal Hemingwayesque couple are engaged in a crisp dialogue on infidelity. It takes the reader only a few exchanges to realize that the "sea change" of the title does not refer to the woman, who is determined to begin (or continue) a lesbian relationship, yet wishes also to return to the man. It is the man who is suffering a sea change, presumably into the writer who will compose the rich and strange *The Garden of Eden*.

"I'm a different man," he twice announces to the uncomprehending bartender, after the woman has left. Looking into the mirror, he *sees* the difference, but what he sees we are not told. Though he remarks to the bartender that "vice is a very strange thing," it cannot be a consciousness of "vice" that has made him a different man. Rather, it is his imaginative yielding to the woman's persuasive defense that has altered him forever. "We're made up of all sorts of things. You've known that. You've used it well enough," she has said to him, and he tacitly acknowledges some crucial element in the sexuality they have shared. He suffers now a sea change, but nothing of him fades in this moment of only apparent loss. Almost too deft for irony, "A Sea Change" is a subtle self-recognition, an erotic autobiography remarkable for its indirection and its nuanced self-acceptance. Only the finest American master of the short story could have placed so much in so slight a sketch.

Flannery O'Connor

D. H. Lawrence, a superb writer of short stories, gave the reader a permanent wisdom in one brief remark: "Trust the tale, not the teller." That seems to me an essential principle in reading the stories of Flannery O'Connor, who may have been the most original tale-teller among Americans since Hemingway. Her sensibility was an extraordinary blend of Southern Gothic and severe Roman Catholicism. So fierce a moralist is O'Connor that readers need to be wary of her tendentiousness: she has too palpable a design upon us, to shock us by violence into a need for traditional faith. As teller, O'Connor was very shrewd, yet I think her best tales are far shrewder, and enforce no moral except an awakened moral imagination.

O'Connor's South is wildly Protestant, not the Protestantism of Europe, but of the indigenous American Religion, whether it calls itself Baptist, Pentecostal, or whatever. The prophets of that religion—"snakehandlers, Free Thinking Christians, Independent Prophets, the swindlers, the mad, and sometimes the genuinely inspired"—O'Connor named as "natural Catholics." Except for this handful of "natural Catholics," the people who throng O'Connor's marvelous stories are the damned, a category in which Flannery O'Connor cheerfully included most of her readers. I think that the best way to read her stories is to begin by acknowledging that one is among her damned, and then go on from there to enjoy her grotesque and unforgettable art of telling.

"A Good Man Is Hard to Find" remains a splendid introduction to O'Connor. A grandmother, her son and daughter-in-law and their three children, are on a car journey when they encounter an escaped convict, the Misfit, and his two subordinate killers. Upon seeing the Misfit, the grandmother foolishly declares his identity, thus dooming herself and all her family. The old lady pleads with the Misfit while her family is taken away to be shot, but O'Connor gives us one of her masterpieces in this natural theologian of a killer. Jesus, the Misfit declares, "thrown everything off balance" by raising the dead, in a cosmos where there is "No pleasure but meanness." Dizzy and hallucinating, the terrified grandmother touches the Misfit while murmuring: "Why you're one of my babies. You're one of my own children!" He recoils, shoots her three times in the chest, and pronounces her epitaph: "She would of been a good woman if it had been somebody there to shoot her every minute of her life."

The tale and the teller came together here, since the Misfit clearly speaks for something fierce and funny in O'Connor herself. O'Connor gives us a hypocritical and banal old lady, and a killer who is, in O'Connor's view, an instrument of Catholic grace. This is meant to be and certainly *is* outrageous because, being damned, *we* are outraged by it. We would be good, O'Connor thinks, if someone were there to shoot us every minute of our lives.

Why do we not resent O'Connor's palpable designs upon us? Her comic genius is certainly part of the answer; someone who can entertain us so profoundly can damn us pretty much as she pleases. In her "Good Country People," we meet the unfortunate Joy Hopewell, who possesses both a Ph.D. in philosophy and a wooden leg, and the fancy first name Hulga, which she has given herself. A brash young Bible salesman, with the improbably phallic name of

Manley Pointer, divests Hulga of her wooden leg in a haystack, and then runs off with it. Hulga accurately knows herself as of the damned (is she not a philosopher?) and we can draw what moral we will from her cruelly hilarious fate. Shall we say of her: "She would of been a good woman if it had been somebody there to seduce her and run off with her wooden leg every minute of her life?"

O'Connor would have disdained my skepticism, and I am aware that my parody is defensive. But her early stories, though lively, are not her greatest. That comes in such later work as "A View of the Woods" and "Parker's Back," and in her second novel, *The Violent Bear It Away.* "A View of the Woods" is a sublimely ugly tale, featuring the seventy-nine-year-old Mr. Fortune, and his nine-year-old granddaughter, Mary Fortune Pitts. Both are dreadful: selfish, stubborn, mean, sullen monuments of pride. At the story's end, a nasty fight between the two closes with the grandfather killing the little girl, having throttled her and smashed her head upon a rock. In his excitement, and exhaustion, Mr. Fortune has a final "view of the woods" during a fatal heart attack. This is all grimly impressive, but how should we interpret it?

O'Connor remarked that Mary Fortune Pitts was saved and Mr. Fortune damned, but she could not explain why, since they are equally abominable persons, and the death struggle might have gone either way. It is splendid that O'Connor was so outrageous, because our skepticism outraged her, and inspired her art. And yet her obsessive spirituality and absolute moral judgments cannot just sustain themselves at the reader's expense. But when I think that, I suddenly recall how close her literary tastes were to my own: she preferred Faulkner's *As I Lay Dying* and Nathanael West's *Miss Lonelyhearts* to all other works of modern American fiction, and so do I. Reading Flannery O'Connor's stories and *The Violent Bear It Away,* I am exhilarated to the brink of fear, as I am by Faulkner and West in their grandest works, and by Cormac McCarthy's *Blood Meridian,* which surely O'Connor would have admired had she survived to read it. Turgenev and Chekhov,

Maupassant and Hemingway, were not ideologues, and the main tradition of the modern short story is certainly theirs, and not O'Connor's. And yet her verve and drive, the propulsive gusto of her comic spirit, is overwhelming. Her Catholicism might as well be Holy Rollerism, so far as the aesthetic effect of her fiction is concerned. There we can locate her natural shrewdness: her mad and damned American religionists can be parodied, but the parody will not touch her assured Roman Catholicism. More than a comedian of genius, she had also the penetrating insight that religion for her countrymen and -women was not the opiate, but rather the poetry of the people.

Vladimir Nabokov

I pass on to a superb story by Vladimir Nabokov, "The Vane Sisters," because the transition refreshes me, going from a vision of spirituality-through-violence to an aestheticism that plays with spiritualism. Nabokov was given to lamenting that his American English could never match the richness of his native Russian style, a lament that seems an irony when the reader confronts the baroquely rich textures of "The Vane Sisters." Our narrator, himself French in origin, instructs in French literature at a New England women's college. Nabokovian through and through, this nameless narrator is a finicky aesthete, a harmless version of Oscar Wilde's Dorian Gray. The Vane sisters are Cynthia and Sybil, whose name and suicide are borrowed from Dorian Gray's victimized girlfriend; though both young women are more Henry Jamesian than Wildean, since they are evanescent and indirect personalities. The nameless French professor was the teacher of Sybil, and the estranged close friend of Cynthia, but the lover of neither.

The narrator begins with a chance hearing of Cynthia's death by heart attack. He is taking his usual Sunday-afternoon stroll, and stops "to watch a family of brilliant icicles drip-dropping from the eaves of a frame house." A long paragraph is devoted to these icicles, and later he observes: "The lean ghost, the elongated umbra cast by a parking meter upon some damp snow, had a strange ruddy tinge." At the story's end, he wakes from a vague dream of Cynthia, but cannot unravel it:

> I could isolate, consciously, little. Everything seemed blurred, yellow-clouded, yielding nothing tangible. Her inept acrostics, maudlin evasions, theopathies—every recollection formed ripples of mysterious meaning. Everything seemed yellowly blurred, illusive, lost.

The self-parody of Nabokov's own style here testifies that Sybil's acrostics are not as inept as Cynthia's. Work out the acrostic formed by the initial letters of this passage and you get: *Icicles by Cynthia, meter from me, Sybil.*

Our narrator is haunted then by both women, but why? Probably because the Vane sisters glided ghostlike through their existence anyway; death seems hardly to alter them. But why the French professor as the object of these charmingly mischievous shades? It is possible that the narrator, being a Nabokovian self-parody, is being punished for Nabokov's own aestheticism and skepticism. Unlike Maupassant's "The Horla," which represents a gathering madness, "The Vane Sisters" is an authentic though highly original ghost story.

Sybil Vane, the day after taking a midyear examination in French literature, given by the narrator, kills herself, in reaction to being abandoned by her married lover. We get to know the older sister, Cynthia, rather better, after Sybil's death. Cynthia is a painter and a spiritualist, and has evolved a "theory of intervenient auras." These auras of the deceased intervene benignly in the lives of their survivors. After the narrator's skepticism alienates Cynthia—she accurately also calls him a prig and a snob—he breaks with her, and forgets her until he is told of her death. Discreetly, she haunts him, until the climactic dream he cannot decipher, and the final acrostic, which we can.

Nabokov's story, though brief, is replete with literary allusions—to Emerson's transparent eyeball (from his *Nature*) and Coleridge's person from Porlock (who supposedly interrupted the composition of "Kubla Khan"). There are also vivid manifestations of Oscar Wilde and of Tolstoy at a séance, and an extraordinary general atmosphere of literary preciosity. What makes "The Vane Sisters" magical is that the reader's own skepticism is overcome by the curious charm of these amiable women whose existences, and after-auras, alike are so tenuous. The reader is separated by Nabokov from the narrator's priggishness, but not necessarily from his skepticism. Pragmatically though, skepticism makes little difference here; these ghosts are persuasive precisely because they are so uninsistent upon persuasion. One doesn't think of the author of *Pale Fire* and *Lolita* as a Chekhovian writer. Nabokov adored Nikolai Gogol, whose spirit was fiercer (and more lunatic) than Chekhov's. But Cynthia and Sybil Vane would be at home in Chekhov; like so many of his women they represent the pathos of the unlived life. Nabokov, not much interested in pathos, prefers them as whimsical ghosts.

Jorge Luis Borges

The modern short story, so long as it remains Chekhovian, is impressionistic; this is as true of James Joyce's *Dubliners* as it is of Hemingway or Flannery O'Connor. Perception and sensation, the aesthetic of Walter Pater, are centered in the impressionistic short story, including the major stories of Thomas Mann and Henry James. Something very different came into modern storytelling with the phantasmagoria of Franz Kafka, a prime precursor of Jorge Luis Borges, who can be said to have replaced Chekhov as the major influence upon the short stories of the second half of our century. Stories now tend to be either Chekhovian or Borgesian; only rarely are they both.

Borges's *Collected Fictions* insist always upon their self-conscious status as artifices, unlike Chekhov's impressionistic glances at the truths of our existence. The reader, encountering Borges and his many followers, is wise to entertain very different expectations than she brings to Chekhov and his vast school. One is not going to hear the lonely voice of a submerged element in the population, but rather a voice haunted by a plethora of literary voices, forerunners. "What greater glory for a God, than to be absolved of the world?" is Borges's great outcry, as he professes his Alexandrianism. If there is a God in Chekhov's stories, then he cannot be absolved of the world, nor can we. But for Borges, the world is a speculative illusion, or a labyrinth, or a mirror reflecting other mirrors.

How to read Borges is necessarily more a lesson in how to read all his precursors than it is an exercise in self-understanding. That does not make Borges less entertaining or less enlightening than Chekhov, but it does make him very different. For Borges, Shakespeare is at once everyone and nobody: he is the living labyrinth of literature itself. For Chekhov, Shakespeare is obsessively the author of *Hamlet,* and Prince Hamlet becomes the ship in which Chekhov sails (quite literally in "At Sea," the first story published under Chekhov's own name). Borges's relativism is an absolute; Chekhov's is conditional. The reader, enthralled by Chekhov and his disciples, can enjoy a personal relation to the story, but Borges enchants the reader into the realm of impersonal forces, where Shakespeare's own memory is a vast abyss into which one can tumble, losing whatever remnants exist of one's self.

Of Borges's fictions, every reader will create a select list: mine includes "Tlön, Ugbar, Orbis Tertius," "Pierre Menard, Author of the *Quixote,*" "Death and the Compass," "The South," "The Immortal," and "The Alephi." Of this half dozen, I will center here only upon the first, in some detail, so as to help culminate this section on how to read the short story, and why we need to go on reading the best examples of it that we can find.

"Tlön, Ugbar, Orbis Tertius" begins with a disarming sentence (in Andrew Hurley's eloquent translation): "I owe the discovery of Ugbar to the conjunction of a mirror and an encyclopedia." That sentence is the purest Borges: add a labyrinth to a mirror and an encyclopedia, and you would have his world. Of all Borges's fictions "Tlön, Ugbar, Orbis Tertius" is the most sublimely outrageous. And yet the reader is seduced into finding the incredible credible, because of Borges's skill at employing real people (his best and most literary friends) and places (a big old country house, the National Library, a familiar hotel). The reader grants the same natural reality to the fictive Herbert Ashe as to the actual Bioy Casares, while Ugbar and Tlön, though phantasmagorias, seem little more marvelous than the National Library. An encyclopedia that deals entirely with an invented world goes a long way towards verifying that world simply because it is an encyclopedia, a work to which we are accustomed to grant authority.

This is disconcerting, but in a diverting way. As Tlönian objects and concepts spread through the nations, reality "caves in." Borges's dry irony is never more imposing:

> The truth is, it wanted to cave in. Ten years ago any symmetry, any system with an appearance of order—dialectical materialism, anti-Semitism, Nazism—could spellbind and hypnotize mankind.

Borges, a firm opponent both of Marxism and of Argentine fascism, indicts what we call "reality," but not his fantasy of Tlön, which is part of the living labyrinth of imaginative literature.

> Tlön may well be a labyrinth, but it is a labyrinth forged by men,
> a labyrinth destined to be deciphered by men.

That is to say, Tlön is a benign labyrinth, where no Minotaur waits at the end of the maze to devour us. Canonical literature is

neither a symmetry nor a system, but a hugely proliferating encyclopedia of human desire, the desire to be more imaginative
rather than to hurt another self. We are not to be spellbound nor
hypnotized by Tlön, and yet as readers we are not given nearly
enough information to decipher it. Tlön remains precisely a vast
cipher, to be solved only by the entire literary universe of fantasia.

Borges's story begins when he and his closest friend (and some-
time collaborator), the Argentine novelist Bioy Casares, sit too late
at dinner, in Borges's rented country house, and together behold
themselves in a mirror, which unsettles them. Bioy remembers a
saying that he attributes to "one of the heresiarchs of Ugbar: *Mirrors and copulation are abominable, for they multiply the number of
mankind.*" We are never told the identity of this Gnostic ascetic,
who necessarily is Borges himself, but Bioy thinks he found the
saying in an article on Ugbar in what purported to be a reprint
(under another title) of the 1902 *Encyclopaedia Britannica*. The
article does *not* appear in the edition available in Borges's rented
house; the next day Bioy brings his own, relevant volume, which
contains four pages on Ugbar. The geography and history of
Ugbar are alike rather vague; the location appears to be Trans-
Caucasian, while the literature of Ugbar is wholly fantasy and
refers to imaginary realms, including Tlön.

There the story, barely begun, would end, but for the aptly
named Herbert Ashe, a reticent British engineer with whom
Borges says he had desultory conversations across eight years, at a
hotel both frequented. After Ashe's death, Borges finds a volume
that the engineer had left in the hotel bar: *A First Encyclopaedia of
Tlön. Vol. XI. Hlaer to Jangr.* The book has no place or date of
publication and contains 1001 pages, in clear allusion to the *Ara-
bian Nights*. Absorbing these mythical pages, Borges discovers
much of the nature (to call it that) of the cosmos that is Tlön.
Bishop Berkeley's fierce philosophical idealism, with its conviction that nothing could be like an idea except another idea, is the
primordial law of existence on Tlön. There are no causes or effects

in that cosmos; the psychology and metaphysics of absolute fantasy prevail.

Such was "Tlön, Ugbar, Orbis Tertius" in 1940, another item in Borges's *Anthology of Fantastic Literature.* A "Postscript," dated 1947, expands on the phantasmagoria. Tlön is explained as a benign conspiracy of Hermetists and Kabbalists across three centuries, but one that took its decisive turn in 1824, when "the reclusive millionaire Ezra Buckley" proposed that an imaginary country be converted into an invented universe. Borges sets the proposal in Memphis, Tennessee, thereby making what we now think of as Elvisland as mysterious as ancient Memphis, Egypt. The forty volumes of the *First Encyclopaedia of Tlön* are completed by 1914, the year that saw the onset of World War I. In 1942, in the midst of World War II, the first objects from Tlön begin to appear: a magnetic compass whose dial letters are in a Tlönian alphabet; a small metal cone of unbearable weight; the discovery in a Memphis library of a complete set of the *Encyclopaedia.* Other objects, made of unearthly material, flood the nations. Reality caves in, and the world in time will be Tlön. Borges, little moved, stays in his hotel, slowly revising a baroque translation of Sir Thomas Browne's *Urne Buriall,* of which my own favorite sentence remains "Life is a pure flame, and we live by an invisible Sun within us."

Borges, a skeptical visionary, charms us even as we accept his warning: reality caves in all too easily. Our individual fantasies may not be as elaborate as Tlön, nor as abstract. Yet Borges has sketched a universal tendency, and fulfilled a fundamental yearning as to why we read.

Tommaso Landolfi

Dostoevsky famously said: "We all came out from under Gogol's 'Overcoat,'" a short story concerning a wretched copying clerk whose new overcoat is stolen. Disdained by the authorities, to whom he duly protests, the poor fellow dies, after which his ghost continues to search vainly for justice. Good as the story is, it is not the best of Gogol, which may be "Old-World Landowners" or the insane "The Nose," which begins when a barber, at breakfast, discovers a customer's nose inside a loaf of bread freshly baked by his wife. The spirit of Gogol, subtly alive in much of Nabokov, achieves its apotheosis in the triumphant "Gogol's Wife," by the modern Italian story-writer Tommaso Landolfi, perhaps the funniest and most unnerving story that I've yet read.

The narrator, Gogol's friend and biographer, "reluctantly" tells us the story of Gogol's wife. The actual Gogol, a religious obsessive, never married, and deliberately starved himself to death at forty-three or so, after burning his unpublished manuscripts. But Landolfi's Gogol (who might have been invented by Kafka or by Borges) has married a rubber balloon, a splendidly inflatable dummy who assumes different shapes and sizes at her husband's whim. Much in love with his wife, in one of her forms or another, Gogol enjoys sexual relations with her, and bestows upon her the name Caracas, after the capital of Venezuela, for reasons known only to the mad writer.

For some years, all goes well, until Gogol contracts syphilis, which he rather unfairly blames upon Caracas. Ambivalence towards his silent wife gains steadily in Gogol through the years. He accuses Caracas of self-gratification, and even betrayal, so that she becomes bitter and excessively religious. Finally, the enraged Gogol pumps too much air into Caracas (quite deliberately) until she bursts and scatters into the air. Collecting the remnants of Madame Gogol, the great writer burns them in the fireplace, where they share the fate of his unpublished works. Into the same fire, Gogol casts also a rubber doll, the son of Caracas. After this final catastrophe, the biographer defends Gogol from the charge of wife-beating, and salutes the memory of the writer's lofty genius.

The best prelude (or postlude) to reading Landolfi's "Gogol's

Wife" is to read some stories by Gogol, on the basis of which we will not doubt the reality of the unfortunate Caracas. She is as likely a paramour as Gogol could ever have discovered (or invented) for himself. In contrast, Landolfi could hardly have composed much the same story and called it "Maupassant's Wife," let alone "Turgenev's Wife." No, it has to be Gogol and Gogol alone, and I rarely doubt Landolfi's story, particularly just after each rereading. Caracas has a reality that Borges neither seeks nor achieves for his Tlön. As Gogol's only possible bride, she seems to me the ultimate parody of Frank O'Connor's insistence that the lonely voice crying out in the modern short story is that of the Submerged Population. Who could be more submerged than Gogol's wife?

Italo Calvino

Other masters of the short story are considered elsewhere in the volume, whether as novelists (Henry James and Thomas Mann) or poets (D. H. Lawrence). Here I wish to close with another great Italian fabulist, Italo Calvino, who died in 1985. My favorite among his books (really a universal favorite) is *Invisible Cities,* translated beautifully by William Weaver in 1974. A description of Calvino's invention, if rendered properly, could show others how and why *Invisible Cities* should be read and reread. Marco Polo is the tale-teller, and the venerable Kublai Khan his audience, as we listen also to stories about imaginary cities. The stories are only a page or two long yet they *are* short stories, in the Borgesian or Kafkan, rather than the Chekhovian, mode. Marco Polo's cities never were, and never could be, and yet most readers would go there, if only we might.

Calvino's *Invisible Cities* come in eleven groupings, scattered rather than bunched: cities and—memory, desire, signs, eyes, names, the dead, the sky—as well as thin cities, trading cities, continuous cities, and hidden cities. Though one can become dizzy keeping all these in mind, it will not do to say that each of these cities is actually the same place. Since they are all named for women, that would amount to saying that all women are one woman, the doctrine of the Spanish philosopher-novelist Miguel de Unamuno, but not Calvino's view. Kublai Khan, listening to Marco Polo, would certainly agree with Calvino and Polo, and not with Unamuno. For Kublai, old and weary of power, finds in Marco Polo's visionary cities a pattern that will endure, after his own empire is dust.

Nostalgia for lost illusions, loves that never quite were, happiness perhaps only tasted—these are the emotions Calvino evokes. In Isidora, one of the Cities of Memory, "the foreigner hesitating between two women always encounters a third," but alas you can arrive at Isidora only in old age. "You leave Tamara without having discovered it," and in Zirma you see "a girl walking with a puma on a leash." Kublai, after many recitals, begins to note a family resemblance among the cities, but that means only that the emperor is learning how to interpret Polo's art of narrative: "There is no language without deceit." In Armilla, one of the Thin Cities, the only activity seems to be that of nymphs bathing: "in the morning you hear them singing." This is bettered by: "A voluptuous vibration constantly stirs Chloe, the most chaste of cities." This is akin to one of Marco Polo's principles as a storyteller: "Falsehood is never in words, it is in the things."

Kublai protests that, from then on, *he* will describe the cities, and Marco Polo will then journey to see if they exist. But Marco denies Kublai's archetypal city and proposes instead a model made up only of exceptions, exclusions, incongruities, contradictions. The reader begins to understand that the true story is the ongoing debate between the visionary Marco and the skeptical Kublai, perpetual youth against eternal age. And so the recital goes on: Esmeralda, where "cats, thieves, illicit lovers move along higher, discontinuous ways dropping from a rooftop to a balcony," or

Eusapia, a city of the dead where "a girl with a laughing skull milks the carcass of a heifer."

Wearying even of this, Kublai orders Marco to cease his travels, and instead engage the great Khan in an endless chess match. But this does not slow Marco down; the movement of the chess pieces becomes the narrative of the invisible cities. We come at last to "Berenice, the unjust city," which has a just city within it, and an unjust within that, and on and on. Berenice is then a sequence of cities, just and unjust, but all the future Berenices are present already, "wrapped one within the other, confined, crammed, inextricable." And since that is where we all live, Marco Polo ceases. There are then no more Invisible Cities.

One final dialogue between Kublai and Marco remains. Where, Kublai asks, are the promised lands? Why has Marco not spoken of New Atlantis, Utopia, the City of the Sun, New Harmony, and all the other cities of redemption? "For these parts I could not draw a route on the map or set a date for the landing," Marco replies, but already the Great Khan, leafing through his atlas, comes upon the cities of "nightmares and maledictions": Babylon, Yahooland, Brave New World, and the others. In despair, the aged Kublai states his nihilism: the current draws us at last to the infernal city. Wonderfully, the last words are given to Polo, who speaks for what is still hopeful in the reader. We are indeed already in "the inferno of the living." We can accept it, and so cease to be conscious of it. But there is a better way, and it might be called the wisdom of Italo Calvino:

> . . . seek and learn to recognize who and what, in the midst of inferno, are not inferno, then make them endure, give them space.

Calvino's advice tells us again how to read and why: be vigilant, apprehend and recognize the possibility of the good, help it to endure, give it space in your life.

SUMMARY OBSERVATIONS

It is useful to consider modern short stories as dividing themselves into rival traditions, Chekhovian and Borgesian.

Flannery O'Connor, despite surface appearances, is as much in Chekhov's tradition as Italo Calvino is in the rival line of Kafka and Borges. The Chekhovian short story is *not* fantasy, however outrageous it turns in the work of Flannery O'Connor. Hemingway, who wanted to be Tolstoy, is very Chekhovian, as was Joyce's *Dubliners,* though Joyce denied he had read Chekhov. Chekhovian stories start off suddenly, end elliptically, and do not bother to fill in the gaps that we would expect to find closed up in the stories (particularly the longer ones) of Henry James. Still, Chekhov expects you to believe in his realism, his faithfulness to our ordinary existence. Kafka, and Borges after him, invest themselves in phantasmagoria. Kafka and Borges do not give you dirges for the unlived life.

It is not always easy to distinguish the Chekhovian-Hemingwayesque mode from the Kafkan-Borgesian, because neither style of narration is necessarily interested in telling you a story, as Tolstoy so thoroughly and completely tells you of the life and death of Hadji Murad, the Chechen hero in the short novel named after him. Chekhov and Kafka create from an abyss or void; Tolstoy's superb sense of reality persuades you as only Shakespeare and Cervantes can. But short stories, whether of the Chekhovian or Borgesian kind, constitute an essential form, as Borges remarked. The best of them demand and reward many rereadings. Henry James observed that short stories are placed "at that exquisite point where poetry ends and reality begins." That puts them between poems and novels, and their characters, as James again said, must be "so strangely, fascinatingly particular and yet so recognizably general."

Plays traditionally imitate actions; short stories frequently do not. Eudora Welty, probably our best living American storyteller, remarked that D. H. Lawrence's characters "don't really speak their words—not conversationally, not to one another—they are *not* speaking on the street, but are playing like fountains or radiating like the moon or storming like the sea, or their silence is the silence of wicked rocks." Lawrence is a visionary extremist, but Welty's eloquent point is well taken for all great stories, which must find their own form, whether Chekhovian or Kafkan. In major short stories, reality becomes fantastic and phantasmagoria becomes disconcertingly mundane. That may be why so many readers, these days, shy away from volumes of stories, and purchase novels instead, even when the stories are of much higher quality.

Short stories favor the tacit; they compel the reader to be active, and to discern explanations that the writer avoids. The reader, as I have said before, must slow down, quite deliberately, and start listening with the *inner* ear. Such listening overhears the characters, as well as hearing them; think of them as *your* characters, and wonder at what is implied, rather than told about them. Unlike most figures in novels, their foregrounding and postgrounding are largely up to you, utilizing the hints subtly provided by the writer.

From Turgenev through Eudora Welty and beyond, short story writers refrain from moral judgments. George Eliot was one of the finest of novelists, and *Middlemarch* (her masterpiece) abounds in fascinating moral judgments. But the most skilled short story writers are as elliptical in regard to moral judgments as they are in regard to continuities of action or the details of a character's past life. You, as reader, are to decide if moral judgment is relevant, and then the judgment will be yours to make.

The reader derives immense benefits from the significant blanks provided both by the Chekhovian and the Borgesian mode. At the same time one has to be wary of supposed symbolism, which is more often absent than present in a masterful short story. Even the great horror story "The Horla" of Maupassant does not overtly render the Horla symbolic, though I have suggested above that there may be some relation between Maupassant's syphilitic madness and his nameless protagonist's obsession with the Horla. To a certain degree, symbolism is as foreign to the good short story as literary allusion should be: Nabokov is a superbly outrageous exception to my attempt to formulate a Bloom's Law for short fiction. Nabokov is frequently allusive, though rarely symbolic. Symbolism is dangerous for short stories, since novels can have world enough and time to mask emblems naturalistically, but stories, necessarily more abrupt, have difficulty in rendering them unobtrusive.

I conclude this epilogue to the how and why of reading the short story by offering the double judgment that the Chekhovian-Hemingwayesque and Borgesian modes need never be preferred one to the other. We want them for different needs; if the first gratifies our hunger for reality, the second teaches us how ravenous we still are for what is beyond supposed reality. Clearly, we read the two schools differently, questing for truth with Chekhov, or for the turning-inside-out of truth with the Kafkan-Borgesians. Landolfi's Gogol destroys his rubber doll of a wife, and we are as strongly affected as we are when Chekhov's student stops by the campfire of the two bereft women and tells them the tale of St. Peter. Our energies of response are different in quality, but they are equally intense.

II

Poems

Introduction

I have not organized this section chronologically, but thematically and by juxtaposition, because poetry tends to be freer from history than are prose fiction or drama. And even as I emphasize poetic argument rather than societal context, so I do not discuss poetic form. On all questions of the schemes, patterns, forms, meters, rhymes of poetry in English, the indispensable authority is John Hollander's *Rhyme's Reason: A Guide to English Verse*, readily available in paperback. My concern here, as elsewhere in this book, is how to read and why, which in regard to poems, generally and specifically, is for me a quest for the larger created presences of the imagination. Poetry is the crown of imaginative literature, in my judgment, because it is a prophetic mode.

I begin with instances of pure lyric, by A. E. Housman, William Blake, Walter Savage Landor, and Tennyson's fragment "The Eagle." These represent poetry at its most economical and poignant, and lead me into two of the greatest of dramatic monologues, Tennyson's eloquent "Ulysses" and Robert Browning's extraordinary "Childe Roland to the Dark Tower Came." Whitman's *Song of Myself* is then juxtaposed to these monologues, as the major instance of the American replacement of dramatic monologue by the epic of Self-Reliance, to employ Emerson's term.

Emily Dickinson's lyric of Self-Reliance follows, after which I
return to Victorian England for a fierce lyric of the self by Emily
Brontë. The mood and spirit of Dickinson and of Brontë is related
to the so-called Popular Ballad or Border Ballad. I analyze here my
two favorite ballads, "Sir Patrick Spence" and "The Unquiet
Grave," before turning to the greatest anonymous poem in the language, the astonishing "Tom O'Bedlam," a mad song worthy of
Shakespeare himself.

That leads on to three of Shakespeare's most powerful sonnets.
Shakespeare's greatest successors in English poetry, Milton and the
Romantics, follow in a natural sequence. I wish I had more space
for *Paradise Lost,* but I have sketched how and why Milton's Satan
needs to be read, and reread.

Two lyrics by Wordsworth, the true inventor of modern
poetry, are followed by Coleridge's uncanny *The Rime of the
Ancient Mariner,* and by Shelley and Keats at their most haunting.
I have reserved a brief discussion of my four favorite modern
poets—W. B. Yeats, D. H. Lawrence, Wallace Stevens, and Hart
Crane—for the start of my "Summary Observations," since these
four poets inherit, between them, all of the crucial elements in the
poems I discuss here.

Housman, Blake, Landor, and Tennyson

> Into my heart an air that kills
>   From yon far country blows:
> What are those blue remembered hills,
>   What spires, what farms are those?
>
> That is the land of lost content,
>   I see it shining plain,

The happy highways where I went
And cannot come again.

That is the fortieth lyric of A. E. Housman's *A Shropshire Lad* (1896). Like many of Housman's poems, it has been in my head for sixty years. As a boy of eight, I would walk about chanting Housman's and William Blake's lyrics to myself, and I still do, less frequently yet with undiminished fervor. How to read a poem can best be introduced by reading Housman, whose concise and economical mode appeals by its apparent simplicity. This artful simplicity conceals the depth, the reverberation, that helps define great poetry. "An air that kills" is a superb irony, since whether as aria or as the remembered sensation of a breeze, the song or breath paradoxically slays, precisely where it should enhance life. Himself born in Worcestershire, Housman as a child loved Shropshire "because its hills were our western horizon." The poem's "blue remembered hills," part for whole, represent not just an idealized Shropshire but a transcendent "beyond," a happiness that the frustrated Housman never achieved. There is a plangent emptying out of the self in the declaration "That is the land of lost content," since the content was only an aspiration. And yet, in a sublime affirmation, the poet insists: "I see it shining plain," as a pilgrim might insist he indeed beholds Jerusalem. Those "happy highways" belonged only to futurity, which is why Housman cannot come there again. The accent of belatedness is caught and held perfectly, in what we finally see is the saddest kind of love lyric, one that memorializes only a dream of youth.

Housman's directness helps to suggest a first principle for how to read poems: closely, because a true criterion for any good poem is that it will sustain a very close reading indeed. Here is William Blake, far grander than Housman, but giving us a lyric that again seems simple and direct, "The Sick Rose":

O rose, thou art sick!
The invisible worm
That flies in the night,
In the howling storm,

Has found out thy bed
Of crimson joy,
And his dark secret love
Does thy life destroy.

Blake's tone, unlike Housman's, is difficult to describe. "Dark secret love" has become a permanent phrase for almost any clandestine erotic relation and whatever destructiveness it entails. The ironies of "The Sick Rose" are fierce, perhaps cruel in their relentlessness. What Blake depicts is altogether natural, and yet the poem's perspective renders the natural itself into a social ritual in which phallic menace is set against female self-gratification (the rose's bed is one of "crimson joy" before the worm finds it out). Like Housman's Shropshire lyric, "The Sick Rose" is best chanted aloud, which may suggest it is a kind of spell, a prophetic outcry against nature and against human nature.

Perhaps only William Blake would have weighted so brief a lyric, only thirty-four words, with so dark a visionary burden, but something in poets likes to manifest its creative exuberance by packing much into little. By "visionary" I mean a mode of perception in which objects and persons are seen with an augmented intensity that has spiritual overtones. Poetry, so frequently visionary, tries to domesticate the reader in a world where what she gazes upon has a transcendental aura.

The Romantic poet Walter Savage Landor, whose frequent literary feuds and incessant lawsuits ironically confirmed his middle name, composed remarkable quatrains that were marvelously self-deceptive, like this one, "On His Seventy-fifth Birthday":

I strove with none, for none was worth my strife.
    Nature I loved and, next to Nature, Art:
I warmed both hands before the fire of life;
    It sinks, and I am ready to depart.

If one reaches seventy-five, one will want to go about murmuring this epigram on one's birthday anyway, cheerfully knowing its untruth, for oneself as well as for Savage Landor. Very good short poems are particularly memorable, and with that, I have arrived at a first crux in how to read poems: wherever possible, *memorize them.* Once a staple of good teaching, memorization was abused into repeating by rote, and so was abandoned, wrongly. Silent intensive rereadings of a shorter poem that truly *finds* you should be followed by recitations to yourself, until you discover that you are in possession of the poem. You might start with Tennyson's beautifully orchestrated "The Eagle":

He clasps the crag with crooked hands;
Close to the sun in lonely lands,
Ringed with the azure world, he stands.

The wrinkled sea beneath him crawls;
He watches from his mountain walls,
And like a thunderbolt he falls.

The poem is an exercise (triumphant) in matching sound to sense, yet has a sublime aspect also. The eagle beckons to our imaginative capacity for identification. Robert Penn Warren, who composed astonishing dramatic lyrics about hawks and eagles, once recited Tennyson's eloquent fragment to me at the end of a lunch, and then said: "I wish I had written that." If you memorize "The Eagle," you may come to feel that you *have* written it, so universal is the poem's proud longing.

73

When I was younger, and rather more a patient teacher than I am now, I once persuaded my Yale class in Victorian poetry to join me in memorizing Tennyson's superb dramatic monologue "Ulysses," a poem that gives itself to memorization, and to the critical insights that possession-by-memory can yield.

Hovering in the margins of Tennyson's passionate meditation are other versions of Ulysses: from Homer's *Odyssey* through Dante's *Inferno* on to Shakespeare's *Troilus and Cressida* and even to Milton's transformation of Ulysses into the Satan of the earlier books of *Paradise Lost.* Allusive and contrapuntal, Tennyson's "Ulysses" is eloquently memorable, and very available for memorization, perhaps because something in many readers is tempted so readily to make an identification with this equivocal hero, a permanently central figure in Western literature. Ambivalence, perfected by Shakespeare, is the arousal in us of powerful feelings, both positive and negative, towards an individual. Tennyson's "Ulysses," in what appear to have been the poet's intentions, represents the need to go onwards with life, despite Tennyson's own extraordinary grief for the early death of his closest friend, Arthur Henry Hallam. Much of Tennyson's finest poetry comprises elegies for Hallam, including "In Memoriam" and the "Morte d'Arthur." Yet a profound ambivalence is evoked by Ulysses the monologist, who begins with what seems a harsh and unloving portrait of his home, the wife and the subjects to whom he had returned, after so many adventures:

> It little profits that an idle king,
> By this still hearth, among these barren crags,
> Matched with an aged wife, I mete and dole
> Unequal laws unto a savage race,
> That hoard, and sleep, and feed, and know not me.

That last reproach appears to be the heart of Ulysses' malaise, transcending his ungallant reference to the faithful Penelope's decline, and his unpersuasive protest at the laws he administers but scarcely desires to improve. The rude Ithacans "know not me," the greatness and glory that alone can define Ulysses, in his own view. Yet how superb an expression of memorable discontent these five opening lines constitute! How many aging males, throughout the centuries, have reflected in just this mode, heroic to themselves though not necessarily to others. But Ulysses, however selfish, is already eloquent, and our negative or muted response is swiftly altered as he continues:

> I cannot rest from travel: I will drink
> Life to the lees: all times I have enjoyed
> Greatly, have suffered greatly, both with those
> That loved me, and alone; on shore, and when
> Through scudding drifts the rainy Hyades
> Vexed the dim sea: I am become a name;
> For always roaming with a hungry heart
> Much have I seen and known; cities of men
> And manners, climates, councils, governments,
> Myself not least, but honoured of them all;
> And drunk delight of battle with my peers,
> Far on the ringing plains of windy Troy.
> I am a part of all that I have met;
> Yet all experience is an arch wherethrough
> Gleams that untravelled world, whose margin fades
> For ever and for ever when I move.
> How dull it is to pause, to make an end,
> To rust unburnished, not to shine in use!
> As though to breathe were life. Life piled on life
> Were all too little, and of one to me
> Little remains: but every hour is saved
> From that eternal silence, something more,
> A bringer of new things; and vile it were
> For some three suns to store and hoard myself,
> And this grey spirit yearning in desire

To follow knowledge like a sinking star,
Beyond the utmost bound of human thought.

Heroic identification is proffered to the reader, and is very difficult to resist. The ethos here prophesies the code of Hemingway: to live one's life all the way up, except that bullfighters and big-game hunters hardly compete with this hero of heroes. The reader notes that Ulysses speaks of "those / That loved me," but never of those he loved or loves. Yet how moving it is to read: "I am become a name," since mere egoism vanishes when we reflect that the name is Ulysses, with all its power of evocation. "Myself not least, but honoured of them all" loses its stigma by merging into "I am a part of all that I have met." That monosyllabic line distributes its emphases, so that the double "I" is partly subdued to the "all" sought, and found, by the quester. A Shakespearean vitalism, echoing Hamlet's restless spirit, reverberates in this Ulysses' "As though to breathe were life." An old man is speaking, in rejection of the wisdom of age.

The poem is taking us to the verge of a last voyage, not foretold by the uncanny Tiresias in the *Odyssey* (XI, 100–152), when he prophesies the hero's death in "rich old age, / your country folk in blessed peace around you" (Robert Fitzgerald's version). Tennyson's source, so unlike this dramatic monologue in spirit, is Dante's *Inferno*, canto 26, where Ulysses is depicted as a transgressive quester. Dante's Ulysses leaves his long sojourn with the sorceress Circe not to return to Penelope and Ithaca, but to sail beyond the known limits of the world, to break out of the Mediterranean into the chaos of the Atlantic Ocean. Dante silently is aware of the deep identity between his own voyage in the *Comedy* and Ulysses' final quest, but the Christian poet has compelled himself to place Ulysses at the eighth circle down of Hell. Close by is Satan, archetype of Ulysses' sin as a fraudulent counselor. Tennyson's Ulysses makes the mad, final voyage of Dante's sinner, but Tennyson's protagonist is not a hero-villain. The Victorian Ulysses discovers the proper Victorian in his son, Telemachus, whom he pictures as rather a prig:

> This is my son, mine own Telemachus,
> To whom I leave the sceptre and the isle—
> Well-loved of me, discerning to fulfill
> This labour, by slow prudence to make mild
> A rugged people, and through soft degrees
> Subdue them to the useful and the good.
> Most blameless is he, centred in the sphere
> Of common duties, decent not to fail
> In offices of tenderness, and pay
> Meet adoration to my household gods,
> When I am gone. He works his work, I mine.

"Well-loved" there is not convincing, compared to the expressive power of "He works his work, I mine." The reader hears the relief with which Ulysses turns away from his virtuous son to address his aged fellow mariners, who will make the suicidal voyage with him.

> There lies the port; the vessel puffs her sail:
> There gloom the dark broad seas. My mariners,
> Souls that have toiled, and wrought, and thought with me—
> That ever with a frolic welcome took
> The thunder and the sunshine, and opposed
> Free hearts, free foreheads—you and I are old;
> Old age hath yet his honour and his toil;
> Death closes all: but something ere the end,
> Some work of noble note, may yet be done,
> Not unbecoming men that strove with Gods.
> The lights begin to twinkle from the rocks:
> The long day wanes: the slow moon climbs: the deep
> Moans round with many voices. Come, my friends,
> 'Tis not too late to seek a newer world.

Push off, and sitting well in order smite
The sounding furrows; for my purpose holds
To sail beyond the sunset, and the baths
Of all the western stars, until I die.
It may be that the gulfs will wash us down:
It may be we shall touch the Happy Isles,
And see the great Achilles, whom we knew.
Though much is taken, much abides; and though
We are not now that strength which in old days
Moved earth and heaven; that which we are, we are;
One equal temper of heroic hearts,
Made weak by time and fate, but strong in will
To strive, to seek, to find, and not to yield.

"Death closes all" is more like Hamlet than Dante (or Tennyson), and augments in force as a declaration when juxtaposed with this Ulysses' extraordinary sensitivity to light and sound:

The lights begin to twinkle from the rocks:
The long day wanes: the slow moon climbs: the deep
Moans round with many voices.

Tennyson ends his poem with another clash of antithetical voices, one that is universally human ("Though much is taken, much abides") and the other that unmistakably echoes Milton's Satan ("To strive, to seek, to find, and not to yield"). Satan asks the great question: "And courage never to submit or yield: / And what is else not to be overcome?" Dante and Milton, respectively the major Catholic and Protestant poets, would have spoken of yielding to God, but then Tennyson's Ulysses, after a lifetime of struggle with the sea god, was not likely to yield to any divinity. The reader, wherever she or he stands in regard either to God or to the possibilities of heroism, is moved by Tennyson's extraordinary eloquence, whatever skepticism towards Ulysses the poem subtly suggests to us.

Something of how to read this sublime poem has been indicated, but why should we go on reading it? The pleasures of great poetry are many and varied, and Tennyson's "Ulysses" is, for me, an endless delight. Only rarely can poetry aid us in communing with others; that is a beautiful idealism, except at certain strange moments, like the instant of falling in love. Solitude is the more frequent mark of our condition; how shall we people that solitude? Poems can help us to speak to ourselves more clearly and more fully, and to *overhear* that speaking. Shakespeare is the largest master of such overhearing; his women and men are our forerunners, as they are also of Tennyson's Ulysses. We speak to an otherness in ourselves, or to what may be best and oldest in ourselves. We read to find ourselves, more fully and more strange than otherwise we could hope to find.

Robert Browning

For many years I taught that self-overhearing was the particular originality of the major Shakespearean personalities, without recalling where I first encountered the notion. Writing the previous paragraph suddenly reminds me of Tennyson's contemporary, the philosopher John Stuart Mill, whose essay "What Is Poetry" (1833) says of a Mozart aria: "We imagine it *overheard.*" Poetry, Mill implies, is also overheard rather than heard. I turn to a masterpiece by Tennyson's true rival, Robert Browning, now much neglected because of his authentic difficulty. "Childe Roland to the Dark Tower Came" takes its title from a song fragment sung by Edgar in Shakespeare's *King Lear,* act 3, as scene 4 closes:

> *Childe Rowland to the dark tower came,*
> *His word was still,* "Fie, foh, and fum,
> I smell the blood of a British man."

That is Edgar in his abject disguise of a wandering "roaring mad Tom," a Tom O'Bedlam beggar, sometimes called an Abraham man. Supposedly Edgar quotes a fragment of an old ballad, but that ballad has not been found, and I suspect that Shakespeare himself wrote these horrid nursery lines. Later in this chapter I will quote and discuss the greatest "mad song" in the language, the anonymous "Tom O'Bedlam," discovered in a literary scrapbook of 1620, and so magnificent a poem that I wish I could ascribe it to Shakespeare, simply upon merit! Whether Edgar's chant was Shakespeare's or not, Browning was inspired by it to the most astonishing of all his dramatic monologues:

I
My first thought was, he lied in every word,
   That hoary cripple, with malicious eye
   Askance to watch the working of his lie
On mine, and mouth scarce able to afford
Suppression of the glee, that pursed and scored
   Its edge, at one more victim gained thereby.

II
What else should he be set for, with his staff?
   What, save to waylay with his lies, ensnare
   All travelers who might find him posted there,
And ask the road? I guessed what skull-like laugh
Would break, what crutch 'gin write my epitaph
   For pastime in the dusty thoroughfare.

III
If at his counsel I should turn aside
   Into that ominous tract which, all agree,
   Hides the Dark Tower. Yet acquiescingly
I did turn as he pointed: neither pride

Nor hope rekindling at the end descried,
　　So much as gladness that some end might be.

IV

For, what with my whole world-wide wandering,
　　What with my search drawn out through years, my hope
　　Dwindled into a ghost not fit to cope
With that obstreperous joy success would bring,—
I hardly tried now to rebuke the spring
　　My heart made, finding failure in its scope.

Who exactly is this eloquently despairing speaker? A "childe" is a noble youth not yet a knight, but still a candidate for knighthood, though this Roland wants only to be fit to fail in the tradition of those who have preceded him in his quest for the Dark Tower. We are never told who or what inhabits the Dark Tower, but presumably it is that ogre whose word was "Fie, foh, and fum, / I smell the blood of a British man." A grisly prospect, but no more dismal than the appalling wasteland through which the negatively heroic childe makes his way:

X

So, on I went. I think I never saw
　　Such starved ignoble nature; nothing throve:
　　For flowers—as well expect a cedar grove!
But cockle, spurge, according to their law
Might propagate their kind, with none to awe,
　　You'd think; a burr had been a treasure-trove.

XI

No! penury, inertness and grimace,
　　In some strange sort, were the land's portion. "See
　　Or shut your eyes," said Nature peevishly,

"It nothing skills: I cannot help my case:
'Tis the Last Judgment's fire must cure this place,
  Calcine its clods and set my prisoners free."

XII
If there pushed any ragged thistle-stalk
  Above its mates, the head was chopped; the bents
  Were jealous else. What made those holes and rents
In the dock's harsh swarth leaves, bruised as to baulk
All hope of greenness? 'tis a brute must walk
  Pashing their life out, with a brute's intents.

XIII
As for the grass, it grew as scant as hair
  In leprosy; thin dry blades pricked the mud
  Which underneath looked kneaded up with blood.
One stiff blind horse, his every bone a-stare,
Stood stupefied, however he came there:
  Thrust out past service from the devil's stud!

XIV
Alive? he might be dead for aught I know,
  With that red gaunt and colloped neck a-strain,
  And shut eyes underneath the rusty mane;
Seldom went such grotesqueness with such woe;
I never saw a brute I hated so;
  He must be wicked to deserve such pain.

Whether we, if we rode by this Roland's side, would see a landscape as deformed and broken as he does is open to question. That
terrifying horse, neither quite alive nor dead, seems incontrovert-
ibly described, but would we cry out "Thrust out past service
from the devil's stud!" or go on to the childlike reflection "I never

saw a brute I hated so; / He must be wicked to deserve such pain"?

You don't leave a small child alone with a wounded kitten, and one wonders how safe it is to let Childe Roland ride alone. Desperate at his own vision, Roland tries to summon up images of his forerunners in the quest for the Dark Tower, but remembers only dear friends disgraced as traitors. "Back therefore to my darkening path again!" he cries out, yet we should know that the reader ought to question what the childe sees. T. S. Eliot's harsh *The Waste Land* can seem mild compared to this landscape:

XX
So petty yet so spiteful! All along,
　Low scrubby alders kneeled down over it;
　Drenched willows flung them headlong in a fit
Of mute despair, a suicidal throng:
The river which had done them all the wrong,
　Whate'er that was, rolled by, deterred no whit.

XXI
Which, while I forded,—good saints, how I feared
　To set my foot upon a dead man's cheek,
　Each step, or feel the spear I thrust to seek
For hollows, tangled in his hair or beard!
—It may have been a water-rat I speared,
　But, ugh! it sounded like a baby's shriek.

XXII
Glad was I when I reached the other bank.
　Now for a better country. Vain presage!
　Who were the strugglers, what war did they wage,
Whose savage trample thus could pad the dank
Soil to a plash? Toads in a poisoned tank,
　Or wild cats in a red-hot iron cage—

XXIII

The fight must so have seemed in that fell cirque.
　　What penned them there, with all the plain to choose?
　　No foot-print leading to the horrid mews,
None out of it. Mad brewage set to work
Their brains, no doubt, like galley-slaves the Turk
　　Pits for his pastime, Christians against Jews.

XXIV

And more than that—a furlong on—why, there!
　　What bad use was the engine for, that wheel,
　　Or brake, not wheel—that harrow fit to reel
Men's bodies out like silk? with all the air
Of Tophet's tool, on earth left unaware,
　　Or brought to sharpen its rusty teeth of steel.

XXV

Then came a bit of stubbed ground, once a wood,
　　Next a marsh, it would seem, and now mere earth
　　Desperate and done with; (so a fool finds mirth,
Makes a thing and then mars it, till his mood
Changes and off he goes!) within a rood—
　　Bog, clay and rubble, sand and stark black dearth.

XXVI

Now blotches rankling, coloured gay and grim,
　　Now patches where some leanness of the soil's
　　Broke into moss or substances like boils;
Then came some palsied oak, a cleft in him
Like a distorted mouth that splits its rim
　　Gaping at death, and dies while it recoils.

That which we are, that only we can see (an Emersonian reflection), prompts the reader to find in Browning's Roland a quester so

ruined that the literary equivalent would be difficult to uncover.
Dante, marching through his Inferno, avoids effects as horrifyingly
equivocal as "But, ugh! it sounded like a baby's shriek." The harrow
of stanza XXIV may be an instrument of torment, but the reader
has grown skeptical. It appears to be Roland himself who breaks
and deforms everything he sees, and who, in consequence, fails to
see the object of his quest until it is too late:

XXVII
And just as far as ever from the end!
   Nought in the distance but the evening, nought
   To point my footsteps further! At the thought,
A great black bird, Apollyon's bosom friend,
Sailed past, nor beat his wide wing dragon-penned
   That brushed my cap—perchance the guide I sought.

XXVIII
For, looking up, aware I somehow grew,
   'Spite of the dusk, the plain had given place
   All round to mountains—with such name to grace
Mere ugly heights and heaps now stolen in view.
How thus they had surprised me,—solve it, you!
   How to get from them was no clearer case.

XXIX
Yet half I seemed to recognize some trick
   Of mischief happened to me, God knows when—
   In a bad dream perhaps. Here ended, then,
Progress this way. When, in the very nick
Of giving up, one time more, came a click
   As when a trap shuts—you're inside the den!

   That great black bird is by no means likely to be bosom friend
to the Apollyon who in the Revelation of St. John the Divine (9:11)

is named "the angel of the bottomless pit." I know of only a few other effects in English poetry as sublimely stirring as the concluding stanzas of this poem:

XXX
Burningly it came on me all at once,
    This was the place! those two hills on the right
    Crouched like two bulls locked horn in horn in fight;
While to the left, a tall scalped mountain . . . Dunce,
Dotard, a-dozing at the very nonce,
    After a life spent training for the sight!

XXXI
What in the midst lay but the Tower itself?
    The round squat turret, blind as the fool's heart,
    Built of brown stone, without a counterpart
In the whole world. The tempest's mocking elf
Points to the shipman thus the unseen shelf
    He strikes on, only when the timbers start.

XXXII
Not see? because of night perhaps?—why, day
    Came back again for that! before it left,
    The dying sunset kindled through a cleft:
The hills, like giants at a hunting, lay,
Chin upon hand, to see the game at bay,—
    "Now stab and end the creature—to the heft!"

XXXIII
Not hear? when noise was everywhere! it tolled
    Increasing like a bell. Names in my ears
    Of all the lost adventurers my peers,—
How such a one was strong, and such was bold,

And such was fortunate, yet each of old
    Lost, lost! one moment knelled the woe of years.

XXXIV
There they stood, ranged along the hill-sides, met
    To view the last of me, a living frame
    For one more picture! in a sheet of flame
I saw them and I knew them all. And yet
Dauntless the slug-horn to my lips I set,
    And blew. *"Childe Roland to the Dark Tower came."*

From "burningly" at the start of stanza XXX through "in a sheet of flame / I saw them and I knew them all," you stand with Roland in what William Butler Yeats was to call the Condition of Fire. After training a lifetime so as to recognize your ultimate place of trial, you fail utterly to see where you are until it is too late. What or who is the ogre whom Roland now confronts? This magnificent poem tells you that there is no ogre, there is only the Dark Tower: "What in the midst lay but the Tower itself?" And the tower is a kind of Kafkan or Borgesian perplexity; it is windowless ("blind as the fool's heart") and is at once utterly commonplace, and yet unique. What rings Roland at the Tower are not ogres, but the shades of his forerunners, the band of brothers who set out upon the doomed quest. Roland was seeking, perhaps only half-unknowingly, not just failure, but a direct confrontation with all the failed questers before him. In the dying sunset he hears what seems a great bell tolling, but magnificently he rallies his will and courage for what should be his final moment. The slug-horn (the eighteenth-century boy poet–forger Thomas Chatterton had mistaken that spelling of *slogan* to mean a trumpet) is sounded defiantly, in the mode of Shelley's "trumpet of a prophecy" in the closing lines of his "Ode to the West Wind":

Drive my dead thoughts over the universe
Like withered leaves to quicken a new birth!
And, by the incantation of this verse,

Scatter, as from an unextinguished hearth
Ashes and sparks, my words among mankind!
Be through my lips to unawakened earth

The trumpet of a prophecy! O, Wind,
If Winter comes, can Spring be far behind?

Browning puts a period, not a colon, after "And blew," which evidently means that the concluding *"Childe Roland to the Dark Tower came"* is not the message of the slug-horn. Since this poem came to Browning in a nightmare, that may mean that the entire poem is cyclic, and that Roland must undergo it again and again. But I don't believe that the common reader takes it that way, and the common reader is right. Browning's greatest dramatic monologue does not resolve itself in cyclic despair, and the quester, though nihilistic and self-ruined, recovers honor in his final confrontation with all those who have failed at the Dark Tower before him. There is no ogre; there are only other selves, and the self. Exultation surges in the last four stanzas, and this glory is as much the sympathetic reader's as it is Childe Roland's. We have renewed and augmented the self, despite its despair, and its suicidal courting of failure. The depth of the poem's descent becomes an authentication of its final music of triumph.

Walt Whitman

The dramatic monologues of Tennyson and Browning represent one major mode of poetry: introspective and ultimately despairing of everything except the strong self and its powers of endurance and defiance. English poetic tradition, from Shakespeare's Hamlet and Milton's Satan on through Romanticism, shapes both "Ulysses" and "Childe Roland to the Dark Tower Came." The two great American contemporaries of Tennyson and Browning were Walt Whitman and Emily Dickinson, both originals, with a much more equivocal relationship to English tradition. If, as I maintain, a prime reason why we should read is to strengthen the self, then both Whitman and Dickinson are essential poets. The American religion of Self-Reliance, crucially invented by Ralph Waldo Emerson, triumphs in Whitman and Dickinson, in startlingly different ways. Emerson teaches self-trust: do not seek yourself outside yourself. Walt Whitman's *Song of Myself* is a direct consequence of Emerson's directive. More evasively, Emily Dickinson's lyrics carry Self-Reliance to a higher pitch of consciousness than nearly any other post-Shakespearean poetry.

In Shakespeare (as I have noted) the extraordinary consciousnesses excel at self-overhearing: Hamlet, Iago, Cleopatra, Prospero. Dickinson maintains this Shakespearean attribute, but Whitman frequently tries to go beyond it. The shock of overhearing yourself is that you apprehend an unexpected otherness. Whitman, particularly in *Song of Myself,* and in the *Sea-Drift* elegy "As I Ebb'd with the Ocean of Life," divides his being into three: my self, the "real me" or "Me myself," and my soul. This psychic cartography is highly original, and difficult to assimilate to the Freudian model, or to any other map of the mind. Yet it is one of the prime reasons why we should read Whitman, who is a subtle and nuanced poet, very unlike what most of his exegetes, past and present, take him to be.

Though he proclaims himself to be the poet of democracy, Whitman at his best and most characteristic is a difficult poet, hermetic and elitist. We need never doubt his love for his projected readers, but his self-portrayal frequently is a persona, a mask through which he sings. There is no single *real* Walt Whitman; the poet (as opposed to the man) is frequently more autoerotic than homoerotic, and much more "the solitary singer" than the cele-brant of the insulted and injured (though he takes care to be that also). I am not suggesting that Whitman is a sleight-of-hand man, but what he gives, his sense of democratic vistas, he sometimes takes away, his art being a shuttle. Yet there is always a richness; only he and Dickinson among American poets manifest the "florabundance" that Wallace Stevens later imitated in them.

We know (or think we know) Walt Whitman best as "Walt Whitman, one of the roughs, an American," but that is the persona or mask of the bard of *Song of Myself*. Whitman knew far better, because he is a surprisingly difficult poet, though he says otherwise. His work can *look* easy, but is delicate and evasive:

These come to me days and nights and go from me again,
But they are not the Me myself.

Apart from the pulling and hauling stands what I am,
Stands amused, complacent, compassionating, idle, unitary,
Looks down, is erect, or bends an arm on an impalpable certain rest,
Looking with side-curved head curious what will come next,
Both in and out of the game and watching and wondering at it.

As graceful as it is solitary, this charming "Me myself" is at peace, yet also is a touch wary of intrusion. Whitman begins *Song of Myself* with an embrace, more gymnosophical than homoerotic, between his outer self and his soul, which appears to be largely an enigma to him, but can be regarded as character or ethos in con-trast to personality or the rough "masculine" self. Yet the real me or "Me myself" can have only a negative relationship to the Whit-manian soul:

I believe in you my soul, the other I am must not abase itself to you,
And you must not be abased to the other.

"I" is the "Myself" of *Song of Myself*, or Whitman's poetic personality. "The other I am" is the "Me myself," his true, inner personality. Whitman fears mutual abasement between his character and his real self, who seem capable only of a master-slave relationship, sadomasochistic and ultimately destructive to both. The reader can surmise that "Walt Whitman, one of the roughs, an American" comes into being in order to prevent such an assured mutual destruction. Whitman knows his poetic persona very well, since (according to Vico) we know only what we ourselves have made. His inner self or "real me" he also knows, astonishingly well when we reflect how few among us have such knowledge. What Whitman scarcely knows is what he calls "my soul"; to "believe in" is not to know, but to take a leap of faith. The Whitmanian soul, rather like the perpetual soul of America, is an enigma, and the reader never feels that Whitman is comfortable with it, despite the harmonious embrace that opens *Song of Myself.* We come to feel that the "Me myself" is the best and oldest part of Whitman, going back before the Creation, whereas the soul belongs to nature, is the unknown element in nature. We learn explicitly by reading Whitman what so many Americans seem to know implicitly, that the American soul does not feel free unless it is alone, or "alone with Jesus," as our evangelicals put it. Whitman, who was his own Christ, nevertheless shared that impulse of the American soul, and converts it into what may be the greatest of his many varied powers, a strength that defies nature, in unison with his soul, as mutually they find their own strength:

Dazzling and tremendous how quick the sun-rise would kill me,
If I could not now and always send sun-rise out of me.

We also ascend dazzling and tremendous as the sun,
We found our own O my soul in the calm and cool of the day-break.

The movement from I, the persona Walt Whitman, to We, self and soul together, is the triumph of this sublime sunrise. Grandest of all American writers (surpassing even Emily Dickinson and Henry James), Whitman transcends the limitation of finding his own soul unknowable. Mastery is the issue between nature and Whitman, and the resolution here favors the poet. How to read this passage should emphasize the audacity of "now and always," an extraordinary declaration of titanic self-reliance. Now and always, I find the question "Why read?" yet more absorbing. A patient, deep reading of *Song of Myself* helps us to the truth that "the what is unknowable." A child asks Whitman: *What is the grass?* and the poet cannot answer: "I do not know what it is any more than he." And yet the not-knowing stimulates the poet to a wonderful series of similitudes:

I guess it must be the flag of my disposition, out of hopeful
    green stuff woven.

Or I guess it is the handkerchief of the Lord,
A scented gift and remembrancer designedly dropt,
Bearing the owner's name someway in the corners, that we
    may see and remark, and say *Whose?*

Or I guess the grass is itself a child, the produced babe
    of the vegetation.

Or I guess it is a uniform hieroglyphic,
And it means, Sprouting alike in broad zones and narrow zones,
Growing among black folks as among white,
Kanuck, Tuckahoe, Congressman, Cuff, I give them the
    same, I receive them the same.

And now it seems to me the beautiful uncut hair of graves.

Tenderly will I use you curling grass,
It may be you transpire from the breasts of young men,
It may be if I had known them I would have loved them,
It may be you are from old people, or from offspring taken
    soon out of their mothers' laps,
And here you are the mothers' laps.

This grass is very dark to be from the white heads of old mothers,
Darker than the colorless beards of old men,
Dark to come from under the faint red roofs of mouths.

"The flag of my disposition, out of hopeful green stuff woven" suggests that the fresh green is an emblem of what Ralph Waldo Emerson had termed "the Newness." By "the Newness," Emerson meant a transcendental influx of fresh spiritual energy. Such Newness, for Whitman, had ensued in the symbolic embrace between assumed self and unknown soul that opens his poem, and life's work. His relation to his soul is hopeful, but accepting of limits, in the Epicurean manner. *Leaves of Grass,* his enigmatic title, combines the leaf, a central metaphor of Western poetry, a Homeric acceptance of the brevity of an individual life, with the image from Isaiah and the Psalms of all flesh being as the grass, poignantly brief in duration. And yet the title, *Leaves of Grass,* transcends its somber intimations of mortality, and becomes an affirmation of a substance in us that prevails. "And limitless are leaves stiff or drooping in the fields," Whitman writes, just before his series of guesses as to "What is the grass?" The immense charm of the flirtatious "handkerchief of the Lord" yields to visions of the grass as itself a child, as a uniform hieroglyphic dissolving racial and social differences, and a wonderfully original yet Homeric "And now it seems to me the beautiful uncut hair of graves."

An American style, prophetic of Hemingway's, emerges from

the most surrealistic of these transmutations of the grass: "This grass is very dark to be from the white heads of old mothers." We need to read Whitman for the shock of new perspectives that he affords us, but also because he still prophesies the unresolved enigmas of the American consciousness. A world that becomes always more American also needs to read Whitman, not only to understand America, but to apprehend better exactly what it is in the process of becoming.

Dickinson, Brontë, Popular Ballads, and "Tom O'Bedlam"

Emily Dickinson, socially in the genteel tradition, breaks with much of the Western continuity of thought and culture in many of her strongest poems. She contrasts in this with her greatest contemporary, Whitman, who followed his mentor, Emerson, and who was an innovator primarily in form and in poetic stance. Dickinson, like Shakespeare and like William Blake, thought everything through again for herself. One has to read Dickinson prepared to struggle with her cognitive originality. The reward is unique, for Dickinson educates us to think more subtly, and with more awareness of how hard it is to break with conventions of response that have been deeply instilled into us.

So original is Dickinson that accurately categorizing her is nearly as impossible as categorizing Shakespeare. Are they Christian or nihilist poets? Shakespeare is hidden within his characters, and seems to take care that we should never know whether even Hamlet and Falstaff speak for him, or uniquely to him. Which of Dickinson's scores of strong poems particularly represent her agile and mobile consciousness? Her letters will not help to answer that (any more than they can aid in deciphering her psychosexuality), because they are not letters in any ordinary sense but rather prose poems, as shrewdly written as her lyrics.

The Resurrected Christ and Christ the Redeemer meant little to Dickinson; Christ's sufferings however were very close to her, and any suggestion of a triumph over suffering was even closer, suffering being one of her prime modes. Bible-soaked though never a formal Christian, Dickinson could write of herself as "Empress of Calvary" and "Bride of the Holy Ghost." These metaphors are ambiguous, and very much part of a personal myth that she insisted upon living, particularly in her final years. She read the Bible pretty much as she read Shakespeare and Dickens, in search of characters she could absorb into her own drama. So formidable an ironist is Dickinson that no part of that story can be interpreted at its face value. We have enough biographical data to see that Dickinson's is a drama of erotic loss: perhaps of Charles Wadsworth, and of her sister-in-law, Susan; more likely, of Samuel Bowles and of Judge Otis Phillips Lord. Yet even erotic loss is converted by Dickinson into images for poems. Of all these magnificences of human loss, I am most haunted by Poem 1260:

> Because that you are going
> And never coming back
> And I, however absolute
> May overlook your Track—
>
> Because that Death is final,
> However first it be,
> This instant be suspended
> Above Mortality—
>
> Significance that each has lived
> This other to detect
> Discovery not God himself
> Could now annihilate

Eternity, Presumption
The instant I perceive
That you, who were Existence
Yourself forgot to live—

The "Life that is" will then have been
A thing I never knew—
As Paradise fictitious
Until the Realm of you—

The "Life that is to be," to me,
A Residence too plain
Unless in my Redeemer's Face
I recognize your own—

Of Immortality who doubts
He may exchange with me
Curtailed by your obscuring Face
Of everything but He—

Of Heaven and Hell I also yield
The Right to reprehend
To whoso would commute this Face
For his less priceless Friend.

If "God is Love" as he admits
We think that he must be
Because he is a "jealous God"
He tells us certainly

If "All is possible with" him
As he besides concedes
He will refund us finally
Our confiscated Gods—

Whether Judge Lord is the particular instance of "Our confiscated Gods," we do not know, but any of us might cringe when we read: "That you, who were Existence / Yourself forgot to live." "Absolute" there might mean "perfect," that is to say "unmixed" and therefore "complete." One thinks of this fierce poem as absolute Dickinson: strong, uncompromising, and marching to the soul's own music. She calls upon her perhaps dying lover to be, for the poem's instant, "suspended / Above Mortality." Her quarrel is neither with death nor God, but at first with the departing beloved, and then with all of the traditional wisdom of comforting bereavement. A reader chanting this great poem out loud to herself may gain something of Dickinson's preternatural strength, which in part is a defiance of premature consolations. Yet the poem's largest powers are in its extraordinary self-reliance, in which Dickinson rivals Whitman and their common precursor, Ralph Waldo Emerson. Hymnlike, Poem 1260 strides through its ten quatrains with an achieved sense of what love has discovered, beyond the power even of an annihilating God.

The best analogue to Emily Dickinson's passionate authority is in the handful of enduring poems by Emily Brontë, the seer of *Wuthering Heights*:

> Often rebuked, yet always back returning
>   To those first feelings that were born with me,
> And leaving busy chase of wealth and learning
>   For idle dreams of things which cannot be:
>
> Today, I will seek not the shadowy region;
>   Its unsustaining vastness waxes drear;
> And visions rising, legion after legion,
>   Bring the unreal world too strangely near.
>
> I'll walk, but not in old heroic traces,
>   And not in paths of high morality,

And not among the half-distinguished faces,
  The clouded forms of long-past history.

I'll walk where my own nature would be leading—
  It vexes me to choose another guide—
Where the grey flocks in ferny glens are feeding,
  Where the wild wind blows on the mountainside.

What have those lonely mountains worth revealing?
  More glory and more grief than I can tell:
The earth that wakes one human heart to feeling
  Can centre both the worlds of Heaven and Hell.

This is essentially the visionary cosmos of heaven and hell in *Wuthering Heights,* where Heathcliff and the first Catherine share, in childhood, "those first feelings," a world at once "unreal" and yet also richer than any social reality. Emily Brontë subtly chooses a third realm, neither the "busy chase" that rebukes her nor "the shadowy region" of a sublime "unsustaining vastness." Instead she chooses to walk, by wild impulse, "where my own nature would be leading," something utterly her own, neither social nor purely visionary. Her "Stanzas" are difficult because they go neither the way of Wuthering Heights, nor of Thrushcross Grange, the opposing locales of her one novel. Her concern is only with "one human heart," her own, in its reception of revelation, not of creed but of the "lonely mountains." Her final image, audacious and vital, salutes her northern landscape as centering within her own creative spirit the antinomies of heaven and hell. At once as antinomian and self-reliant as Dickinson's "Because That You Are Going," Emily Brontë's stanzas suggest an even lonelier freedom than Emily Dickinson's, since Dickinson commemorates erotic loss while Brontë's romance is altogether visionary. Solitude is the state of the soul that Emily Dickinson and Emily Brontë passionately share.

The world of *Wuthering Heights* and of Emily Brontë's lyrics has much in common with that of the English and Scottish Popular Ballads, which share the creative exuberance of the wild freedom that pervades Emily Brontë's work, though the Popular Ballads are even more dramatic and abrupt in their effects. Brief narrative poems, always anonymous, the Ballads existed in all nations, and frequently passed from land to land. They came out of the later Middle Ages and were performed by singers of tales, but many were not written down until the eighteenth century. We have a body of poetry composed between roughly 1200 and 1700, no doubt severely revised in transition. Since they are among the best poems in English, they immensely reward reading, both for themselves and because they have been imitated by William Blake, Robert Burns, William Wordsworth, Samuel Taylor Coleridge, and John Keats, and later by D. G. Rossetti, William Morris, A. C. Swinburne, and, in the modern period, by Housman, Kipling, and Yeats.

Most of us have favorite ballads; I myself love best "Sir Patrick Spence":

> The king sits in Dumferling toune>,   town
>   Drinking the blude-reid> wine: blood-red
> "O whar> will I get a guid> sailor,   where / good
>   To sail this schip of mine?"

> Up and spak an eldern> knicht,   old
>   Sat at the king's richt> kne   right
> "Sir Patrick Spence is the best sailor,
>   That sails upon the se."

> The king has written a braid letter,
>   And signed it wi' his hand;
> And sent it to Sir Patrick Spence,
>   Was walking on the sand.

The first line that Sir Patrick red,
  A loud lauch> lauched he: laugh
The next line that Sir Patrick red,
  The teir> blinded his ee>.   tear / eye

"O wha> is this has don this deid>,   who / deed
  This ill deid don to me;
To send me out this time o' the yeir>,   year
  To sail upon the se!

"Mak haste, mak haste, my mirry men all,
  Our guid schip sails the morne."
"O say na sae>, my master deir>,   not so / dear
  For I feir> a deadlie storme.   fear

"Late, late yestreen> I saw the new moone   last evening
  Wi' the auld> moone in hir arme;   old
And I feir, I feir, my dear master,
  That we will cum to harme."

O our Scots nobles wer richt laith>   loath
  To weet> their cork-heil'd schoone;   wet
Bot lang owre a'> the play wer played,   ere all
  Thair hats they swam aboone.

O lang, lang may thair ladies sit
  Wi' thair fans into their hand,
Or eir> they se Sir Patrick Spence   before
  Com sailing to the land.

O lang, lang may the ladies stand
  Wi' thair gold kems> in their hair,   combs
Waiting for thair ain> deir lords,   own
  For they'll se thame> na mair>.   them / more

Haf owre>, haf owre to Aberdour,	halfway over
It's fiftie fadom deip>:	deep
And thair lies guid Sir Patrick Spence	
Wi' the Scots lords at his feit>.	feet

Coleridge, fascinated by "Sir Patrick Spence," used it as a model for his *Rime of the Ancient Mariner.* There is something prophetic of cinematic technique—of montage in particular—in the Popular Ballads, as in the sudden transition in the last line of stanza 3, and in the final line of stanza 8. As a narrative poem, "Sir Patrick Spence" could scarcely be bettered; the story vaults to its inevitable conclusion, and makes us wonder about the opening dialogue between the wine-drinking king and his elderly counselor. Certainly Sir Patrick, first laughing and then crying, judges the consequence of that dialogue to be a successful plot against his life.

The ballad leaps wonderfully from the dire presage of a deadly storm in stanza 7, to stanzas 8–10, thus excluding the actual shipwreck and drownings. High irony contrasts the finery of the drowned Scots nobles—the cork-heeled shoes they were reluctant to wet; their hats bobbing in the water—with the ornamental fans and golden combs of their widows. And the best stanza, a tribute to Sir Patrick, is reserved for the last: we end with a picture of the deep sea, and then a vision of the heroically dutiful Sir Patrick, with the Scots lords stationed where they should be, at the great seaman's feet.

I love "Sir Patrick Spence" because it has a tragic economy almost unique in its stoic heroism. There is a sense throughout the poem that heroism is necessarily self-destructive, and yet remains admirable. When I recite "Sir Patrick Spence" out loud to myself, I always think of the lonely heroism of Emily Dickinson and of Emily Brontë, both of whom learned the cost of their confirmation as imaginative creators.

One of the most poetically accomplished of the Popular Ballads is "The Unquiet Grave," which may have been written in the later eighteenth century, at least in the version I will quote:

> The wind doth blow today, my love,
>   And a few small drops of rain;
> I never had but one true-love,
>   In cold grave she was lain.
>
> I'll do as much for my true-love
>   As any young man may:
> I'll sit and mourn all at her grave
>   For a twelvemonth and a day.
>
> The twelvemonth and a day being up
>   The dead began to speak:
> "Oh who sits weeping on my grave
>   And will not let me sleep?"
>
> "'Tis I, my love, sits on your grave
>   And will not let you sleep;
> For I crave one kiss of your clay-cold lips
>   And that is all I seek."
>
> "You crave one kiss of my clay-cold lips,
>   But my breath smells earthy strong;
> If you have one kiss of my clay-cold lips
>   Your time will not be long.
>
> "'Tis down in yonder garden green,
>   Love, where we used to walk,
> The finest flower that ere was seen
>   Is withered to a stalk.
>
> "The stalk is withered dry, my love,
>   So will our hearts decay;

So make yourself content, my love,
    Till God calls you away."

The eloquent chill of this lovers' exchange is hard to match.
Many traditions tell us it is unsafe to maintain erotic mourning for
longer than a year, and "The Unquiet Grave" memorably enforces
such wisdom: just one day too much, and the lost beloved is startled out of her sleep. It is a kind of sinister delight that the bereaved
young man knows precisely what he risks, and also that his true
love offers him no illusions, but only fatality. No deception exists
on either side; only a mutual awareness that after a year and a day,
mourning is dangerous to the survivor and troublesome to the
dead. But that dark burden of meaning is somewhat at variance
with the sensual music of this deliciously unwholesome ballad.
The reader is at first shocked upon hearing the complaint "And
will not let me sleep." Still, this is equaled by the young man's grim
accuracy in craving one kiss of her clay-cold lips. The triple repetition of that "kiss of clay-cold lips" dominates the poem, and
heightens its strongest quatrain:

"You crave one kiss of my clay-cold lips,
    But my breath smells earthy strong;
If you have one kiss of my clay-cold lips
    Your time will not be long.

One wonders if this fatal woman had that direct a style of
truth-telling while she was still alive. This is no impersonal ghost
or undead speaking, but a personality of some considerable interest. Her theme is the death of love: in nature, in herself, and in her
lover, to whom she will give (at his knowing request) the kiss of
death. Love dies, hearts decay. She is superbly ironic: "So make
yourself content, my love," which refers to the kiss she is about to
grant. As in "Sir Patrick Spence," the intense irony of the ballad
tempers its otherwise enormous pathos.

Part of the fascination of the Popular Ballads is their anonymity. Not even the best among them is quite of the eminence of the greatest anonymous lyric in the language, "Tom O'Bedlam," first discovered in a commonplace book of about 1620, four years after the death of Shakespeare:

From the hag and hungry goblin
That into rags would rend ye,
The spirit that stands by the naked man
In the Book of Moons defend ye,
That of your five sound senses
You never be forsaken,
Nor wander from yourselves with Tom
Abroad to beg your bacon,
    While I do sing, Any food, any feeding,
    Feeding, drink, or clothing;
    Come dame or maid, be not afraid,
    Poor Tom will injure nothing.

Of thirty bare years have I
Twice twenty been enragèd,
And of forty been three times fifteen
In durance soundly cagèd
On the lordly lofts of Bedlam
With stubble soft and dainty,
Brave bracelets strong>, sweet whips ding dong   handcuffs
With wholesome hunger plenty,
    And now I sing, Any food, any feeding,
    Feeding, drink, or clothing;
    Come dame or maid, be not afraid,
    Poor Tom will injure nothing.

With a thought I took for Maudlin>   Magdalene or prostitute
And a cruse of cockle pottage>,   weed stew

With a thing thus tall, sky bless you all,
I befell into this dotage.
I slept not since the Conquest,
Till then I never wakèd,
Till the roguish boy of love where I lay
Me found and strip'd me nakèd.
    And now I sing, Any food, any feeding,
    Feeding, drink, or clothing;
    Come dame or maid, be not afraid,
    Poor Tom will injure nothing.

When I short have shorn my sow's face
And swigged my horny barrel>,   *leather flask*
In an oaken inn I pound> my skin   *impound or pawn*
As a suit of gilt apparel;
The moon's my constant mistress
And the lovely owl my marrow>;   *mate*
The flaming drake> and the night crow> make   *dragon / owl*
Me music to my sorrow.
    While I do sing, Any food, any feeding,
    Feeding, drink, or clothing;
    Come dame or maid, be not afraid,
    Poor Tom will injure nothing.

The palsy plagues my pulses
When I prig your pigs or pullen>,   *steal chicken*
Your culvers> take, or matchless make   *doves*
Your Chanticleer or Sullen>.   *rooster*
When I want provant> with Humphrey   *provender, food*
I sup, and when benighted,
I repose in Paul's> with waking souls   *St. Paul's Churchyard*
Yet never am affrighted.
    But I do sing, Any food, any feeding,
    Feeding, drink, or clothing;

Come dame or maid, be not afraid,
Poor Tom will injure nothing.

I know more than Apollo,
For oft when he lies sleeping
I see the stars at bloody wars
In the wounded welkin weeping;
The moon embrace her shepherd,
And the Queen of Love her warrior,
While the first doth horn the star of morn,
And the next the heavenly Farrier>.   Vulcan
    While I do sing, Any food, any feeding,
    Feeding, drink, or clothing;
    Come dame or maid, be not afraid,
    Poor Tom will injure nothing.

The gypsies, Snap and Pedro,
Are none of Tom's comradoes,
The punk> I scorn and the cutpurse> sworn, whore / pickpocket
And the roaring boy's> bravadoes.   street gangster
The meek, the white, the gentle
Me handle, touch, and spare not;
But those that cross Tom Rynosseross
Do what the panther dare not.
    Although I sing, Any food, any feeding,
    Feeding, drink, or clothing;
    Come dame or maid, be not afraid,
    Poor Tom will injure nothing.

With an host of furious fancies
Whereof I am commander,
With a burning spear and a horse of air,
To the wilderness I wander.
By a knight of ghosts and shadows

I summoned am to a tourney
Ten leagues beyond the wide world's end:
Methinks it is no journey.
    Yet will I sing, Any food, any feeding,
    Feeding, drink, or clothing;
    Come dame or maid, be not afraid,
    Poor Tom will injure nothing.

I mentioned this astonishing poem in relation to Browning's dramatic monologue "Childe Roland to the Dark Tower Came." "Tom O'Bedlam" is one of a number of "mad songs," though nothing else in the genre compares to it, not even the "Mad Song" of William Blake. Try chanting the poem aloud, repeatedly. Its surging power is deeply energizing for the attentive reader, and I strongly recommend the poem for memorization. The singer, supposedly a former inmate of Bedlam (Bethlehem Hospital, London), begs by protesting his harmlessness, tells a version of his personal history, and finally expresses a visionary perspective only rarely achieved in poetic history. I know few other poems that open with the speed, directness, and dramatic intensity of Tom O'Bedlam's song:

    From the hag and hungry goblin
    That into rags would rend ye,
    The spirit that stands by the naked man
    In the Book of Moons defend ye,
    That of your five sound senses
    You never be forsaken,
    Nor wander from yourselves with Tom
    Abroad to beg your bacon,
        While I do sing, Any food, any feeding,
        Feeding, drink, or clothing;
        Come dame or maid, be not afraid,
        Poor Tom will injure nothing.

The Book of Moons probably was a work of popular astrology, as current then as now, and the naked man might be Hermes, a frequent figure in such handbooks. Rent into rags by his madness, which he interprets as a spell put upon him by hag or by goblin, Tom yet invokes the visionary protection for us, his auditors, of the Hermetic naked man. The function of his song, for the reader, is to ward off madness, the condition described, with bitter irony, in the second stanza, with its memories of "the lordly lofts of Bedlam": handcuffs, whippings, near-starvation.

Whether the erotic element in Tom's "dotage" is imaginary or not, we cannot know, though for him it has become another vision: "With a thought I took for Maudlin" refers either to a particular Magdalene or prostitute, or to all womankind, but either way a pure phantasmagoria has prevailed in him:

> I slept not since the Conquest,
> Till then I never wakèd,
> Till the roguish boy of love where I lay
> Me found and strip'd me nakèd.

A victim of Cupid, though of no certain time or place, from the Norman Conquest of 1066 onwards, Tom sings of an eternal Romanticism, as little trapped in a particular era as was Shakespeare:

> The moon's my constant mistress
> And the lovely owl my marrow;
> The flaming drake and the night crow make
> Me music to my sorrow.

One can think of many Shakespearean plays where this could be sung and be altogether worthy of the context. The owl, or "night crow," is mated to Tom by the illumination of the meteor, the "flaming drake," and yet the moon remains the Bedlamite's "constant mistress," emblem of an unattainable love. Mixed in with the pathos of Tom's hungry life are moments of pure vision, Shakespearean and prophetic of Blake and of Shelley:

> I know more than Apollo,
> For oft when he lies sleeping
> I see the stars at bloody wars
> In the wounded welkin weeping;
> The moon embrace her shepherd,
> And the Queen of Love her warrior . . .

To know more than the sleeping sun god, Apollo, is also to know more than the rational. Tom looks up at the night sky of falling stars ("wounded welkin weeping") and contrasts these battles to the embraces of the moon, Diana, with her shepherd-lover Endymion, and of the planet Venus with her warrior, Mars. A mythological poet, Mad Tom is also a master of intricate images: the crescent moon enfolds the morning star within the crescent horns, while the Farrier, Vulcan, husband of Venus, is horned in quite another sense, being cuckolded by the lustful Mars. Once these allusions are absorbed, the stanza is magical in its effect, adding strangeness to beauty, a High Romantic formula that the anonymous poet of "Tom O'Bedlam" seems to have learned from Shakespeare. I think I hear Shakespeare himself in the extraordinary transitions of the next stanza, in the sudden tonal drop into tenderness of the fifth and sixth lines, followed by the defiant roar of lines seven and eight:

> The gypsies, Snap and Pedro,
> Are none of Tom's comradoes,
> The punk I scorn and the cutpurse sworn,
> And the roaring boy's bravadoes.
> The meek, the white, the gentle
> Me handle, touch, and spare not;
> But those that cross Tom Rynosseross
> Do what the panther dare not.

There is a marvelous pathos in "The meek, the white, the gentle / Me handle, touch, and spare not."

The poet of "Tom O'Bedlam" attains a visionary height in the brilliant final stanza, suggestive of Cervantes as well as Shakespeare. I can think of nothing else in the language where the spirits of Don Quixote and of Hamlet seem to meld:

> With an host of furious fancies
> Whereof I am commander,
> With a burning spear and a horse of air,
> To the wilderness I wander.
> By a knight of ghosts and shadows
> I summoned am to a tourney
> Ten leagues beyond the wide world's end:
> Methinks it is no journey.

Sometimes, when out walking, quite involuntarily this stanza returns to me, and if I am alone, I recite it. In itself, this proudly self-conscious closure is a touchstone for poetic quality. Hamlet, summoned to revenge by "a knight of ghosts and shadows," would have preferred a Quixotic tourney, "Ten leagues beyond the wide world's end." Death, to Hamlet, was that undiscovered country from whose bourn, or limit, no traveler returned. With Mad Tom, Hamlet might have said of a more visionary summons: "Methinks it is no journey."

William Shakespeare

"Tom O'Bedlam," if it can be bettered at all, as poetry, would have to find its rivals in the sonnets and plays of William Shakespeare. Later in this book I will discuss at some length how to read *Hamlet,* here I turn to a few of the Sonnets. Since Shakespeare was, as Borges said, everyone and no one, we can say of the Sonnets that they are, at once, autobiographical and universal, personal and impersonal, ironical and passionate, bisexual and heterosexual, wounded and integral. This is a good place to warn the reader against the increasingly useless literary dogma that the "I" speaking a poem is always a mask or persona, rather than a human being. The "I" of Shakespeare's Sonnets is the playwright-actor William Shakespeare, creator of Falstaff, Hamlet, Rosalind, Iago, and Cleopatra. When we read the Sonnets we are listening to a dramatic voice, one both like and unlike Hamlet's. The unlikeness is that we are listening to Shakespeare himself, who is not entirely his own creation. Yet there remains a similarity between "Will" in the Sonnets and Hamlet or Falstaff; Shakespeare ruefully rough-hews his self-presentation, even if he cannot wholly shape it. The meditative voice of the Sonnets takes great care to distance itself from its own suffering, sometimes even from its own humiliation. We hear a story in the Sonnets that could be called betrayal, and yet we never hear of the death of love, though there is every reason why it ought to die.

Of all literature's uncanny effects, to me the uncanniest is Shakespeare's balance, in the Sonnets, between self-alienation and self-affirmation.

'Tis better to be vile than vile esteemed,
When not to be receives reproach of being,
And the just pleasure lost, which is so deemed
Not by our feeling, but by others' seeing.
For why should others' false adulterate eyes
Give salutation to my sportive blood?
Or on my frailties why are frailer spies,
Which in their wills count bad what I think good?
No, I am that I am, and they that level
At my abuses reckon up their own;
I may be straight though they themselves be bevel.
By their rank thoughts my deeds must not be shown.

Unless this general evil they maintain:
All men are bad and in their badness reign.

This is Sonnet 121 in a sequence of 154; we do not know whether Shakespeare himself arranged them in their present order, but it seems likely. We are nearing the end of the 126 sonnets addressed to a fair young nobleman, presumably Shakespeare's patron (some think also his lover), the Earl of Southampton. One might want to recommend this sonnet to President William Jefferson Clinton, but will have no occasion to do so. It is the most powerful expression in the language of being condemned for erotic activity by the "false adulterate eyes" of others who "themselves be bevel," that is to say, crooked, and I wish the poem could have been read aloud, frequently, on television during our recent national orgy of virtue alarmed, as manifested by talking heads and congressmen. But my concern is how to read it as well as why, so I turn to a closer examination of its magnificently charged diction.

By "vile" Shakespeare may intend a state of moral baseness, yet the word (as he knew) held in it the notion of being cheap, of low value or price, and so there may be an overtone of social inferiority as well. Part of the complexity of the opening quatrain turns upon "which is so deemed." Is the reference to "vile" or to "the just pleasure"? Shakespeare deliberately allows this to be ambiguous, and so we must read it both ways. The bitter irony of "'Tis better to be vile than vile esteemed, / When not to be receives reproach of being" partly means that one may as well be debased in one's behavior, because even if one is actually virtuous, others will see it differently. They will deem one vile, which will end the pleasure one's love ought to give. Yet the other reading is more interesting, because even more ironically bitter. "Just pleasure" can be deemed such by observers, but that will be their judgment, and not Shakespeare's, who knows that his love is chaste. Nothing in the remaining ten lines of Sonnet 121 will resolve this ambiguity.

The beholders are mocked for their mockery, when they intrusively "give salutation to my sportive blood," as if they were cheering Shakespeare on to his supposed sexual performance, which they make into their spectator sport. More advanced in their frailties than those they salute in Shakespeare, they are guilty of ill will, whether they are counting as bad an innocent relationship or moralizing against an actual liaison. Again, Shakespeare does not tell us exactly what he wants us to believe. Instead, he startles us with an extraordinary declaration: "No, I am that I am." Shakespeare, and his readers then and now, could not miss the allusion to Exodus 3:14, where Moses requests Yahweh's name, and Yahweh replies: "I am that I am." In the Hebrew, *ehyeh asher ehyeh*—that is an audacious pun upon Yahweh, as a name, and literally means something like "I will be [wherever and whenever] I will be." Shakespeare presumably did not know that, and so probably his "No, I am that I am" primarily means "I am what I am," but by way of a considerable blasphemy. Shakespeare himself did not publish the Sonnets, and 121 just may be an independent poem, with no necessary reference to any homoerotic relationship with the fair young nobleman. We do not know, and the poem may be stronger for it. As in his sublimely rancid farewell to comedy, *Measure for Measure,* Shakespeare neither endorses nor denies the dark formula: *All men are bad and in their badness reign.*

Anger becomes controlled frenzy in the superb Sonnet 129, a lament that only hints at betrayal by the famous and nameless Dark Lady of the Sonnets:

> Th' expense of spirit in a waste of shame
> Is lust in action; and, till action, lust
> Is perjured, murd'rous, bloody, full of blame,
> Savage, extreme, rude, cruel, not to trust;
> Enjoyed no sooner but despisèd straight;
> Past reason hunted, and no sooner had,
> Past reason hated as a swallowed bait
> On purpose laid to make the taker mad;

Mad in pursuit, and in possession so;
Had, having, and in quest to have, extreme;
A bliss in proof, and proved, a very woe,
Before, a joy proposed; behind, a dream.
 All this the world well knows, yet none knows well
 To shun the heaven that leads men to this hell.

The furious energy of this is almost a drumroll, a litany for desire that prophesies only further desire, further erotic disaster. There are no personages in this poem; the fair youth is far off, and even the Dark Lady is present only by implication. Lust is the hero-villain of this night-piece of the spirit, male lust for the "hell" that concludes the sonnet, *hell* being Elizabethan-Jacobean slang for the vagina. The ancient commonplace of sadness-after-coition achieves its apotheosis in Sonnet 129, but at more than the expense of spirit. So impacted is this sonnet's language that it evades its apparent adherence to the Renaissance belief that each sexual act shortens a man's life. The reader may hear in Sonnet 129 an intimation of venereal disease in that "hell," foreshadowing a Shakespearean preoccupation in many of the plays, *Troilus and Cressida* and *Timon of Athens* in particular. That seems the final burden also of the more-than-ironic Sonnet 144:

Two loves I have, of comfort and despair,
Which like two spirits do suggest me still;
The better angel is a man right fair,
The worser spirit a woman colored ill.
To win me soon to hell, my female evil
Tempteth my better angel from my side,
And would corrupt my saint to be a devil,
Wooing his purity with her foul pride.
And whether that my angel be turned fiend
Suspect I may, yet not directly tell;
But being both from me, both to each friend,

I guess one angel in another's hell.
    Yet this shall I ne'er know, but live in doubt,
    Till my bad angel fire my good one out.

"Suggest me still" means something like "tempt me perpetually." The fair, young "better angel" is clearly not renowned for his purity, and "the devil in hell" is vernacular for copulation. "Guess" is laconic, as no guess is involved, while "Till my bad angel fire my good one out" refers less to the end of that affair, than to the bestowal of syphilis upon the youth by the Dark Lady, with an implication that Shakespeare has already received that gift from her.

Why read Sonnet 144? Shakespeare's ironies and lyric genius certainly give the reader more pleasure in scores of the other sonnets, but the subdued yet terrifying pathos of the poem is a unique aesthetic value, troublingly memorable and all but universal in its suggestiveness. The sonnets are a unique element in Shakespeare's awesome achievement. It is appropriate that the central Western writer, inventor of the human as we continue to know it, should also be the most piercing lyric and meditative poet in the English language. I do not believe that we necessarily come to know the inner or innermost Shakespeare in the Sonnets, where he seems to veil himself quite as enigmatically as he does in the plays. Walt Whitman, as we've seen, presents us with three metaphors of his being: my self, my soul, the real me or me myself. There are nearly as many metaphors of Shakespeare's being in the Sonnets as there are sonnets. Somehow Shakespeare contrives to make all of these images of self persuasive yet tentative. His questioning tribute to the fair young nobleman at the start of Sonnet 53 might better be asked of Shakespeare himself:

What is your substance, whereof are you made,
That millions of strange shadows on you tend?

John Milton

Though I have space here only for a brief account of Milton's *Paradise Lost*, I feel that a book on how to read and why ought to say something useful about the greatest poet, after Chaucer and Shakespeare, in the English language. Satan, the hero-villain of *Paradise Lost*, is a very Shakespearean character, whose "sense of injured merit," at being passed over by God for Christ, clearly echoes Iago's psychic wound at being passed over by Othello for Cassio. Macbeth and Hamlet also filter into Satan. Shelley remarked that the devil owed everything to Milton; he could have added that Milton's devil owed a great deal to Shakespeare. *Adam Unparadised* was to have been a stage tragedy about the Fall, as Milton originally conceived what instead became the epic *Paradise Lost*. I suspect that Milton encountered the strange shadows of Shakespeare's hero-villains and drew back, realizing that the English heroic epic was still open to him, but that tragic drama in English had been usurped forever.

The late C. S. Lewis, revered by many American Fundamentalists as the author of the dogmatic tract *Mere Christianity*, advised the reader of *Paradise Lost* to begin with "a Good Morning's Hatred of Satan." That, in my own judgment, is *not* how to start reading *Paradise Lost*. Milton was not as heretical as Christopher Marlowe or William Blake, but he was clearly a "sect of one" and a very heretical Protestant indeed. He was a Mortalist, and believed that the soul and body died together, and would be resurrected together, and he also denied the orthodox account of creation out of nothing. *Paradise Lost* identifies energy with spirit; Satan abounds in both, but then so does Iago. And so, overwhelmingly, does John Milton, though he takes care to make his Satan both his double and his parody. One could argue ironically, against C. S. Lewis and other churchwardenly critics, that Satan is a more orthodox Christian (however inverted) than Milton is. Satan does not identify energy with spirit, even though he incarnates their melding, but cries: "Evil be thou my good!" One would expect Milton, very nearly a Muggletonian (a visionary, radical sect of heretical Protestants), to have slyly made Satan both authentically heroic (more in the Shakespearean than the classical mode) and also a scheming Papist, with a low view of both human and angelic nature.

How to read the splendid Satan is the key to opening *Paradise Lost,* which to most current readers may seem like a vast work of science fiction performed in cosmic cinema. The great Russian film director Sergey Eisenstein first pointed out how prophetic of cinema *Paradise Lost* is, since the poem brilliantly exploits montage. I passionately love *Paradise Lost,* but worry whether it will survive our visual age of information, where only Shakespeare, Dickens, and Jane Austen seem able to survive television and cinematic treatment. Milton requires mediation; he is learned, allusive, and profound. Like James Joyce and Borges in our century, blindness helped to stimulate both a baroque verbal richness and a visual clarity, neither of which are easily transferable to the screen. The blurred montages of our cinema would not accommodate *Paradise Lost.*

Primarily Milton, more than ever, needs mediation for the common reader because his characters, despite their Shakespearean colorings, are not recognizable human beings, as in Shakespeare and Jane Austen. Nor are they grand Dickensian grotesques. Either they are gods and angels, or idealized humans (Adam, Eve, the Samson of *Samson Agonistes*). Here is Satan at his most impressive: He wakes up, on a burning lake in Hell, to find himself surrounded by his stunned and traumatized followers. He, with them, has been defeated by Christ in the War in Heaven. Milton's Christ, a kind of General Patton leading an angelic armored attack, has mounted the flaming Chariot of Paternal Deity, a cosmological version of the Israeli Merkabah tank, and with fire and fury has thrown the rebel angels out into the Abyss. When the flaming fallen angels hit bottom, the impact burns Hell into the realm of what had been Chaos. The reader is to conceive of her own sensations were she waking up with Satan and his catastrophic legions in so sublimely uncomfortable a condition! She will then better admire Satan's authentic heroism, when he returns to consciousness and regards the blasted features of his lover Beelzebub (the Miltonic angels are androgynous, fallen and unfallen).

Contemplating Beelzebub, Satan has to overcome, with superb immediacy, a narcissistic crisis, since Milton makes clear that Satan had been the most beautiful of the angels. If the beloved Beelzy now looks like Hell, what do I look like? Satan must be thinking it, but as a heroic (though defeated) general, he will not say it:

> If thou beest he; but O how fall'n how chang'd
> From him, who in the happy Realms of Light
> Cloth'd with transcendent brightness didst outshine
> Myriads though bright: If he whom mutual league,
> United thoughts and counsels, equal hope
> And hazard in the Glorious Enterprize,
> Joynd with me once, now misery hath joynd
> In equal ruin: into what Pit thou seest
> From what highth fall'n, so much the stronger prov'd
> He with his Thunder: and till then who knew
> The force of those dire Arms? yet not for those,
> Nor what the Potent Victor in his rage
> Can else inflict, do I repent or change,
> Though chang'd in outward lustre; that fixt mind
> And high disdain, from sense of injur'd merit,
> That with the mightiest rais'd me to contend,
> And to the fierce contention brought along
> Innumerable force to Spirits arm'd
> That durst dislike his reign, and me preferring,
> His utmost power with adverse power oppos'd

In dubious Battle on the Plains of Heav'n,
And shook his throne. What though the field be lost?
All is not lost; th' unconquerable Will,
And study of revenge, immortal hate,
And courage never to submit or yield:
And what is else not to be overcome?
That Glory never shall his wrath or might
Extort from me. To bow and sue for grace
With suppliant knee, and deifie his power,
Who from the terrour of this Arm so late
Doubted his Empire, that were low indeed,
That were an ignominy and shame beneath
This downfall; since by Fate the strength of Gods
And this Empyreal substance cannot fail,
Since through experience of this great event
In Arms not worse, in foresight much advanc't,
We may with more successful hope resolve
To wage by force or guile eternal Warr
Irreconcileable, to our grand Foe,
Who now triumphs, and in th' excess of joy
Sole reigning holds the Tyranny of Heav'n.

Miltonic scholars who consider themselves to be of God's party (the pompous, tyrannical God who appears as a character in *Paradise Lost,* but who is *not* Milton's own, heretical vision of God) always comment on this passage by saying it is untrue. If God's throne shook, it was the effect of Christ's ferocious armored attack. This orthodox argument has its own charm, but Satan is in despair, as any defeated commander would be, and his hyperbole is therefore understandable. What is best in his grand oration is not hyperbolical:

And courage never to submit or yield:
And what is else not to be overcome?

119

That is to say: the field *is* lost, but courage remains, and what else matters provided one does not acknowledge being overcome? You can deny heroism to Satan, if you are a partisan of Milton's God, but not if you are Milton's authentic reader. Milton himself editorializes that Satan is "vaunting aloud," but acknowledges that the apostate angel is in pain. The "sense of injur'd merit" is no more to be scoffed at in Satan than in Iago. Satan has considerably less genius than Iago, yet works on a grander scale, bringing down all mankind rather than one brave but limited general.

I have acknowledged that the common reader now requires mediation to read *Paradise Lost* with full appreciation, and I fear that relatively few will make the attempt. This is a great sorrow, and true cultural loss. Why read so difficult and so erudite an epic poem? One could make the merely historical plea; Milton is as much the central Protestant poet as Dante is the central poet-prophet of Catholicism. Our culture and sensibility, even our religion, in the United States are in many subtle respects more post-Protestant than Protestant, yet hardly to be comprehended without some clear sense of the Protestant spirit. That spirit achieved its apotheosis in *Paradise Lost,* and an adventurous reader would be well counseled to brave the difficulties.

William Wordsworth

If you read modern poetry at all, then in some sense you have read William Wordsworth, even if you have never read him. But everyone (who still reads) ought to read Wordsworth, and not only because he has influenced nearly every poet writing in English after him (again, whether they have read him or not). If you were asked, or commanded, to write a poem, most likely it would turn upon yourself, rather than upon some subject external to the self. William Hazlitt, who was Wordsworth's younger contemporary (and whose personal feelings towards Wordsworth were mixed), understood the poet's wonderful originality:

> He takes a subject or a story merely as pegs or loops to hang thought and feeling on; the incidents are trifling, in proportion to his contempt for imposing appearances; the reflections are profound, according to the gravity and aspiring pretensions of his mind.

The aspirations of Wordsworth's mind indeed were crucial; he distrusted the bodily eye, "the most tyrannical of our senses," and relied always upon the power of his imagination. This might have been less than successful had Wordsworth not had a preternatural gift for emotional accuracy:

> A slumber did my spirit seal;
>   I had no human fears:
> She seemed a thing that could not feel
>   The touch of earthly years.
>
> No motion has she now, no force;
>   She neither hears nor sees;
> Rolled round in earth's diurnal course
>   With rocks, and stones, and trees.

Wordsworthian "nature" is not very naturalistic, but rather a spirit that beckons us to sublime intimations, or else to terrors, as in this remarkable lyric of loss, which stops well short of transcendence. This is one of the five "Lucy" poems, which Wordsworth himself never grouped as a sequence. They elegize (probably) Margaret Hutchinson, the younger sister of Mary, whom Wordsworth married, and of Sara, whom Coleridge wished to marry but could not (being married already). Margaret Hutchinson died in 1796, in her early twenties, and evidently was, at least in Wordsworthian imagination, a lost or unfulfilled love.

The lyric's first stanza describes the young woman as a visionary being "that could not feel / The touch of earthly years." The reader will experience the shock, well-nigh traumatic, as the second stanza opens. In a sense, Margaret Hutchinson remains, as she was, a visionary figure; Wordsworth cannot bring himself to say, literally, that she has died. Daily the earth rolls round in its course, and her buried remnants roll "With rocks, and stones, and trees." Is the poet too numb to express his grief? Trauma seems the principal affect of the poem, and yet that might be only a label by which we push the poem aside.

How to read this "Lucy" poem, and read it well, is a considerable exercise in patience and receptivity, yet also an exercise in pleasure. The poet Shelley, who was in some respects Wordsworth's involuntary disciple, once defined the poetic Sublime as an experience that persuaded readers to give up easier pleasures for more difficult pleasures. Since the reading of the best poems, stories, novels, and plays necessarily constitutes more difficult pleasure than most of what is given to us visually by television, films, and video games, Shelley's definition is crucial to this book. The second stanza of "A Slumber Did My Spirit Seal" is an economical venture into the poetic Sublime. "The Sublime," as a literary notion, originally meant "lofty," in an Alexandrian treatise on style, supposedly composed by the critic Longinus. Later, in the eighteenth century, the Sublime began to mean a visible loftiness in nature and art alike, with aspects of power, freedom, wildness, intensity, and the possibility of terror. Something of that idea of the Sublime has gotten into Wordsworth's curious elegy for Margaret Hutchinson. Motion and force belong to the daily movement of the earth; Margaret now has the status of rocks, and stones, and trees. This is not a consolation, and yet it opens to a larger process of which the death of one lovely young woman forms just a part.

Let us try another short poem by Wordsworth, equally celebrated but less Sublime:

My heart leaps up when I behold
   A rainbow in the sky:
So was it when my life began;
So is it now I am a man;
So be it when I shall grow old,
   Or let me die!
The Child is Father of the Man;
And I could wish my days to be
Bound each to each by natural piety.

"My Heart Leaps Up," remarkable in itself, is also the seed of the great *Ode: Intimations of Immortality from Recollections of Early Childhood,* where Wordsworth employs as an epigraph the last three lines of this fragment (if it is that). "My Heart Leaps Up," remembering that Noah's covenant with Yahweh was symbolized by the rainbow, employs the rainbow to celebrate another covenant, the continuity in Wordsworth's consciousness of self. Certainly this little poem is simple both in structure and in language, but the reader can come to uncover some perplexities in it. The child's ecstatic rainbow is primary, almost instinctive. "So is it now I am a man" is necessarily secondary, since it depends upon memory of the child's joy. "So be it when I shall grow old" is clearly tertiary, since it depends both upon memory and the renewal of memory. The shock of the poem commences with "Or let me die!" Wordsworth does not wish to survive if his days—past, present, and future—cannot be "Bound each to each" in the double sense of *bound* as "connected" and as "bond" or covenant. "Or let me die!" testifies both to a potential despair and a desperation for faith, the belief in his own poetic election that Wordsworth perhaps misleadingly calls "natural piety," by which he does not mean the "natural religion" of the Enlightenment that opposed natural reason to revelation. William Blake, reacting to Wordsworth's misnomer, memorably snapped: "There is no such

Thing as Natural Piety Because the Natural Man is at Enmity with God."

Wordsworth's reply to Blake probably is implicit in the one line of "My Heart Leaps Up" we have not considered, the flat paradox "The Child is Father of the Man." Sigmund Freud would have had little trouble with that formulation, but Wordsworth may mean by it a rather un-Freudian irony. Noah, seeing the rainbow, accepted it as the sign of the covenant: no more floods, and the blessing of more life on into a time without boundaries. Wordsworth, though he borrows the Yahwistic sign, intends the survival of his poetic gift, which depends upon the renewal of the child's joy. Memory, Wordsworth's great resource, is also his source of poetic anxiety. He will have to go on questing for evidences of poetic election, which became very scarce after 1807, when he was just thirty-seven. Wordsworth lived another forty-three years, and wrote very bad poetry indeed, by the ream. His superb originality, and his subsequent decline, between them set the parameters for modern poetry.

Samuel Taylor Coleridge

Wordsworth's closest friend was Samuel Taylor Coleridge, poet, critic, philosopher, lay theologian, political theorist, and occasional plagiarist. His great poem is the 625-line ballad in seven parts: *The Rime of the Ancient Mariner.* This magnificent nightmare of a ballad remains one of the essential poems, yielding pleasures that a good reader may not find elsewhere.

At the root of Coleridge's poem is the popular ballad "The Wandering Jew," but the Ancient Mariner has more in common with Franz Kafka's characters in "The Hunter Gracchus" or "A Country Doctor" than with the traditional mocker of Christ. In literature prior to Coleridge, the Ancient Mariner's ancestors are Shakespeare's Iago and Milton's Satan. Between Coleridge and

Kafka there are Poe's Pym, Melville's Ahab, and Dostoevsky's Svidrigailov and Stavrogin. After Kafka come Gide, Camus, Borges, and many others, for Coleridge's magically eloquent ballad is the centerpiece of the Western tradition of the gratuitous crime, the "motiveless malignity" that Coleridge (wrongly, I think) attributed to Iago.

The ship upon which the Mariner serves is storm-driven towards the south pole, and is trapped in a frozen sea. An albatross comes to the aid of the ship, is hailed and fed by the crew, and magically causes the ice to split, saving everyone. Domesticated, the albatross stays with the ship, until the Ancient Mariner, altogether gratuitously, shoots the albatross with his crossbow. After that, we accompany the Mariner and crew in their descent into Hell.

The bald summary omits not less than everything that poetically matters, since Coleridge achieves a unique art:

> "And now there came both mist and snow,
> And it grew wondrous cold:
> And ice, mast-high, came floating by,
> As green as emerald.
>
> "And through the drifts the snowy clifts
> Did send a dismal sheen:
> Nor shapes of men nor beasts we ken—
> The ice was all between.

This is superb phantasmagoria, mediated for us by the unimaginative Mariner, who can see and describe admirably, yet rarely knows what it is he sees. Coleridge wants it that way; we are dependent upon the Ancient Mariner, a literalist adrift in what Coleridge called "a work of pure imagination." The wretched Mariner becomes a fundamentalist of what we now like to call ecology:

> He prayeth best who loveth best
> All things both great and small;
> For the dear God who loveth us,
> He made and loveth all.

That is the moral as the Mariner sees it; since he is crazed and monomaniac, we need not identify him with Coleridge. Here actually we have Coleridge's own support. When the celebrated Bluestocking (or premature feminist critic) Mrs. Barbauld objected to Coleridge that the poem lacked a moral, the poet replied brilliantly:

> I told her that in my own judgment the poem had too much; and that the only or chief fault, if I might say so, was the obtrusion of the moral sentiment so openly on the reader as a principle or cause of action in a work of pure imagination. It ought to have had no more moral than the *Arabian Nights'* tale of the merchant's sitting down to eat dates by the side of a well and throwing the shells aside, and lo! a genie starts up and says he *must* kill the aforesaid merchant *because* one of the date shells had, it seems, put out the eye of the genie's son.

Now *there* is your truly gratuitous crime, and one feels Coleridge, a third of a century after writing his greatest poem, would have done it even more wickedly. But it is quite sublimely wicked enough, if we learn to trust the tale, and *not* its ancient teller. Do not shoot albatrosses, and don't scatter your date shells, and still you will go down to Hell in your ship of death:

> All in a hot and copper sky,
> The bloody Sun, at noon,
> Right up above the mast did stand,
> No bigger than the Moon.
>
> Day after day, day after day,
> We stuck, nor breath nor motion;

As idle as a painted ship
Upon a painted ocean.

Water, water, every where,
And all the boards did shrink;
Water, water, every where,
Nor any drop to drink.

The very deep did rot: O Christ!
That ever this should be!
Yea, slimy things did crawl with legs
Upon the slimy sea.

If you compare these four stanzas to the two I quoted earlier concerning the emerald ice, then clearly the wretched crew is worse off, but only in degree. Being in a cosmos of glare ice is hellish enough, even though it lacks the grisly panache of "Yea, slimy things did crawl with legs / Upon the slimy sea."

My suggestion is that the Mariner, and his poem, were compulsive enough *before* he murdered the amiable albatross. What the reader will grasp is that we indeed are in a poem of "pure imagination" from the start, so that the entire voyage is necessarily visionary. But *why* does the Ancient Mariner murder the humanized albatross? He is shockingly passive throughout, not least when he performs the slaughter. His only other actions are to drink his own blood in order to cry out that he has seen a sail, and later when he delivers a single blessing. He is reminiscent of Swift's Lemuel Gulliver and Defoe's Robinson Crusoe; like them, the Mariner seems an accurate observer who is lacking in affect and in sensibility. I once believed that Coleridge's protagonist was desperately trying to establish a self by his gratuitous crime, but I no longer find any evidence for so "modernist" a view. After all, the Ancient Mariner at the close of the poem does not have any heightened sense of his identity. He is a machine for dictating always the one story.

As Coleridge later observed, there is no moral, and ought not to be. There is then no answer to the question as to *why* the albatross was slain. I urge the reader not to baptize the poem; it isn't about Original Sin and the Fall of Man. Those involve disobedience and depravity; *The Rime of the Ancient Mariner* is not *Paradise Lost*. In a way, Coleridge's poem is Shakespearean in its detachment of tone, while its visionary language sometimes has an affinity to the chant "Tom O'Bedlam":

> The moving Moon went up the sky,
> And no where did abide:
> Softly she was going up,
> And a star or two beside—
>
> Her beams bemocked the sultry main,
> Like April hoar-frost spread;
> But where the ship's huge shadow lay,
> The charmed water burnt alway
> A still and awful red.
>
> Beyond the shadow of the ship,
> I watched the water-snakes:
> They moved in tracks of shining white,
> And when they reared, the elfish light
> Fell off in hoary flakes.
>
> Within the shadow of the ship
> I watched their rich attire:
> Blue, glossy green, and velvet black,
> They coiled and swam; and every track
> Was a flash of golden fire.
>
> O happy living things! No tongue
> Their beauty might declare:

A spring of love gushed from my heart,
And I blessed them unaware:
Sure my kind saint took pity on me,
And I blessed them unaware.

The self-same moment I could pray;
And from my neck so free
The Albatross fell off, and sank
Like lead into the sea.

This is not only the resolution of *The Rime of the Ancient Mariner* (insofar as it can have one) but poetically it is also the strongest effect that Coleridge achieved. The Mariner, elsewhere so desperately inadequate, is so moved by the beauty and apparent happiness of the water snakes that he blesses them, in his heart, and attains whatever liberation from his curse that will be available to him. The sympathetic reader, enjoying the *Rime* for its intricate addition of strangeness to beauty, will emerge from this dark voyage with an enhanced sense of freedom, another reason why we should read.

Shelley and Keats

Shelley and Keats were very different poets, and were not quite friends (Keats being suspicious of Shelley's wealth and flamboyant career), but are forever linked by Shelley's *Adonais,* his elegy for Keats. They are the last poets I will consider at any length in this book, since I must content myself with some briefer observations on the twentieth-century poets I most admire: W. B. Yeats, D. H. Lawrence, Wallace Stevens, and Hart Crane.

On Shelley, I will confine myself to a few passages from his superb, unfinished death poem, *The Triumph of Life,* which seems to me as close as anyone has come to persuading us that this is how Dante would sound had the poet of *The Divine Comedy* composed in English. *The Triumph of Life* is an infernal vision, a fragment of about 550 lines in Dantesque *terza rima,* and in my judgment is the most despairing poem, of true eminence, in the language. Shelley, in his final days though only twenty-nine, gives us his vision of human nature and destiny before he sails on his final voyage, to a death by drowning, whether accidental or not we still do not certainly know. The most High Romantic of all poets, Shelley abandons *The Triumph of Life* to us, his readers, as his testament, one that would bewilder and depress us were it not for its augmented poetic power.

Methought I sate beside a public way

   Thick strewn with summer dust, & a great stream
Of people there was hurrying to & fro
   Numerous as gnats upon the evening gleam,

All hastening onward, yet none seemed to know
   Whither he went, or whence he came, or why
He made one of the multitude, and so

   Was borne amid the crowd as through the sky
One of the million leaves of summer's bier.—
   Old age & youth, manhood & infancy,

Mixed in one mighty torrent did appear,
   Some flying from the thing they feared & some
Seeking the object of another's fear,

   And others as with steps towards the tomb
Pored on the trodden worms that crawled beneath,
   And others mournfully within the gloom

Of their own shadow walked, and called it death . . .
　　And some fled from it as it were a ghost,
Half fainting in the affliction of vain breath.

　　But more with motions which each other crost
Pursued or shunned the shadows the clouds threw
　　Or birds within the noonday ether lost,

Upon that path where flowers never grew;
　　And weary with vain toil & faint thirst
Heard not the fountains whose melodious dew

　　Out of their mossy cells forever burst
Nor felt the breeze which from the forest told
　　Of grassy paths, & wood lawns interspersed

With overreaching elms & caverns cold,
　　And violet banks where sweet dreams brood, but they
Pursued their serious folly as of old . . .

This Dance of Death is the "serious folly" of our competitive
lives: "with motions which each other crost." *The Triumph of Life*
is a bitterly ironic title, since the "life" that triumphs over all of us
in this poem is death-in-life, annihilator of all individuality and
integrity:

　　And as I gazed, methought that in the way
The throng grew wilder, as the woods of June
　　When the South wind shakes the extinguished day.—

And a cold glare, intenser than the noon
　　But icy cold, obscured with light
The Sun as he the stars. Like the young moon—

When on the sunlit limits of the night
Her white shell trembles amid crimson air
    And whilst the sleeping tempest gathers might

Doth, as a herald of its coming, bear
    The ghost of her dead Mother, whose dim form
Bends in dark ether from her infant's chair,

    So came a chariot on the silent storm
Of its own rushing splendour, and a Shape
    So sate within as one whom years deform

Beneath a dusky hood & double cape
    Crouching within the shadow of a tomb,
And o'er what seemed the head, a cloud-like crape,

    Was bent a dun & faint aetherial gloom
Tempering the light; upon the chariot's beam
    A Janus-visaged Shadow did assume

The guidance of that wonder-wingèd team.
    The Shapes which drew it in thick lightnings
Were lost: I heard alone on the air's soft stream

    The music of their ever moving wings.
All the four faces of that charioteer
    Had their eyes banded . . . little profit brings

Speed in the van & blindness in the rear,
    Nor then avail the beams that quench the Sun
Or that his banded eyes could pierce the sphere

    Of all that is, has been, or will be done.—
So ill was the car guided, but it past
    With solemn speed majestically on . . .

Heralded by the image of the old moon in the new moon's arms (from the ballad of "Sir Patrick Spence," quoted by Coleridge as the epigraph to his "Dejection" ode), Life's chariot bursts upon us. Shelley audaciously parodies the Divine Chariot in the Book of Ezekiel, Revelation, Dante, and Milton, while the Shape called Life the Conqueror is guided by a demonic coachman who is a fearsome parody of the four cherubim or angels of the Divine Chariot. Janus-visaged, looking before and after like the Roman god Janus, this infernal charioteer can see nothing, and the icy glare emanating from his chariot blinds us. The reader gradually comes to understand that Shelley is distinguishing between three realms of light—the stars (poetry), the sun (nature), and the chariot's glare (life). Nature outshines imagination, to our loss, and then the chariot's destructive splendor outshines nature, to our ruin.

Behind the triumphal chariot stumble its innumerable host of captives, the last among these mixing young lovers in erotic madness, and the old, "foully disarrayed," still trying to keep up with Life's chariot. Desperately seeking to understand, Shelley confronts his guide in Rousseau, Virgil to his Dante, who speaks to the poet with prophetic eloquence and urgency:

> "Before thy memory
>
> "I feared, loved, hated, suffered, did, & died,
> And if the spark with which Heaven lit my spirit
> Earth had with purer nutriment supplied
>
> "Corruption would not now thus much inherit
> Of what was once Rousseau—nor this disguise
> Stained that within which still disdains to wear it.—

This is the most difficult poetry that I have introduced to any reader, but we have been learning how to read and why to read it. The terrible pride of Rousseau emerges mingled with his sense of

133

dreadful degradation, but the statement is universally human, and transcends the historical Rousseau. Shelley's belated guide speaks for something concealed within every reader, for who among us does not fear that she or he is not disguised, blocked from true selfhood (the spark) by the corruption of death-in-life?

I hope that the reader will go on to the remainder of this great torso of a poem without me, remembering always to slow down and read very slowly, and preferably out loud, whether to oneself or to others. The intensity and vividness of Shelley's final utterance will reward the reader's labor, both by its bitter eloquence and by insight into the human condition.

Here I want to juxtapose to Shelley's tragic epilogue a magnificent ballad by Keats, "La Belle Dame Sans Merci," which for all its haunting wistfulness is ultimately as despairing a work as *The Triumph of Life:*

> O, what can ail thee, knight-at-arms,
>   Alone and palely loitering?
> The sedge has withered from the lake,
>   And no birds sing.
>
> O, what can ail thee, knight-at-arms,
>   So haggard and so woe-begone?
> The squirrel's granary is full,
>   And the harvest's done.
>
> I see a lily on thy brow,
>   With anguish moist and fever dew;
> And on thy cheeks a fading rose
>   Fast withereth too.
>
> I met a lady in the meads,
>   Full beautiful—a faery's child,

Her hair was long, her foot was light,
 And her eyes were wild.

I made a garland for her head,
 And bracelets too, and fragrant zone;
She looked at me as she did love,
 And made sweet moan.

I set her on my pacing steed,
 And nothing else saw all day long;
For sidelong would she bend, and sing
 A faery's song.

She found me roots of relish sweet,
 And honey wild, and manna dew,
And sure in language strange she said—
 "I love thee true."

She took me to her elfin grot,
 And there she wept and sighed full sore,
And there I shut her wild wild eyes
 With kisses four.

And there she lullèd me asleep
 And there I dreamed—Ah! woe betide!
The latest dream I ever dreamed
 On the cold hill side.

I saw pale kings and princes too,
 Pale warriors, death-pale were they all;
They cried—"La Belle Dame Sans Merci
 Hath thee in thrall!"

I saw their starved lips in the gloom,
  With horrid warning gapèd wide,
And I awoke and found me here,
  On the cold hill's side.

And this is why I sojourn here
  Alone and palely loitering,
Though the sedge has withered from the lake,
  And no birds sing.

This may be the most poetically successful ballad in the language since the Popular Border Ballads of the later Middle Ages. For an alerted reader, it becomes an extraordinary occasion for learning better how to read a poem. Something goes very wrong in "La Belle Dame Sans Merci," which is not at all a celebratory poem, as the late poet-novelist Robert Graves took it to be. To Graves the Belle Dame was, at once, consumption (which killed Keats at twenty-five); Fanny Brawne (whom Keats loved, but never possessed); love, death, poetry, and the White Goddess, the mythological Muse who mothered, married, and buried her true poets. Graves was an accomplished reader of poetry, but he read into Keats's ballad his own sublimely destructive relationship to the American poet Laura Riding.

Keats's "Beautiful Lady without Pity" takes its title from a French medieval poem, but remains so original and subtle that we can never be certain we are reading it right. Yet reading attentively, we may well doubt that the "faery's child" is without pity, though evidently she has had a long progression of victimized lovers: pale kings, princes, and warriors who presumably starved to death because they could not go back to earthly food after faery fare. But that is the knight's dream, and should we credit it?

We are in late autumn or early winter, and the knight-at-arms is anguished, ill, and perhaps starving. The first three stanzas are spoken by Keats; the remaining nine by the faery's bereft lover.

When the final stanza comes full circle back to the first, we realize that Keats has avoided framing his ballad with a return to himself as narrator. Subtly, does that suggest an identity between Keats and the knight, which was Graves's reading?

What is most crucial in the poem is that the Belle Dame and the knight do not understand one another's language, and he may be misinterpreting her gestures and facial expressions. The knight has fallen in love with the beautiful enchantress at first sight; we feel he could hardly do less! Yet the knight's own words make us doubtful that he read her correctly: "She looked at me *as she did love,* / And made sweet moan." That moan may be more ominous than amorous, and we sense the knight's own uncertainty when he sings: "And *sure* in language strange she said— / 'I love thee true.'" His interpretation seems wrong, and we rightly worry that "she wept and sighed full sore" as another deluded lover dooms himself.

Among the saddest lines in the language, perfectly expressive of all forlorn lovers, these nevertheless may involve further self-deception:

> And I awoke and found me here,
> On the cold hill's side.

He fell asleep in "her elfin grot," to what effectual purpose we are not told, but those "kisses four" may be the sum of his gratification. How was he transported from her bower of bliss (if it was that) to the cold hill's side of his awakening? The agency could be magical, but can we be certain that his entire experience was not delusional? When did his dream begin?

The ballad is too adroit to firmly answer any of these questions. We are left in doubt, yet ourselves enchanted, as Keats here seems also to have enchanted himself. Why read "La Belle Dame Sans Merci"? For its marvelous expression of the universal longing for romance, and its deep awareness that all romance, literary and human, depends upon incomplete and uncertain knowledge.

SUMMARY OBSERVATIONS

The major poets in English, in the century just ended, would certainly include the American Robert Frost, the Anglo-American T. S. Eliot, and the English poet-novelist Thomas Hardy. But I want to frame my observations here with four poets of at least equal eminence: the Anglo-Irish W. B. Yeats, the Americans Wallace Stevens and Hart Crane, and the English prophetic poet-novelist D. H. Lawrence. Yeats inherits from William Blake's symbolic lyrics, from the Victorian dramatic monologue, and from the visionary stances of Keats and Shelley. Stevens and Crane share in part of that lineage, but are also legatees of the American tradition of Whitman and Dickinson. Lawrence, close to both Blake and Whitman, is a culmination of the visionary despair that seems to me central to the greatest poetry of the English language.

"But where are the poems of a different character?" a reader may ask. "Must all superb poetry be despairing?" Certainly not, but a rereading of my commentaries on Tennyson's "Ulysses," on Whitman and on Dickinson, on "Tom O'Bedlam" and on Shakespeare's Sonnets, on Milton and Wordsworth, will demonstrate that "a visionary despair" is not despair as you and I may experience it in our daily lives. I have chosen a group of my favorite poems precisely because their visionary quality transcends the mundane dark. Poetry, as I urge the reader to see, can be a mode of transcendence, secular or spiritual, depending upon how you receive it. But I will illustrate this first, briefly, in these four modern poets.

Yeats, who played with occultism, saying that the spirits brought him "metaphors for poetry," wrote the powerful "The Man and the Echo," as one of his death poems. Tormented by personal remorse ("I lie awake night after night"), the old man receives only stony answers from the echo: "Lie down and die" and "Into the night." Yet the poet concludes with stoic, agnostic courage, by answering his own question "Shall we in that great night rejoice?" with the unanswerable truth of the human condition:

> What do we know but that we face
> One another in this place?

The reader, of whatever age, can find in this a quality beyond despair, akin to Childe Roland setting the slug-horn to his lips and sounding the Shelleyan trumpet of a prophecy. Another death poem that confronts ultimates is D. H. Lawrence's majestic "Shadows," where the middle-aged poet, dying of tuberculosis like the young Keats, also finds the courage for a new vision:

> And if tonight my soul may find her peace
> in sleep, and sink in good oblivion,
> and in the morning wake like a new opened flower
> then I have been dipped again in God, and new created.

Lawrence's poetic voice, liberated by Whitman's heroic cadences (which John Hollander points out are not "free verse," since no authentic verse is free), opens itself to "good oblivion," rather than our ordinary ideas of death as being either annihilation or a supernatural survival. As a quester for what it might mean to be "new created," Lawrence eloquently admits the horror of self-defeat: "my wrists are broken." Yet what rises out of "Shadows" is the quickening sense of Lawrence's spirit, *sustained by the poem that he is writing.* I myself believe that poetry is the only "self-help" that works, because reciting "Shadows" aloud strengthens my own spirit. The reader will be reminded that all great poetry should be read aloud, whether in solitude or to others.

Wallace Stevens, facing his death by cancer, beheld a vision of "The Palm at the End of the Mind," in the most exalted poem of his final days: "Of Mere Being." Confronting what he knows to be phantasmagoria, the dying poet attains the knowledge "that it is not the reason / That makes us happy or unhappy." At the end of the mind, a palm tree rises. I do not know whether or not Stevens was aware of the beautiful Shiite Sufi myth that Allah, after fashioning Adam from the clay, had a remnant and used it to mold the palm tree, "Adam's sister." Does it matter whether Stevens knew this lovely fancy? This raises the issue of why difficult, allusive poets require mediation, if the common reader is to fully comprehend them. Milton, perhaps the most learned of all poets, ever, certainly benefits by mediation. So does Stevens, but not to so intense a degree. Shakespeare is almost unique among poets in being both the grandest of popular entertainers, and ultimately supremely difficult, because of the unrivaled power of his mind. Stevens is allusive, sometimes withdrawn, but his final vision is both simple and enigmatic:

> The bird sings. Its feathers shine.

> The palm stands on the edge of space.
> The wind moves slowly in the branches.
> The bird's fire-fangled feathers dangle down.

The phoenix, originally an Egyptian myth, lived for five hundred years, and then burned up by an inner fire, and in time rose up again out of its own ashes. Stevens does not know (nor do we) whether the gaudy bird of his vision is a phoenix. Does it matter? The bird *sings,* its feathers *shine,* the tree *stands* (however precariously), the wind *moves:* these are assured phenomena, a comfort at the end. The dangling-down is ambiguous; the reader may remember the death image in Stevens's much earlier poem "Sunday Morning," written forty years before "Of Mere Being": "Downward to darkness, on extended wings." But this last line— "The bird's fire-fangled feathers dangle down"—is far more exuberant, a final assertion of a strong consciousness. Again, it is the reader's choice whether we are given an image of secular transcendence, or an intimation of the spiritual.

My personal favorite among all modern poets is Hart Crane, who drowned himself by leaping off shipboard into the Caribbean, when he was just thirty-two. His death poem (probably not intended as such) is the extraordinary self-elegy "The Broken Tower," one of whose stanzas has haunted me daily for almost sixty years, since I was ten:

> And so it was I entered the broken world
> To trace the visionary company of love, its voice
> An instant in the wind (I know not whither hurled)
> But not for long to hold each desperate choice.

The aesthetic dignity of this is overwhelming, partly because Crane was a master of incantation, capable of holding us in a spell, which is one of the indubitable powers of poetry. Entering the broken world is a birth that is also a catastrophe creation, condemning Crane to a lifelong "trace" that is also a tracking and a depiction of "the visionary company of love," which certainly included, for Crane, Blake and Shelley and Keats. Crane's long series of homoerotic relationships, each choice desperate and momentary, is the hopeless but valid pursuit of a voice whose direction and duration alike are marred by the wind, a wind identical with his own indubitable inspiration.

Hart Crane, more even than most poets, yields you his secret and his value most readily when you memorize him. I return here to my early emphasis upon the joys of memorization, which is an immense aid to the reading of poetry. Committed to memory, the poem will possess you, and you will be able to read it more closely, which great poetry demands and rewards. First readings of Hart Crane are likely to be a glorious rush of sound and rhythm, but difficult to absorb. Repeated rereading of "The Broken Tower" or the "Proem: To Brooklyn Bridge" will give you the poem forever.

I know many people who continually recite poems to themselves in the awareness that the possession of and by the poem helps them to live their lives.

Help of that kind is provided by Emily Dickinson, whose intellectual originality allows her close readers to break with the conventions of response that have been deeply instilled in us. In this, she is Shakespeare's disciple. The supernal value of Hamlet's meditations, as I will show later in this book, is another strengthening of the reader's autonomy. Like *Hamlet,* Shakespeare's Sonnets are a perpetual refreshment in the pleasures of change in meaning, each time we reread.

There is a shock of recognition when we read Walt Whitman at his strongest. Poetry, at the best, does us a kind of violence that prose fiction rarely attempts or accomplishes. The Romantics understood this as the proper work of poetry: to startle us out of our sleep-of-death into a more capacious sense of life. There is no better motive for reading and rereading the best of our poetry.

III

NOVELS, PART I

Introduction

In some respects, reading a novel ought not to differ much from reading Shakespeare or reading a lyric poem. What matters most is who you are, since you cannot evade bringing yourself to the act of reading. Because most of us also bring definite expectations, a difference enters with the novel, where we think to encounter, if not our friends and ourselves, then a recognizable social reality, whether contemporary or historical. The arrival of the latest novel by Iris Murdoch aroused sensations in me different from the advent of a new book of poems by John Ashbery. Bad writing is all one; great writing is scandalously diverse, and genres constitute authentic divisions within it. There are still some dramatic and narrative poets alive and worth reading, but they are few indeed: I read Ashbery to reencounter Ashbery, a solitude who yearns for others and for otherness. One went to Murdoch, who was the most traditional of our good novelists, for people, for story, for metaphysical and erotic reflections, and for an ironic social wisdom. I did not ask Murdoch to give me a *Bleak House* or a *Middlemarch,* but to extend a continuity with them that may make their equivalents possible again, someday. Perhaps Murdoch's lively new characters will fade away into the continuum, as they have before. There will still remain the pleasures of repetition, and of keeping alive civilized tradition.

The audience for high lyric poetry is necessarily tiny. This causes grief to our best poets, but they have pragmatic precursors in William Blake and Walt Whitman, Emily Dickinson and Gerard Manley Hopkins, who reached so few in their own lifetimes. Whitman was self-published, as Blake was, while Dickinson and Hopkins were brought out posthumously. Elizabeth Bishop found fit audience though few, and a handful or two of our best contemporaries follow her. Even if the millennium brings us a *ricorso* of a Theocratic Age (as Giambattista Vico prophesied in his *New Science*) one expects an elitist poetry to survive, but the novel may have a darker fortune. Novels require more readers than poems do, a statement so odd that it puzzles me, even as I agree with it. Tennyson, Browning, and Robert Frost had large audiences, but perhaps did not need them. Dickens and Tolstoy had vast readerships, and needed them; multitudes of overhearers are built into their art. How do you read a novel differently if you suspect you are one of a dwindling elite rather than the representative of a great multitude?

Unless you read out loud and to others, then even the presence of others does not transform reading from a solitary to a social act. For fifty years I have read novels for their characters, their stories, and for the beauty of their authorial and narrative voices. If novels are indeed fated to vanish, then let us honor them for their aesthetic and spiritual values, perhaps even for their heroism, in both the protagonists and as an aspect of the authors. Let us read them, in the coming years of the third millennium, as they were read in the eighteenth and nineteenth centuries: for aesthetic pleasure and for spiritual insight.

Characters in great novels are not marks upon the page, but are post-Shakespearean portraits of the reality of men and women: actual, probable, and possible ones. The novel is still there to be read, and has added, in our century, Proust and Joyce and Beckett and a host of Americans, Hispanic and Northern, to the wealth of Austen, Dickens, Flaubert, Stendhal, and the other classic practitioners. Joyce in *Finnegans Wake* prophetically lamented that he lacked Shakespeare's audience at the Globe Theater, and I fear that the *Wake* will vanish in the visual new age. Perhaps Proust will vanish also, a peculiar irony because no novel seems to me to gain so much in these bad days, when we reread it against the darkening background of all novels waning away.

Miguel de Cervantes:
Don Quixote

Any discussion of how to read novels and why must include the *Don Quixote* of Cervantes, the first and best of all novels, which nevertheless is more than a novel. To my favorite critic of Cervantes, the Basque writer Miguel de Unamuno, the book was the true Spanish Bible, and "Our Lord Don Quixote" was the authentic Christ. If I may be wholly secular, Cervantes seems to me Shakespeare's only possible rival in the imaginative literature of the past four centuries. Don Quixote is the peer of Hamlet, and Sancho Panza is a match for Sir John Falstaff. Higher praise I do not know how to render. Exact contemporaries (they may have died upon the same day), Shakespeare had evidently read *Don Quixote,* but it is most unlikely that Cervantes had ever heard of Shakespeare.

Novelists who have loved *Don Quixote* include Henry Fielding, Tobias Smollett, and Laurence Sterne in eighteenth-century England; none of their work is conceivable without Cervantes. The influence of Cervantes is intense upon Stendhal and Flaubert, whose Madame Bovary is "the female Quixote." Herman Melville and Mark Twain are Cervantine, and so are Dostoevsky, Turgenev, Thomas Mann, and virtually all modern Hispanic writers of fiction.

Don Quixote is so vast a book (though, with Dr. Samuel Johnson, I would not wish it any shorter) that I will confine my advice on how to read it to just its central relationship, the friendship between Don Quixote and Sancho Panza. There is nothing like it in Shakespeare, since Prince Hal, when he becomes King Henry V, destroys his friendship with Falstaff, which had become highly ambivalent by the time we first encounter them together, at the start of *Henry IV, Part One*. Horatio is merely a straight man for Hamlet, and every other close male relationship in Shakespeare has its equivocal aspects, particularly in the Sonnets. Shakespeare's women are capable of maintaining authentic friendships with one another, but not his men. Sometimes this seems to me as true of life as of Shakespeare, or is it another instance of Shakespeare's influence upon life?

The Don and Sancho have many fallings-out, but always reconcile, and never fail one another in love, loyalty, and in the Don's great unwisdom and Sancho's admirable wisdom. Everyone in Shakespeare (as in life?) has real difficulty in listening to one another. King Lear scarcely listens to anyone, while Antony and Cleopatra (sometimes hilariously) can't listen to one another at all. Shakespeare himself must have been the most preternaturally gifted of listeners, particularly in the company of Ben Jonson, who never stopped talking. Cervantes, one suspects, was also an unwearied listener.

Though very nearly everything that *can* happen does happen in *Don Quixote*, what matters most are the ongoing conversations between Sancho and the Don. Open the book at random, and you are likely to find yourself in the midst of one of their exchanges, angry or whimsical, but ultimately always loving, and founded upon mutual respect. Even when they argue most fiercely, their courtesy is unfailing, and they never stop learning from listening to the other. And by hearing, they change.

I think we can establish the principle that change, the deepening and internalization of the self, is absolutely antithetical when we bring Cervantes and Shakespeare together. Sancho and the Don develop newer and richer egos by hearing one another, but

Falstaff and Hamlet perform the same process only by overhearing themselves. The major Western novelists owe as much to Shakespeare as they do to Cervantes. Melville's Ahab, in *Moby-Dick*, has no Sancho; he is as isolated as Hamlet or Macbeth. Otherwise quixotic, poor Emma Bovary also possesses no Sancho, and dies ultimately of self-overhearing. Huckleberry Finn finds his Sancho in Jim and so is saved from withering gloriously in the air of solitude. Raskolnikov, in Dostoevsky's *Crime and Punishment*, confronts what might be termed the anti–Sancho Panza in the nihilistic Svidrigailov's Iago. Prince Myshkin in Dostoevsky's *Idiot* clearly owes much to the noble "madness" of Don Quixote. Mann, highly conscious of his debt to Cervantes, deliberately repeats the poet Goethe's complex homage to the author of *Don Quixote,* as well as Sigmund Freud's tribute to Cervantes.

In the affectionate (though frequently testy) debates between the Don and Sancho, they gradually take on some of each other's attributes. Quixote's visionary madness begins to acquire a cannier dimension, and Panza's commonsensical shrewdness starts to mutate into the play world of quest. Their natures never fuse, but they learn to depend upon one another (up to a comic point). Explaining his purposes to Sancho, the Don enumerates the erotic madness of his jealousy-ridden precursors—Amadis and Orlando—and sensibly adds that perhaps he will simply imitate Amadis, who unlike Orlando rose to fame by inflicting insane injuries upon everyone who came near.

> "It seems to me," said Sancho, "that the knights who did all these things were driven to them . . . but . . . why should you go crazy? What lady has rejected you . . . ?"
>
> "That is exactly it," replied Don Quixote, "that's just how beautifully I've worked it all out—because for a knight errant to go crazy for good reason, how much is *that* worth? My idea is to become a lunatic for no reason at all . . ."
>
> (Translated by Burton Raffel)

Like Hamlet, the Don is but mad north-northwest, and he is anything but a fool, nor is Sancho. Like Prince Hal and Falstaff, they are playing a very complex game, happily without ambivalence. So complex indeed is their play that the reader is fated to read her own *Don Quixote,* because Cervantes, like Shakespeare again, is as impartial as he is complex. Against my favorite Cervantes critic, Unamuno, many scholars uphold Erich Auerbach, who found in the book a nonproblematical gaiety. Unamuno's Quixote rather embodies the tragic sense of life, and the Don's "madness" is a protest against the necessity of dying, you might even say a rebellion against the Spanish temperament, which in different epochs makes a cult of death. Something in Cervantes, battered warrior as he was (he lost the use of his left hand forever in the sea battle of Lepanto against the Turks), is always on the verge of crying, with Sir John Falstaff: "Give me life!" I think Unamuno was correct in saying that the book's gaiety belonged entirely to the greatness of Sancho Panza, who with Falstaff and the Panurge of Rabelais is another great instance of the undying in us.

In none of Shakespeare's plays do two characters equally carry off the honors of imaginative primacy. Imaginatively, Falstaff triumphs over Hal, Juliet over Romeo, Cleopatra over Antony. Of all Cervantes's splendors, the most wonderful is that he gives us two great souls in the Don and Sancho, and that they love and respect one another.

Refreshingly, they quarrel frequently and robustly, as befits two strong personalities who know who they are. Though Don Quixote, and later Cervantes, are beset by enchanters, self-identity is not jeopardized. What Shakespeare called the "selfsame," his word for coherence of individual identity, endures for the Don, despite the apparent madness of knight-errantry. A crucial element in that selfsame is Don Quixote's passionate devotion to his own imaginative creation, the astonishingly beautiful and outrageously virtuous Dulcinea, whom he invokes so eloquently: "Oh Dulcinea de Tobosa, day of my night, glory of my suffering, true North and compass of every path I take, guiding star of my fate . . ." The merely actual woman is a neighboring peasant girl, Aldonza Lorenzo, who is as coarse as she should be. Enchanters have transformed the peerless Dulcinea into the common Aldonza, yet Don Quixote understands his own fiction, his own gorgeous invention in the order of play: "I perceive everything I say as absolutely true, and deficient in nothing whatever, and paint it all in my mind exactly as I want it to be . . ." The reader is well advised to accept Dulcinea with *some* credence, since in one sense she is to the Don what Beatrice is to Dante, the center of a heterocosm, or alternative world to that of nature. That High Romantic or Shelleyan notion is punctured by Sancho Panza, and in another way by the Don himself, who knows and does not know the limits of play: "I know who I am, and who I may be, if I choose." The reader, who learns to love Don Quixote, and Sancho Panza, will get to know better who she is, because of them. Cervantes, like Shakespeare, will entertain any reader, but again like Shakespeare he will create a more active reader, according to the reader's capabilities. It is Don Quixote, encountering caged lions, who *knows* whether the noble lions have come to attack him or not. It is the active reader, riding along with the Don and Sancho, who comes to share their knowledge that they are characters in a story, and in Part II of the huge book Don and Sancho in turn fully participate in the reader's knowledge, since they become overt critics, appreciating their adventures.

Shakespeare had the supreme art to obliterate himself in his two dozen or so great plays; the reader or playgoer might want to know what Shakespeare thought about it all, but Shakespeare has so arranged it that we cannot reach him, and in many ways thanks to him we don't need him. Cervantes, particularly in Part II of *Don Quixote,* invented just the opposite art, and so arranges things that we can't do without him. He cuts a gap into the illusion he creates for us, because both the Don and Sancho, throughout Part II, comment upon the roles they have played in

Part I. Cervantes, even more baroque and knowing, joins Don Quixote in complaining about enchanters, in Cervantes's case the plagiarist-impostor who would finish his novel for him.

Thomas Mann, writing about *Don Quixote,* admired the uniqueness of a hero who "lives off the glory of his own glorification." Sancho, too shrewd to go that far, nevertheless says that he is "to be found also in the story and is called Sancho Panza." If the reader becomes a little bewildered, she only will need Cervantes himself more. Cervantes, speaking as Miguel de Cervantes Saavedra, assumes and sustains a new kind of story-telling authority, one whose ultimate heir may have been Marcel Proust, who perhaps took the Cervantine novel as far as it could go. Or perhaps the final heir was James Joyce in *Ulysses,* or Joyce's and Proust's disciple, Samuel Beckett, in his trilogy: *Molloy, Malone Dies, The Unnameable.*

Reading *Don Quixote* is an endless pleasure, and I hope I have indicated some aspects of how to read it. We are, many of us, Cervantine figures, mixed blends of the Quixotic and the Panzaesque. Why read *Don Quixote?* It remains the best as well as the first of all novels, just as Shakespeare remains the best of all dramatists. There are parts of yourself you will not know fully until you know, as well as you can, Don Quixote and Sancho Panza.

Stendhal:
The Charterhouse of Parma

Stendhal—the pen name of Marie-Henri Beyle—was born in Grenoble, France, in 1783, and died in Paris in 1842. The Battle of Waterloo (1814), which ended Napoleon's career, began Stendhal's career as a writer. Living in Italy until the Austrian police expelled him in 1821, Stendhal subsequently lived in Paris, where in 1830 he published his first permanent novel, *The Red and the*

Black. Here I will discuss his other great achievement, *The Charterhouse of Parma,* dictated by him, while in poor health, in a little more than seven weeks, and published to Balzac's acclaim in 1839. I choose the *Charterhouse* (as I shall call it for short) over *The Red and the Black,* because I love it even more than Stendhal's prior masterpiece, and also because there is a superb new translation of it by the poet Richard Howard.

Stendhal is, with Balzac and Flaubert, one of the trinity of major French novelists before their summit in Marcel Proust. Unlike Flaubert and Proust, unlike even the massively productive and vastly detailed Balzac, Stendhal is the highest of High Romantics, a partisan of Shakespeare, and to a lesser extent of Lord Byron.

Richard Howard admirably remarks of the *Charterhouse*: "Nothing fixed: . . . [Stendhal] is the anti-Flaubert." *Madame Bovary* is an autonomous work, beautifully closed in upon itself, as James Joyce's *Ulysses* is, on a titanic scale. And yet, as Howard also observes, the relatively formless Stendhal, at his best demands *rereading;* he goes from surprise to surprise. Proust, perhaps more Shakespearean even than Stendhal, loved Stendhal, who did not menace him as Flaubert perhaps did. Why read Stendhal? Because no other novelist (whom I admire) so makes you a co-conspirator; the devoted reader becomes Stendhal's accomplice.

Balzac, celebrating the *Charterhouse,* said that it "often contains a whole book in a single page." That could drive a stolid reader more than a little mad, but if you have some gusto (William Hazlitt's favorite critical term), then the *Charterhouse* is the novel for you. Insanely rational, as only a High Romantic could be, Stendhal nevertheless chronicles in his apparently formless *Charterhouse* the death of the age of Napoleon, and the return of an earlier, eighteenth-century Italy, part of the world that Metternich tried to restore after Waterloo.

I *like* historical novels, from Sir Walter Scott's *Redgauntlet* through Gore Vidal's *Lincoln,* but the *Charterhouse* is not really a historical novel, though it purports to be one, any more than Shakespeare's *Romeo and Juliet* (which deeply influences the *Charterhouse*) is essentially a historical play. Like *Romeo and Juliet,* the *Charterhouse* is tragedy, though Stendhal, always charmingly ironic, never quite abides in a tragic sentiment; he is far too playful, too Quixotic for that. The *Charterhouse* opens joyfully, with the victory of Napoleon's young army in Italy in 1796. If Stendhal had a passion, beyond his unfulfilled lust for certain women who had evaded him, it was for Napoleonic idealism. The child of that idealism is Stendhal's Romantic hero, Fabrice, a dashing, young, disaster-eager scamp who is loved by his aunt-of-marriage (not a blood connection), the fascinating and high-souled Gina. She in turn is loved by the amiable Machiavellian Mosca, minister to the Prince of Parma. Fabrice however is in love with Clélia, daughter of his jailer, and Juliet to his Romeo. A grand, most frustrating time is had by all, except for the reader, who delights in the two triangles, Mosca/Gina/Fabrice and Gina/Fabrice/Clélia.

Stendhal has learned from Shakespeare (and from his own romantic disasters) the arbitrariness of all grand passions, and from Cervantes he has learned that passion, even when it kills, is a mode of play. All is irony, unless you happen to be one of the four lovers caught inside this chess game. The play, as Balzac saw, was of private passions; the age of Napoleon was over. We are postchivalric, and what matters are the four lovers. Romance is everything, once Wellington has triumphed. Julien Sorel, in *The Red and the Black,* pursues his suicidal and more or less heroic erotic career as a Napoleonic clone bound to undergo a *sparagmos* in the Restoration. But post-Congress-of-Vienna Parma is a sublime madness, where everything goes, and nothing works for long, except the sadly noble survivor Mosca, who ends up rich but deprived of his Gina, who has lost her Fabrice, who is divested of his Clélia.

What makes the *Charterhouse* wonderful for the reader is how much unmixed affection is inspired in us by the style and panache of Gina and Fabrice, of Clélia and Mosca. They delight us all:

they have admirable pride, verve, honor, authentic lust, and a superb *sprezzatura:* they truly are Stendhal's unhappy/happy few, whom he can commend to the happy few, ourselves as his readers. Stendhal bravely addresses us as if we were Henry V's cohorts at Agincourt, about to be led on to glory.

The Charterhouse of Parma is itself a puzzle, not a symbol but a red herring. We find it only upon the novel's final page; Fabrice lives out his final year, a saddened Romeo without his lost Juliet, Clélia. As a title, the *Charterhouse* is misleading, but so is everything else in the heroically helter-skelter novel, where all is at once paradox and passion. Stendhal, a scarred amorist, celebrates desire that goes beyond all limits. As in Shakespeare, and Cervantes, we are instructed in the madness that is falling-in-love.

But how delighted the reader is with the chess game or whist game constituted by Gina, Fabrice, Clélia, and Mosca! Stendhal, as in *The Red and the Black,* creates Shakespearean characters who enlist our affections, and move us to woe and wonder. Julien Sorel of *The Red and the Black* is a more finished consciousness than Fabrice is in the *Charterhouse,* but Fabrice's somewhat slapdash psyche adds to his immense charm. The most lovable and persuasive character in the novel is Gina, Mosca's lover but in love with Fabrice, who all but succumbs to Gina until he meets Clélia, daughter of his jailer.

Though Fabrice is the natural son of a Lieutenant Robert (who appears only in the novel's opening pages, as an officer in Napoleon's liberating army), he is the child also of Lieutenant Robert's lover, the Marchesa del Dongo, so henceforward I will call him Fabrizio del Dongo, his name in Richard Howard's lively translation. The young man's supposed aunt Gina del Dongo, the sister of the Marchesa, is about fifteen years his senior, which does not prevent her from falling permanently in love with him.

Fabrice's affection for Gina, though intense, is limited; Romeo-like, he will fall in love with Clélia at first sight, and it will become, as in Shakespeare, a kind of love-death. He is never in love with his quasi-aunt, Gina, though he has more regard for her than for any-one else. The center of Stendhal's concern, and so the focus of the novel, is Gina's unrequited passion, since she is the most remark-able and achieved character in the novel. The *Charterhouse* ulti-mately matters because she does; no other figure in Stendhal is so vital and fascinating, or ultimately as Shakespearean and Cervan-tine. Gina is the glory of Stendhal's career as a writer.

Gina and Fabrice never become sexual lovers, partly because of his wariness (would it be incest?) and partly through the irony of circumstance. The book's poet-translator, Richard Howard, sug-gests that the *Charterhouse* is a novel without a hero and without a heroine. One grants that Fabrice is too metamorphic to be alto-gether a hero, but it seems a little hard-hearted on the translator's part to see Gina, with whom the reader falls in love, as less than the book's heroine.

Gina Pietranera, the Duchess Sanseverina, has giant flaws in her personality and moral character, but they serve only to enhance her interest for us. Rarely prudent, caught up by the pos-sibilities of the moment, Gina captivates (and alarms) us by her passionate (and destructive) sincerity. As a High Romantic, mad about women, Stendhal has earned the approbation of Simone de Beauvoir, who in *The Second Sex* praised him as "a man who lives among women of flesh and blood." Gina is the most persuasive representation of those women that Stendhal achieved.

Stendhal, though always praised as a psychologist of heterosex-ual love, seems to me more a metaphysician in search of the barely conscious truth of desire. Vanity, he finds, is at the center of pas-sionate love, or rather, if you fall in love, then everything in your condition that is not pathology is vanity. The reader, particularly if she is in love, may be unsettled by Stendhal, yet also enlightened.

The pleasures of *The Charterhouse of Parma,* as of *The Red and the Black,* are not those of sustained rapture. Stendhal writes as he is inspired, but he doesn't want to inspire us. Rather, he wishes us to learn to see erotic coldness as vanity, and passion as vanity raised to madness. His men and women are not Quixotic but Napoleonic, and even their most authentic attachments, however heroic, are self-destructive. Byron, though Stendhal might have wished otherwise, is closer to Stendhal than Shakespeare was; the *Charterhouse* attempts to render Fabrice and Clélia into Romeo and Juliet, but sometimes they seem more like lovers in *Don Juan.* Paul Valéry, the most gifted French poet and man of letters in the century that has now ended, remarked that the *Charterhouse* "at times suggests operetta," by which Valéry intended no disparagement. Stendhal's amazingly quick wit, his incessant liveliness, fascinated the intellectual Valéry.

"A skeptic who believed in love," is Valéry's summary of Stendhal accurate for the *Charterhouse?* I doubt that the mature Shakespeare "believed in love," and I am not at all certain about Stendhal.

Valéry though also noted Stendhal's shrewd drawing of the reader into complicity, which I suspect Stendhal had learned from Cervantes. Stendhal's true belief (as Valéry also intimates) was in the natural self, both his own and the reader's. Sometimes the reader may feel that Stendhal flatters her egotism (and his own), but he means well by her. To be made one of his "happy few" is a large benefit, because greater self-clarification will come from it. Personal energy is exalted by him, but always at a remove from self-deception. The greatness of Gina emerges best in her interview with her lover, Count Mosca, in chapter 16, where as a woman of thirty-seven ("I stand on the threshold of old age") she avows the innocence and the despair of her love for Fabrice:

> . . . I love him by instinct . . . I love in him his courage, so simple and so perfect that one might say that he is not even aware of it himself . . . I began to discern a perfect grace in my nephew. His great soul revealed itself to me . . . In short, if he is not happy I cannot be happy.
>
> (Translated by Richard Howard)

Here Stendhal is well beyond skepticism or irony, and he takes us with him. We *want* Gina and Fabrice to be together, and to be happy, but we know it cannot be, since the twenty-two-year-old Fabrice is in love with Clélia. Stendhal is only interested in star-crossed love, and *The Charterhouse of Parma,* madcap and humorous, concludes by turning into a tragedy. Clélia's son by Fabrice dies, and several months later the grieving Clélia also expires. Fabrice retreats to the enigmatic Charterhouse of the title, and himself dies a year later. Unhappy in a world without Fabrice, Gina (who has married Mosca) dies very shortly after him. Mosca remains, and we seem to be onstage at the end of *Romeo and Juliet* or of *Hamlet,* where everyone vital has been swept away.

Balzac, reviewing the *Charterhouse* in 1840, saluted Stendhal for rising well above mere realism, and for portraying only characters of exceptional qualities. This sounds much like Balzac's own praxis, but the same praise is due both novelists, different as they are. Reading Stendhal (or Balzac) is an enlargement of the reader's reality, without in Stendhal's work any yielding to fantasy.

Jane Austen:
Emma

It is easier to ascribe social purposes to novels than to short stories or poems. But the reader should be wary of all those who insist that the novel, to survive, must be an instrument of reform. There may not be a novelist, in English, who surpasses Jane Austen, and what do *Pride and Prejudice, Emma, Mansfield Park,* and *Persuasion* wish to reform? Their heroines require some realignment in personal stances, which Austen provides, and amiable husbands, whom they secure. A profound ironist, who employs her irony to refine aspects of Shakespeare's invention of the human, Austen is too pragmatic to worry about the equivocal sources of the affluence of those amiable husbands. Her pragmatism is commendable, for what difference would it make if the funds were cleaner, scrubbed free say of the exploitation of West Indian slavery? Austen is neither a prophet nor a politician. She is too intelligent not to know that much of social reality could not sustain close scrutiny, but the societal order for her is a given, something to be accepted so that her stories can be told. Henry James, who is in her tradition, makes Isabel Archer in *The Portrait of a Lady* the "heiress of all the ages," but the financial element in that inheritance from the ages is only a concern for him insofar as it leads to Madame Merle's plot against Isabel Archer.

Dickens was a social reformer; Austen and James were not. *Great Expectations* thrives upon its financial and legal perplexities, but we must not pass a law that imposes upon fiction the burden of improving society. What were the social purposes of Cervantes, father of all novelists? Was Spain to be morally improved if everyone gave up reading romances of chivalry? Stendhal, grand Romantic, gave his heart to the Napoleonic myth, but *The Charterhouse of Parma* has more to do with *Romeo and Juliet* than with the titanic career that ended at Waterloo. Only literature can be made into literature, though life must get into the mix, almost always as provender rather than as form.

Though *Persuasion* is my favorite Austen, I have written on it in my book *The Western Canon,* and choose *Emma* here, as it is my second favorite, just ahead of *Pride and Prejudice* and *Mansfield Park.* But I will write about *Emma* with some explicit reference to *Pride and Prejudice,* since both the similarities and the differences between Emma Woodhouse and Elizabeth Bennet are highly useful in the quest to read both novels as they deserve to be read.

Jane Austen died at the age of forty-one, in 1817, after a yearlong illness. Had she lived longer, doubtless we would have received several more novels as splendid as *Emma* and *Persuasion,* which she wrote in her final years. Though Austen began writing fiction when she was eighteen, her full powers were exercised only from 1811 on, when she began to revise *Pride and Prejudice* from a much earlier version, *First Impressions.* Essentially, her four great novels are the work of only five years, and our loss is therefore immense.

It is a truism to remark that Emma Woodhouse has a more powerful imagination than Elizabeth Bennet, while Elizabeth outdoes Emma in wit. Emma's imagination isn't always a virtue (another truism), while Elizabeth's wit sometimes misleads her. Both women have powerful wills, with common failings of self-deception, from which they will emancipate themselves.

There is something ineluctably Shakespearean about both Elizabeth and Emma, even though Austen builds explicitly upon the work of her novelistic precursors: Samuel Richardson's marvelous *Clarissa* and his *Sir Charles Grandison;* Fanny Burney's *Evelina.* Yet the awesome Clarissa Harlowe and Evelina lack the Shakespearean wit and imagination that are manifest in Elizabeth and in Emma. Elizabeth Bennet can remind the reader of Beatrice in *Much Ado About Nothing,* while Emma's high-spiritedness can suggest the Rosalind of *As You Like It.* As an ironist, Austen is not particularly Shakespearean; Hamlet's ironies are more aggressive than defensive. Yet, after Shakespeare, no writer in the language does so well as Austen in giving us figures, central and peripheral, utterly consistent each in her (or his) own mode of speech and consciousness, and intensely different from each other. The strong selves of her heroines are wrought with a fine individuality that attests to Austen's own reserves of power. Had she not died so soon, she would have been capable of creating a Shakespearean diversity of persons, despite her narrowly, deliberately limited social range of representation. She had learned Shakespeare's most difficult lesson: to manifest sympathy towards all of her characters, even the least admirable, while detaching herself even from her favorite, Emma. Austen feared that only she would like Emma, but that fear itself may have been ironic. I do not know any readers who are not deeply fond of the formidable but vastly engaging Emma Woodhouse.

Do Austen's heroines, like Shakespeare's in the comedies, imaginatively speaking, marry down? The dazzling Darcy (*Pride and Prejudice*) and the benign Mr. Knightley (*Emma*) surpass Rosalind's Orlando and Beatrice's Bendick, let alone Helena's caddish Bertram (*All's Well That Ends Well*) and Viola's crazy Duke Orsino (*Twelfth Night*). If Austen evidently is content with Darcy and Mr. Knightley, should we not be? Or ought the reader to yield to current academic fashions, and judge that, in Austen and Shakespeare alike, brilliant heroines are victimized by social tyrannies whose interests are not theirs? I would suggest that careful readers, who do not look everywhere for evidences of humiliation, will not underestimate either Austen or Shakespeare. Nor will they discover, among living women novelists, any genius remotely comparable to Austen's or George Eliot's. It is perhaps a historical peculiarity, but we also lack a living woman poet who can rival Emily Dickinson and Elizabeth Bishop. Ideological cheerleading does not necessarily nurture great, or even good, readers and writers; instead it seems to malform them.

There is no misandry in Jane Austen or George Eliot or Emily Dickinson. Elizabeth Bennet and Emma Woodhouse are not concerned either with upholding or undermining patriarchy. Being vastly intelligent persons, like Rosalind, they do not think ideologically. To read their stories well, you need to acquire a touch of Austen's own wisdom, because she was as wise as Dr. Samuel Johnson. Like Johnson, though far more implicitly, Austen urges us to clear our mind of "cant." "Cant," in the Johnsonian sense, means platitudes, pious expressions, group-think. Austen has no use for it, and neither should we. Those who now read Austen "politically" are not reading her at all.

Like many great writers, male and female, Austen implicitly judged women to be imaginatively superior to men. Shakespeare, though he gave us Hamlet, Falstaff, and Iago, gave us also Rosalind, Portia, and Cleopatra, so I suppose he can be said to have divided the honors. Though Austen, in *Emma*, gives us the admirable Mr.

Woodhouse (called by A. C. Bradley the most perfect gentleman in fiction, except for Don Quixote), Emma herself and Jane Fairfax concern her much more, and are worthy of the imaginative regard of every reader.

Emma is Austen's most complex character. Sir Walter Scott, reviewing *Emma* in 1815, ironically observed that the heroine, "like a good sovereign, preferring the weal of her subjects of Highbury to her own private interest, sets generously about making matches for her friends without thinking of matrimony on her own account." Austen's own stance towards her Emma is an ironic love, and she intends Emma to charm us. Readers *are* charmed, both by Emma and by Jane Fairfax, but Emma is the superior "imaginist" and is finally more charming to us, because she is much more interesting than Jane Fairfax. *Imaginist* is Jane Austen's own word, doubtless ironic, and so far as I know has been used by no other author. To be an imaginist is to be a consciousness not fully aware of the reality of other selves. Emma, endless blunderer at matchmaking, has to undergo considerable self-development before her solipsistic temperament is somewhat healed. Elizabeth Bennet, in contrast, is from the start wholly free of solipsism.

Austen evidently preferred Emma even to Elizabeth, for reasons the reader is obliged to explore. It is Emma's novel; her perspective influences Austen-as-narrator. Emma's flaws, for Austen, are only the excess of her virtues. To imagine more intensely, were Emma to confine herself to her own aspirations, would make her a kind of Wordsworthian visionary. But Emma's obsession with matchmaking is a peculiar mode of imagination; it is in fact a parody of Austen's playing field as an artist. It may seem odd to see Austen as Cervantes to Emma's Quixote, but Emma's preposterous scenarios for Harriet (Elton, Churchill, at last the charming prospect of Knightley) are analogous to the heroic Don sallying forth against windmills, lions, soldiers guarding galley slaves.

Emma's comic scrapes are not painful for the reader, wherever they leave Emma. When she fears that Knightley intends to marry

Harriet, fierce comedy ensues for the reader, humiliating agony for Emma. Undisciplined imagination set free by her, which has harmed others, now subjects her to severe mental suffering. This is Austen upon the height of her genius, detaching herself from Emma, at the demand of the Comic Muse:

> When Harriet had closed her evidence, she appealed to her dear Miss Woodhouse, to say whether she had not good ground for hope.
>
> "I never should have presumed to think of it at first," said she, "but for you. You told me to observe him carefully, and let his behavior be the rule of mine—and so I have. But now I seem to feel that I may deserve him; and that if he does choose me, it will not be any thing so very wonderful."
>
> The bitter feelings occasioned by this speech, the many bitter feelings, made the utmost exertion necessary on Emma's side to enable her to say in reply,
>
> "Harriet, I will only venture to declare, that Mr. Knightley is the last man in the world, who would intentionally give any woman the idea of his feeling for her more than he really does."
>
> Harriet seemed ready to worship her friend for a sentence so satisfactory; and Emma was only saved from raptures and fondness, which at the moment would have been dreadful penance, by the sound of her father's footsteps. He was coming through the hall. Harriet was too much agitated to encounter him. "She could not compose herself—Mr. Woodhouse would be alarmed—she had better go"—with most ready encouragement from her friend, therefore, she passed off through another door—and the moment she was gone, this was the spontaneous burst of Emma's feelings: "Oh God! that I had never seen her!"
>
> The rest of the day, the following night, were hardly enough for her thoughts.—She was bewildered amidst the confusion of all that had rushed on her within the last few hours. Every moment had brought a fresh surprise; and every surprise must be matter of

humiliation to her.—How to understand it all! How to understand the deceptions she had been thus practicing on herself, and living under!— The blunders, the blindness of her own head and heart!—she sat still, she walked about, she tried her own room, she tried the shrubbery—in every place, every posture, she perceived that she had acted most weakly; that she had been imposed on by others in a most mortifying degree; that she had been imposing on herself in a degree yet more mortifying; that she was wretched, and should probably find this day but the beginning of wretchedness.

This exquisite comedy depends upon the contrast between Emma's despairing cry "Oh God! that I had never seen her!" and the marvelous "she sat still, she walked about, she tried her own room, she tried the shrubbery—in every place, every posture, she perceived that she had acted most weakly." Her will, which she had fused with her imagination, suffers the abnegation of the delicious comedy of "she tried the shrubbery." "Every posture" seems now a humiliation of the spirit for Emma, all of whose imaginings have been reduced to mere delusions. Austen, who was close to identifying herself with Emma, rescues her heroine from this purgatory through the agency of Mr. Knightley, who had the maturity to endure Emma's vision, and then be there for her at the end.

Austen's superb heroines—Emma and Elizabeth in particular—approach the splendor of Rosalind in *As You Like It.* They integrate wit and will, and they triumph in that integration.

Charles Dickens:
Great Expectations

Rereading old books, as William Hazlitt recommended, is the highest form of literary pleasure, and instructs you in what is deepest in your own yearnings. I used to reread Dickens's *The Pickwick Papers* twice a year, wearing out several copies in the process. If that was escape, I was glad to escape, though none of the Pickwickians provided me with the joy of identification. In Dickens's world of caricatures and grotesques, the reader generally is not invited (or tempted) to merge into the characters, who share more with Ben Jonson's and Tobias Smollett's fierce cartoons than with the men and women of Shakespeare. And yet there are complexly inward figures in Dickens, in particular Esther Summerson in *Bleak House* and Pip in *Great Expectations.* Pip, certainly the most inward of all Dickens's characters, is particularly useful for my purposes here. To understand Pip in all his shadings is to have read *Great Expectations* well, and is a good start on how to read a novel.

Only three of Dickens's novels have first-person narrators: Pip in *Great Expectations,* David Copperfield in his book, and Esther Summerson in *Bleak House,* where Dickens doesn't always remember to let her do the job. Dickens lovers rarely rank *Great Expectations* first among the novels; it has not joined *Oliver Twist* as popular mythology, and Dickens himself preferred *Copperfield,* while many literary critics (myself included) would vote for *Bleak House.* But, rather like *A Tale of Two Cities, Great Expectations* is grand public entertainment. It joins Jane Austen's *Pride and Prejudice* and *Emma,* and a round dozen of Shakespeare's plays, as works certain to survive our ongoing Information Age, and not just as film or television. We will go on reading *Great Expectations* as we will continue to read *Hamlet* and *Macbeth:*

> My father's family name being Pirrip, and my Christian name Philip, my infant tongue could make of both names nothing longer or more explicit than Pip. So, I called myself Pip, and came to be called Pip.

Pip's sense of his own pathos is unceasing; it begins with his nickname and does not end when he is in the company of his godson, little Pip, as the novel achieves its original (and better) ending:

I was in England—in London, and walking along Piccadilly with little Pip—when a servant came running after me to ask would I step back to a lady in a carriage who wished to speak to me. It was a little pony carriage, which the lady was driving; and the lady and I looked sadly enough on one another.

"I am greatly changed, I know; but I thought you would like to shake hands with Estella too, Pip. Lift up that pretty child and let me kiss it!" (She supposed the child, I think, to be my child.)

I was very glad afterwards to have had the interview; for, in her face and her voice, and in her touch, she gave me the assurance, that suffering had been stronger than Miss Havisham's teaching, and had given her a heart to understand what my heart used to be.

Dickens is not a Shakespearean novelist; his deeper affinities are with Ben Jonson's comedy of humors. The Shakespearean novelists—Jane Austen and Dostoevsky, Goethe and Stendhal, Philip Roth and Cormac McCarthy (among many others)—invest themselves in characters who change, but Pip darkens without development. Yet Dickens manipulates *Hamlet* in *Great Expectations,* by parodying it and then reversing revenge into Pip's universal forgiveness. Magwitch, Pip's surrogate father and Estella's actual progenitor, returns as the Ghost of Hamlet's father, without however converting Pip into a Hamlet.

I am not at all certain whether anyone—*contra* Freud—can have an *unconscious* sense of guilt, but Hamlet and Pip both are quite conscious of an anguish of contamination. Hamlet, as the play progresses, has much about which to be guilty: he is brutal to Ophelia, shows no remorse at having slain Polonius, and gratuitously sends Rosenkrantz and Guildenstern off to their unmerited deaths. But none of this can be said to bother him; his malaise is metaphysical, not psychic, and has a long foreground. Pip indeed is another story, but his narrative never quite accounts for his conviction of guilt. *Great Expectations* is enough of a romance rather than a realistic novel that I think we have to take Pip's complicity in a nameless guilt as a *given,* one of the conditions that the book requires to get started and then keep going. What matters is that the reader loves and trusts Pip, a boy of great goodwill, and accepts his darkness of spirit as a Gothic element in this romance. Kafka, who learned much from Dickens, must have found in Pip (and other Dickens protagonists) another spur to his terrifying formula for the tale "In the Penal Colony," which is "Guilt is never to be doubted." Pip, like Hamlet, does not seem to me one of Freud's "moral masochists" who cannot bear happiness and success. Married to an Estella not ruined by Miss Havisham, Pip would have been happy. Hamlet, the great charismatic, cannot as easily be visualized occupying the Danish throne, with Queen Ophelia by his side. The Prince of Denmark is an aesthete and a malcontent, and something in him would always be casting about for another "Murder of Gonzago" to revise into a "Mousetrap." Pip, always a lost child, is content enough at the end to be fathered by the benign Gargerys, while wandering about with his godson, little Pip. Dickens's revised ending, with its possibility of marriage to Estella, cannot bear surmise. Is Pip to reenact the role of Drummle, her sadistic husband, and beat her regularly? When I remember Pip's affections in the novel, I do not immediately recall his thwarted passion for Estella, or even his profound affection for Joe Gargery. What burns in my memory is the quality of Pip's final love for Magwitch, more his father than Estella's, and the continuous love that Magwitch has manifested towards Pip for so long.

How to read *Great Expectations*? With the deepest elements in one's own fears, hopes, and affections: to read as if one could be a child again. Dickens invites you to do so, and makes it possible for you; that may be his greatest gift. *Great Expectations* does not take us into the Sublime, as Shakespeare and Cervantes do. It wants to return us to origins, painful and guilty as perhaps they must be. The novel's appeal to our childlike need for love, and recovery of self, is nearly irresistible. The "why" of reading it is then self-evident: to go home again, to heal our pain.

Fyodor Dostoevsky:
Crime and Punishment

Raskolnikov, a resentful student, plays with the terrible fantasy of murdering a greedy old woman, who as a pawnbroker exploits him. His phantasmagoria becomes reality when he kills not only her, but her half-witted stepsister as well. Once the crimes have been committed, the fate of Raskolnikov turns upon his encounters with the novel's three major characters. The first is Sonya, a pious and angelic young girl who has sacrificed herself as a prostitute, in order to care for her destitute siblings. Next is Porfiry Petrovich, a wise police investigator, who is Raskolnikov's patient nemesis. The most fascinating is Svidrigailov, a monument to nihilistic solipsism, and to cold lust.

In the intricate movements of the plot, Raskolnikov falls in love with Sonya, gradually realizes that Porfiry knows of his guilt, and increasingly sees his own potential for total degradation in the brilliant Svidrigailov. What the reader comes to understand is that there is deep division in Raskolnikov, between the urge to repent and the inner conviction that his Napoleonic self needs to be expressed in full. Dostoevsky himself is subtly divided, since Raskolnikov does not collapse into repentance until the novel's epilogue.

Crime and Punishment remains the best of all murder stories, a century and a third after its publication. We have to read it—though it is harrowing—because, like Shakespeare, it alters our consciousness. Though many among us deny the nihilism of Shakespeare's high tragedies of blood—*Hamlet, Othello, King Lear, Macbeth*—they are an inescapable origin for Dostoevsky's grand nihilists: Svidrigailov, Stavrogin in *The Possessed (The Devils),* and old Karamazov, the father in *The Brothers Karamazov.* We never will know what Shakespeare's actual belief (or skepticism) was, while Dostoevsky became a clerical reactionary almost beyond our capacity to conceive. But for *Crime and Punishment* in particular, we ought to follow D. H. Lawrence's adage: Trust the tale, and not the teller.

Dostoevsky believed in a Christianity that is yet to come: when all of us would love selflessly, and so sacrifice ourselves to others, as Sonya does in *Crime and Punishment*. In that Christian phase, beyond civilization as we think we know it, could novels be written? Presumably, we would not need them. Tolstoy, who wanted Dostoevsky to be Russia's Harriet Beecher Stowe, insisted that he valued *Uncle Tom's Cabin* over *King Lear*.

Dostoevsky, essentially a tragedian, and not an epic moralist, did not agree with Tolstoy. I muse sometimes that Dostoevsky left the Russian army, at twenty-three, in order to pursue a literary career, and Rodion Raskolnikov is twenty-three in the dreadful summer when he gratuitously murders two women, so as to aggrandize his Napoleonic vision of his self. There is a submerged affinity between Raskolnikov's refusal to swerve from his self-estimate, and Dostoevsky's heroic quest to write eternal fictions, culminating in *The Brothers Karamazov*. Raskolnikov repents truly at last, in the novel's unconvincing epilogue, when he surrenders wholly to the Magdalene-like Sonya, as the hope for his Lazarus-ascension from death to salvation. But since Raskolnikov's tragic recalcitrance is inextricably bound up with Dostoevsky's heroic drive to compose great tragedy, the reader is unlikely to be persuaded by Raskolnikov's belated Christian humility. Dostoevsky is superb at beginnings, astonishing at middle developments, but oddly weak at endings, since his apocalyptic temperament (one might think) would render him adept in last things.

Readers who are open to the experiential darkness of *Crime and Punishment* may well ponder the split not only in Raskolnikov but the implied fissure in Dostoevsky himself, and may conclude that a recalcitrance in the novelist, dramatic rather than moral-religious, renders him reluctant utterly to transform

Raskolnikov into a redeemed being. Happy endings are not consonant with works that feature the awesome nihilists Svidrigailov and Iago. When I think of *Crime and Punishment,* immediately Svidrigailov comes into my mind, and I shudder at his explanation as he pulls the trigger to commit suicide: "Going to America." This is the postnihilist (mere nihilist will not suffice) who tells Raskolnikov that Eternity exists; it is like a filthy bathhouse in the Russian countryside, crawling with spiders. Poor Raskolnikov, confronted with the real thing in Svidrigailov, the Way Down and Out incarnate, can be forgiven when he yearns for a vision more comforting, whether he believes in it or not.

There seems to me a real affinity between Raskolnikov and the murderer Macbeth, as there is between Svidrigailov and the Edmund of *King Lear,* another cold sensualist. Himself born in 1821, Dostoevsky more overtly associates the disturbing Svidrigailov with Lord Byron, made immensely popular in Russia by the national poet Pushkin, who also preceded Dostoevsky and Turgenev in their Shakespearean sympathies. Svidrigailov's criminal lusts, particularly excited by little girls, are a degradation of Edmund's and Byron's proclivities. But Raskolnikov, who is alarming enough, is several verges away from becoming a Svidrigailov, just as the murderous yet still sympathetic Macbeth is also a hero-villain, rather than a peer of Iago and Edmund.

Dostoevsky emulates Shakespeare by identifying the reader's imagination with Raskolnikov, even as Macbeth usurps our imaginations. Porfiry, the police inspector who brilliantly tortures Raskolnikov with uncertainty, presents himself as a Christian, but clearly causes distaste in Dostoevsky, who regards Raskolnikov's nemesis as a Western-influenced "mechanist," a manipulator of Raskolnikov's already tormented psychology. Sonya is as spiritually beyond the reader in the transcendental dimension as uncanny Svidrigailov exceeds us in the demonic mode. We have no place to go but Raskolnikov's consciousness, just as we have to journey with Macbeth into his heart of darkness. *We* might not murder old women or a fatherly monarch, but since in part we *are* Raskolnikov and Macbeth, perhaps in certain circumstances we might. Like Shakespeare, Dostoevsky makes us complicit in his hero-villain's murders. *Macbeth* and *Crime and Punishment* both are authentically frightening tragedies that do not purge us of pity, let alone of fear. Reversing Aristotle's socio-medical idea of catharsis, in which tragedy frees us of emotions not conducive to the public good, both Shakespeare and Dostoevsky have darker designs upon us.

It is this sharing in *Macbeth*'s terrible sublimity that allows *Crime and Punishment* to transcend depressing us, as we are led through a bad Petersburg summer in which a nightmare phantasmagoria becomes reality. Every wall we look at seems a hideous yellow, and the horror of a modern metropolis is portrayed with an intensity that rivals Baudelaire, or Dickens in his least affable moments. We begin to feel that in Raskolnikov's Petersburg, as in Macbeth's bewitched Scotland, we too might commit murders.

The question of how to read *Crime and Punishment* rapidly becomes, what causes Raskolnikov to become a murderer? He is replete with good qualities; his impulses are essentially decent, indeed humane. I marvel at the eminent modern Italian novelist Alberto Moravia, who found Raskolnikov a forerunner of Stalinist commissars, who were better known for oppressing others than for tormenting themselves. Raskolnikov, like his demonic parody Svidrigailov, is a self-punisher, whose masochism is absolutely incompatible with his professed desire to be a Napoleon. In one sense, Raskolnikov kills in order to discover whether he is a potential Napoleon, though he has every reason to believe that he is anything but that. Perhaps deeper is Raskolnikov's fierce guilt, which *precedes his crimes*. Whether he is a coarser version of Sonya's will-to-suffer, I rather doubt. Nor is he a passive double of Svidrigailov, all of whose malevolent sadism is a mask for "going to America" or suicide. It seems impossible to detach Raskolnikov from Dostoevsky, who at twenty-eight endured eight months in solitary confinement for being part of a radical group. Under sentence of death, he and his companions stood before a firing squad, and only then were reprieved. Four years of hard labor in Siberia followed, during which Dostoevsky became a thorough reactionary, a monarchist, and a devout follower of the Russian Orthodox Church.

Raskolnikov goes to Siberia for seven years, a light sentence for a double murder, but he has confessed his crimes, and the court has found him to have been at least in part insane, particularly when he killed. I don't see how an open, common reader could ascribe, with any certainty, any motive to Raskolnikov's transgressions in any ordinary meaning of "motive." Malignancy, deep rooted in Svidrigailov as in Iago and Edmund, has little place in the psyches of Raskolnikov and Macbeth, which makes their descents even more terrifying. Nor does one progress by looking for Original Sin in Raskolnikov and Macbeth. Both men suffer from powerfully proleptic or prophetic imaginations. Once either perceives a potential action to advance the self, he leaps the gap and experiences the crime as having been done, with all the attendant guilt. With so potent an imagination, and so guilty a consciousness, the actual murder is only a copy or a repetition, a self-wounding that lacerates reality, yet just to complete what in a way has already been done.

Absorbing as *Crime and Punishment* is, it cannot be absolved of tendentiousness, which is Dostoevsky's invariable flaw. He is a partisan, whose fierce perspective is always explicit in what he writes. His design upon us is to raise us, like Lazarus, from our own nihilism or skepticism, and then convert us to Orthodoxy. Writers as eminent as Chekhov and Nabokov have been unable to abide him; to them he was scarcely an artist, but a shrill would-be prophet. I myself, with each rereading, find *Crime and Punishment* an ordeal, dreadfully powerful but somewhat pernicious, almost as though it were a *Macbeth* composed by Macbeth himself.

Raskolnikov hurts us because we cannot cut loose from him. Sonya seems to me quite unendurable, but even Dostoevsky did not have the power to create a sane saint; I wince before her. Yet it is extraordinary that Dostoevsky could give us two supporting characters as vivid as Porfiry, the police inspector who is Raskolnikov's mighty opposite, and the amazingly plausible Svidrigailov, whose fascination is endless.

Porfiry, an accomplished investigator, is a kind of pragmatist, and a utilitarian, believing in the greatest good for the greatest number through the exercise of reason. Any reader (I assume), myself included, would rather dine with Porfiry than with the dangerous Svidrigailov, but I suspect Dostoevsky would have preferred Svidrigailov. Quite openly, Porfiry compares himself to a candle, and Raskolnikov to a circling butterfly, in a wonderfully composed waiting game:

> "What if I run away?" asked Raskolnikov, with a strange smile.
>
> "You won't run away. A peasant would run away, or a modern dissenter—the lackey of another's ideas, because you need only show him the end of your finger and, like Mr. Midshipman Easy, he will believe anything you like for the rest of his life. But you, after all, no longer believe even your own theory, why should you run away? What would you do in hiding? The fugitive's life is hard and hateful, and your first need is for a definite position and existence, and a suitable atmosphere, and what sort of atmosphere would you have? If you run away, you would come back of yourself. *You can't get on without us.*"
>
> (Translated by Jessie Coulson)

This is a deservedly classic moment in the history of "detective novels." What could be finer than Porfiry's *"You can't get on without us,"* candle speaking to butterfly. One feels in this instance that even the superb Chekhov was wrong; underestimating Dostoevsky is hazardous, even if you don't esteem him.

More hazardous, and yet more memorable, is Svidrigailov, the authentic nihilist, and the end of what might be called the Shakespearean road in Dostoevsky (if one adds Stavrogin in *The Devils*).

So strong and strange a character is Svidrigailov that I almost have to retract my assertion as to Dostoevsky's tendentiousness. Raskolnikov has confronted Svidrigailov, who has been pursuing Dunya Raskolnikov, the protagonist's sister. This is Svidrigailov on the woman who will reject him, then and always:

> In spite of Avdotya Romanovna's real aversion for me, and my persistently gloomy and forbidding aspect, she grew sorry for me at last, sorry for a lost soul. And when a girl's heart begins to feel *pity* for a man, then of course she is in the greatest danger. She begins to want to "save" him, and make him see reason, and raise him up, and put before him nobler aims, and awaken him to a new life and new activities—well, everybody knows what can be dreamt of in such circumstances. I realized at once that the bird had flown into the net of its own accord, and I began to make preparations in my turn. You seem to be frowning, Rodion Romanovich. There is no need; the affair, as you know, came to nothing. (Devil take it, what a lot of wine I'm drinking!) You know, from the very beginning I always thought it was a pity that your sister had not chanced to be born in the second or third century of our era, as the daughter of a ruling prince somewhere, or some governor or proconsul in Asia Minor. She would doubtless have been one of those who suffered martyrdom, and she would, of course, have smiled when they burnt her breast with red-hot pincers. She would have deliberately brought it on herself. And in the fourth or fifth century she would have gone into the Egyptian desert and lived for thirty years on roots, ecstasies, and visions. She is the kind of person who hungers and thirsts to be tortured for somebody, and if she does not achieve her martyrdom she is quite capable of jumping out of a window.

It is after Avdotya Romanovna's (Dunya Raskolnikov) failure to kill Svidrigailov (something he desires, rather more desperately even than he does her) that Svidrigailov "goes to America"—shoots himself. Svidrigailov's freedom, like Stavrogin's in *The Devils*, is absolute, and also is absolutely terrifying. Raskolnikov never repents, though in the epilogue he breaks down and yields to Sonya's saintliness. But it is Svidrigailov, not Raskolnikov, who runs away from Dostoevsky's ferocious ideology, and indeed runs out of the book. A reader may well want to murmur to herself: "Svidrigailov lives," though we probably won't scrawl that on subway walls.

Henry James:
The Portrait of a Lady

The Portrait of a Lady, my favorite among all of Henry James's novels, originally appeared in 1880–81. James revised extensively, more than a quarter century later, in 1908, for the definitive New York edition of *The Novels and Tales of Henry James*. Thirty-seven when he first sketched his portrait of Isabel Archer, James was sixty-five when he revised it.

There are almost two Isabel Archers, so that the reader is well advised to choose a reprint carefully, the later version being preferable. No novelist—not even Cervantes or Austen or Proust—had James's vast consciousness. One would have to go back to Shakespeare to find, as Emily Dickinson phrased it, a larger demonstration that the brain is wider than the sky. Isabel Archer, always a heroine of consciousness, manifests a palpably expanded consciousness in the revision of 1908.

Why read *The Portrait of a Lady*? We ought to read for many purposes, and to gain copious benefits, but the cultivation of an individual consciousness is certainly a prime purpose, and a major benefit, of deep reading. Zest and insight: these are the attributes of the solitary reader's consciousness that are most enhanced by reading. Social information, whether past or contemporary, seems to me a peripheral gain of reading, and political awareness an even more tenuous dividend.

As James revises *The Portrait of a Lady,* his near identity with Isabel Archer is augmented. Since Isabel is James's most Shakespearean character, her identity is placed in the reader's perspectives upon her. We are more guided by James in the revised version, so that it could be argued that Isabel was a richer, more enigmatic personality in 1881 than in 1908. Put another way, the most masterful of all American novelists seems to trust his readers less, and himself more, as his own perspectives upon Isabel changed.

Isabel, in 1881, is a victim of her drive for autonomy. By 1908, James converts her partial loss of autonomy, caused by her errors of judgment, into a gain in her consciousness. She *sees* much more, at the apparent cost of much of her freedom. To adopt one of our current modes, a feminist reader might be happier with the Isabel of 1881 than with the more Jamesian figure of 1908, whose prime concern is to stand beyond being deceived. Isabel's earlier attempt at *Self*-Reliance, brave but mistaken, is replaced by an emphasis upon the self's superior optics. Self-Reliance is Ralph Waldo Emerson's prime doctrine, and Isabel Archer is one of Emerson's children, as James, on some interior level, must have been aware. Since Henry James Sr. never achieved independence from Emerson, his son's comments upon the Sage of Concord require wary reading:

> It is hardly too much, or too little, to say of Emerson's writings in general that they were not composed at all.

> But no one has had so steady and constant, and above all so natural, a vision of what we require and what we are capable of in the way of aspiration and independence.

> . . . the rarity of Emerson's genius, which has made him so, for the attentive peoples, the first, and the one really rare, American spirit in letters . . .

The first remark is absurdly condescending; read Emerson's essay "Experience" and you may not agree with Henry James. But the second excerpt is pure Isabel Archer: that is precisely her vision. Whether James really meant the third extract, I rather doubt; he preferred Hawthorne, Emerson's uneasy walking companion. The passionate Hester Prynne, in Hawthorne's *The Scarlet Letter,* seems to me even more an Emersonian heroine than does Isabel Archer, who flees passion, as did Henry James. Emerson was in love with both his wives, Ellen and Lidian; perhaps more passionately with Ellen, who died so young. James, not Emerson, is responsible for Isabel's repression of her sexual nature. Never much of a novel reader, Emerson read *The Scarlet Letter* but underesteemed it; and I doubt that he would have admired *The Portrait of a Lady.* Yet he would have recognized in the idealistic Isabel a true child, and would have deprecated the aestheticism that led her to choose for a husband the dreadful Gilbert Osmond, a parody both of Emerson and of Walter Pater, high priest of the Aesthetic Movement in England.

Reading *The Portrait of a Lady* for the first time, you may find it useful to realize that Isabel Archer is always mediated for you by the narrator, Henry James, and by her admirers—Ralph Touchett, Lord Warburton, and Caspar Goodwood (unforgivably outrageous name!). Of Isabel as a dramatic personality, in the Shakespearean sense, James is able to give us very little. We take her on faith, because James's skill at studying her consciousness is so elaborate and artful, and because she has so strong an effect upon everyone else in the novel, male or female, with the ironic exception of her husband, the poseur Osmond. For Osmond, she ought to be only a portrait or a statue; her largeness of soul offends his narrowness. The crucial enigma of the novel, as every reader recognizes, is why did she marry the tiresome Osmond, and even more, why does she return to him at the end?

Why do so many readers, women as well as men, fall in love with Isabel Archer? If you are an intense enough reader when you are still very young, your first love is likelier to be fictive than actual. Isabel Archer, famously termed by Henry James "the heiress of all the ages," attracts many among us because she is the archetype of all those young women, in fiction or in actuality, who are pragmatically doom-eager because they seek complete realization of their potential while maintaining an idealism that rejects selfishness. George Eliot's Dorothea Brooke in *Middlemarch* aspires bravely, but her transcendental yearnings do not have the element added by Isabel Archer's Emersonianism, which is to drive for inward freedom almost at any cost.

Since Isabel is Henry James's self-portrait as a lady, her consciousness has to be extraordinarily large, almost the rival of her creator's. This renders any reader's moral judgment of her character rather irrelevant. The novelist Graham Greene, a Jamesian disciple, insisted that James's moral passion in *The Portrait of a Lady* centers upon the idea of treachery, as exemplified by Madame Merle, who plots successfully to marry Isabel to Osmond so that he, and Pansy, her daughter by Osmond, can enjoy Isabel's wealth. But Madame Merle, despite her deception, makes very little of a mark upon Isabel's capacious consciousness. Treachery obsessed Graham Greene, far more than it did Henry James.

Though *The Portrait of a Lady* is a kind of tragicomedy, few readers are going to be moved to laughter by the book. Despite the nasty vividness of Osmond and Madame Merle, and the different types splendidly exemplified by Isabel's admirers—Touchett, Warburton, Goodwood—James carefully sees to it that Isabel Archer is always at the center of our concern. It is indeed her portrait that matters; everyone else exists only in relation to her. The figure of Isabel means too much to James, and to the sensitive reader, for any comic perspective upon her to be adequate. Nor is irony allowed to dominate James's account of her odyssey of consciousness, though her situation is almost absurdly ironic. She took Osmond in the delusion that she was choosing—and granting—freedom. He knew everything worth knowing, she had thought, and in turn he would wish her to know all that could be known of life. Her terrible error might almost seem to be a cruelty towards her on James's part, but he suffers with her and for her, and her mistake is absolutely central for the book. "Error about life is necessary for life," Nietzsche remarked. Neither Henry James nor Isabel Archer is at all Nietzschean, but his adage illuminates Isabel's enormous blunder.

What is it that has blinded Isabel? Or, to ask that another way, why does James inflict such a catastrophe upon his own self-portrait as a woman? In James's revisions for the 1908 edition, Osmond is considerably darkened into authentic snobbishness, uselessness, and fakery, which makes Isabel's bad judgment all the more peculiar. James's first description of Gilbert Osmond is enough to warn the reader that Isabel's future husband is very bad news:

> He was a man of forty, with a high but well-shaped head, on which the hair, still dense, but prematurely grizzled, had been cropped close. He had a fine, narrow, extremely modeled and composed face, of which the only fault was just this effect of its running a trifle too much to points; an appearance to which the shape of the beard contributed not little. This beard, cut in the manner of the portraits of the sixteenth century and surmounted by a fair mustache, of which the ends had a romantic upward flourish, gave its wearer a foreign, traditionary look and suggested that he was a gentleman who studied style. His conscious, curious eyes, however, eyes at once vague and penetrating, intelligent and hard, expressive of the observer as well as of the dreamer, would have assured you that he studied it only within well-chosen limits, and that in so far as he sought it he found it. You would have been much at a loss to determine his original clime and country; he had none of the superficial signs that usually render the answer to this question an insipidly easy one. If he had English blood in his veins it had probably received some French or Italian comixture; but he suggested, fine gold coin as he was, no stamp nor emblem of the common mintage that provides for general circulation; he was the elegant complicated medal struck off for a special occasion.

He had a light, lean, rather languid-looking figure, and was apparently neither tall nor short. He was dressed as a man who takes little other trouble about it than to have no vulgar things.

Osmond, an American permanently settled in Italy, "studied style" but "only within well-chosen limits, and . . . in so far as he sought it he found it." Wonderfully Jamesian, that tells the reader how narrow and dubious Osmond is. Contrast that to the novel's opening description of Isabel Archer:

> She had been looking all round her again—at the lawn, the great trees, the reedy, silvery Thames, the beautiful old house; and while engaged in this survey she had made room in it for her companions; a comprehensiveness of observation easily conceivable on the part of a young woman who was evidently both intelligent and excited. She had seated herself and had put away the little dog; her white hands, in her lap, were folded upon her black dress; her head was erect, her eye lighted, her flexible figure turned itself easily this way and that, in sympathy with the alertness with which she evidently caught impressions. Her impressions were numerous, and they were all reflected in a clear, still smile. "I've never seen anything beautiful as this."

Isabel studies, not style, but people and places, and never within self-chosen limits. Intelligent and excited, knowingly beautiful, alert to her numerous impressions, amiably amused: it is no wonder that Ralph Touchett, Lord Warburton, and old Mr. Touchett have fallen in love with her at first sight, and that we will also, as we get to see her more clearly. The two initial descriptions in the 1908 edition are 170 pages apart, but the juxtaposition, though delayed, is direct and disconcerting. The sublime Isabel Archer— like the Shakespearean heroines Rosalind, Viola, Beatrice, Helena, and others—is compelled to marry down, but Ralph Touchett, Lord Warburton, and Caspar Goodwood are none of them potential disasters; Gilbert Osmond is a catastrophe. Each reader must judge for herself whether Henry James really makes Isabel's choice of Osmond persuasively inevitable. Much as I love James, Isabel, and *The Portrait of a Lady*, I have never been persuaded, and it seems to me the one flaw in an otherwise perfect novel. Isabel's blindness is necessary if the book is to work, but the more Jamesian Isabel of the 1908 revision simply seems too perceptive to be deceived by Osmond, particularly since James revises him into someone who quite definitely is *not* "the heir of all the ages."

James, subtlest of novelistic masters (excepting Proust), exerts all his art to make Isabel's misjudgment plausible. Osmond is, as he says, "convention itself," whose theoretic function is to liberate us from chaos, but whose pragmatic effect is to stifle Isabel's possibilities. His daughter, Pansy, is, for him, primarily a work of art to be sold, preferably to "a rich and noble husband." Osmond, a walking "gold coin," sees in Isabel not only her fortune (bequeathed to her by her kinspeople, the Touchetts) but also "material to work with," a portrait to be painted. But Isabel recognizes none of that until it is too late to save herself. Why? James gives us many hints, none definitive. There is Pansy, who awakens her maternal instincts (her boy, by Osmond, dies at six months, and James intimates that the sexual relation between Osmond and Isabel dies soon after). And there is Isabel's growing obsession to "choose" a form of life: Ralph Touchett is her kinsman and is ill; Lord Warburton represents English aristocracy, which her Americanness shuns; Caspar Goodwood, her early Albany suitor, is too possessive and passionate, too much in love with her. Like Henry James, Isabel wants to be loved, but not to be the object of another's overwhelming sexual passion.

James in addition ascribes Isabel's acceptance of Osmond, whose tastes are expensive but whose income is slight, to the girl's (she is still very young) generous idealism, and to her guilt as to the Touchett inheritance. Is all this enough? I think not, as I've said already, but James is quite Shakespearean and perhaps realistic in regard to the mysteries of marital choice. Shakespeare married

Anne Hathaway, and then lived apart from her in London for twenty years, sending money to Stratford for her and the children, and going home as little as possible. James, homoerotic to the core, but not acting on it, expressed an extraordinary regard for the value and sanctity of heterosexual marriage, while dryly observing that he himself thought too little of life to venture upon the blessed state himself.

I find more soluble, though still enigmatic, why Isabel returns to Rome and Osmond at the end of the story. Again rejecting Goodwood, she nevertheless experiences (and fears) the force of his passion:

> He glared at her a moment through the dusk, and the next instant she felt his arms about her and his lips on her own lips. His kiss was like white lightning, a flash that spread, and spread again, and stayed; and it was extraordinary as if, while she took it, she felt each thing in his hard manhood that had least pleased her, each aggressive fact of his face, his figure, his presence, justified of its intense identity and made one with this act of possession. So had she heard of those wrecked and under water following a train of images before they sink. But when darkness returned she was free.

She is free a take "a very straight path" back to Rome and Osmond. That will keep her free of Goodwood, but life with Osmond can be at best only an armed truce. Is *that* to be the final fate of James's heiress of all the ages? James will not tell us, because his part in the story is over; he knows no more, and probably, at the close, Isabel does not know either. But what will become of her potential for greatness of spirit, for amplitude of consciousness, without which the book must sink? James has declined to give her alternatives to Osmond; Goodwood threatens her sense of autonomy, as somehow the wretched Osmond does not. But even in 1908, Isabel could have been her own alternative: divorce, and a financial settlement, would free her from Osmond. Perhaps that yet may happen, but James gives us no clues towards this.

Osmond, however mean-spirited, is not so formidable as Isabel. She goes back, I surmise, to work through the consequences of her idealistic blunder, and thus assert a continuity in her own consciousness. That is quite Jamesian, though readers are not wrong to protest against it. *The Portrait of a Lady*, in its final form, demands close and sympathetic reading. We may not be satisfied by Isabel's choice, but her story tells us again one motive for why we read: to know better the consciousness too valuable for us to ignore.

Marcel Proust:
In Search of Lost Time

"How to read a novel" now means to me how to read Proust, the final splendor of the classical novel. What shall we do when confronted by the absolute inventiveness of *In Search of Lost Time*?

Proust's vast novel is narrated by the almost unnamed Marcel, a portrait of the novelist mostly as a young man, who gives us a labyrinthine recollection of French society from the closing decade of the nineteenth century down to 1922 (the year of Proust's death). The novel's great themes, alphabetically listed, include aestheticism and beauty, brothels, the dead (who annex the living), dress, the Dreyfus Affair (and its immersion in anti-Semitism), friendship, habits, inversion (homosexuality, both female and male), jealousy (above all!), literature itself and the gradual evolution of the narrator into a novelist, lying, memory (as prevalent as sexual jealousy), sadomasochism, the sea, sleep, and time (about as omnipresent as jealousy, and memory).

In Search of Lost Time tells three love stories (*erotic* might be a better word than *love*). Charles Swann, of Jewish origin but a leading socialite, becomes erotically obsessed with Odette de Crécy, whom he eventually marries, after suffering all the torments of love and jealousy. Their daughter, Gilberte, is the narrator Marcel's first infatuation, before she marries his best friend, Saint-Loup, whose early passion was for the actress Rachel. Gilberte Swann is only a forerunner of the narrator's overwhelming love, Albertine Simonet, with whom Marcel has a long, complex affair, terminated by her flight, and subsequent death in a riding accident.

Marvelous as are Proust's accounts of the jealous sufferings of Swann, in regard to Odette, and of Saint-Loup in relation to Rachel, the apotheosis of what could be called the jealous sublime is achieved in Marcel's retrospective quest for the lost time of Albertine's lesbian "betrayals" of her possessive lover. One would have to turn to the Bible, Shakespeare, and Dante to find apt analogues for the narrator's zeal, intensity, and suffering as he searches for what Norman Mailer might call "the time of Albertine's time." Shakespearean tragicomedy, as in *Measure for Measure* and *Troilus and Cressida,* comes closest to the superb irony and charmed rancidity of Marcel's grand quest.

These days there are mutterings that the nameless narrator (twice rather teasingly referred to as Marcel in the 3,300 pages of the novel) is a Proustian evasion, since the narrator is heterosexual and Christian. The mutterings are obtuse; the gays and lesbians who abound throughout, like the Jews and Dreyfusards, gain in sympathy by the apparent disinterestedness of the narrator (Proust himself was of course homosexual, a Dreyfusard, and the son of a beloved Jewish mother). As a surrogate for the magnificent author, the narrator has the privilege of presenting the largest, most vital, and most varied constellation of characters to be encountered outside of Shakespeare. How to read a novel, and Proust in particular, is in the first place how to read and appreciate literary character. Alphabetically listed, the indispensable personalities in Proust are Albertine, Charlus, Françoise, Oriane de Guermantes, the narrator's Mamma, Odette, Saint-Loup, Swann, Madame Verdurin. Add a tenth in the narrator himself, and you have a roster more vivid, inward, and titanically comic than any other novel whatsoever affords us. Proust's cosmos is as ironic as Jane Austen's, yet the

Proustian irony is less defensive and perhaps less an aid to invention. We can say that irony, in Proust, does not so much say one thing while meaning another, but rather makes intimations that are too large for any social context whatsoever. These intimations reach out to the corners of our consciousness, and search for the principles of right action in us. It seems peculiar to call such irony mystical or quietistic, and yet it is the secular equivalent of a profound spirituality. One doesn't want to confuse Proust with Krishna in the Bhagavad Gita, and yet Proustian memory finally seems a mode of right action that cures the narrator, and the reader, of what the ancient Hindu work warns against as "dark inertia." We read novels (the greater ones) to treat ourselves for dark inertia, the sickness-unto-death. Our despair requires consolation, and the medicine of a profound narration. Character in Proust's novel, as in Shakespeare, does the healing work implicitly prescribed for it by a literary culture. It is a wretched social irony of our moment that a culture failed by all its conceptual modes—philosophy, politics, religion, psychoanalysis, science—is compelled to become literary, rather in the mode of ancient Alexandria. Proust, like Shakespeare a better physician than Freud, offers us his characters as humanely as Chaucer and Shakespeare presented theirs. All of Proust's characters are essentially comic geniuses; as such they give us the option of believing that the truth is as funny as it is grim.

Nietzsche, in one of his most Hamlet-like formulations, advised us that what we could find words for was something already dead in our hearts, so that there was always a kind of contempt in the act of speaking. Proust, unlike Shakespeare, is free of that contempt, and his grandest characters manifest his generosity. The deadness of our hearts, our selfish egoism, is an intense concern, manifested more by sexual jealousy than by any other human affect, in Proust as in Shakespeare. I venture that novel-reading now performs the labor of assuaging envy, of which a most virulent form is sexual jealousy. Since the two Western authors most supreme at dramatizing sexual jealousy are Shakespeare and Proust, the quest for how to read a novel can provisionally be reduced to how to read sexual jealousy. I sometimes feel that the best literary training my students at Yale and NYU can obtain is only an enhancement of their pragmatic training by sexual jealousy, the most aesthetic of all psychic maladies, as Iago knew. That must be why Proust compares the quests of his jealous lovers to the obsessions of the art historian, as when Swann reconstructs the details of Odette's sexual past with "as much passion as the aesthete who ransacks the extant documents of fifteenth-century Florence in order to penetrate further into the soul of the Primavera, the fair Vanna or the Venus of Botticelli." Presumably art historians revel in this ransacking, whereas poor Swann gazes "in impotent, blind, dizzy anguish over the bottomless abyss." Yet Swann provokes our comic pleasure by his sufferings, even as we wince. Reading about the fictive jealous agonies of others may not heal our parallel torments, and may never teach us a comic perspective applicable to ourselves, and yet the sympathetic pleasure aroused seems close to the center of aesthetic experience. In Proust as in Shakespeare, the art itself is nature, an observation crucial to *The Winter's Tale*, which rivals *Othello* as Shakespeare's vision of sexual jealousy. Proust does not make us into Iago as we read, and yet we revel in his narrator's self-ruinings, for in Proust every major character, but Marcel in particular, becomes his own Iago. Of all Shakespeare's villains, Iago is the most inventive at stimulating sexual jealousy in his prime victim, Othello. The genius of Iago is that of a great playwright who delights in tormenting and mutilating his characters. In Proust, many of the protagonists become instances of an Iago turned against himself. What gives more aesthetic pleasure than a pride of self-mutilating Iagos? My favorite passage in all of Proust comes after the narrator's beloved Albertine is dead, and results from his minute investigations into every detail of her lesbian passions:

> Albertine no longer existed; but to me she was the person who had
> concealed from me that she had assignations with women in Bal-

bec, who imagined that she had succeeded in keeping me in ignorance of them. When we try to consider what will happen to us after our own death, is it not still our living self which we mistakingly project at that moment? And is it much more absurd, when all is said, to regret that a woman who no longer exists is unaware that we have learned what she was doing six years ago than to desire that of ourselves, who will be dead, the public shall still speak with approval a century hence? If there is more real foundation in the latter than in the former case, the regrets of my retrospective jealousy proceeded none the less from the same optical error as in other men the desire for posthumous fame. And yet, if this impression of the solemn finality of my separation from Albertine had momentarily supplanted my idea of her misdeeds, it only succeeded in aggravating them by bestowing upon them an irremediable character. I saw myself astray in life as on an endless beach where I was alone and where, in whatever direction I might turn, I would never meet her.

(Translated by C. K. Scott Moncrieff
and Terence Kilmartin)

"How to read a novel" might be epitomized as "how to read this passage," which is Proust's *Search* in miniature, and so is a model also of the traditional novel. Proust's vision of jealousy, quite Shakespearean, is that indeed it is in search of lost time, and of lost space as well. Othello, Leontes, Swann, and Marcel all suffer "the same optical error," the jealous resentment that there will never be enough time and enough space for themselves to enjoy Desdemona, Hermione, Odette, and Albertine. Such resentment is another mode of the ultimate outrage, the death of the lover rather than of the beloved. As a writer, Proust necessarily desires literary immortality, baldly reduced to public approval a century hence. Shakespeare's Sonnets hover on the edge of associating sexual jealousy with the envy of rival poets, but only Proust genially ascribes both resentments to the wonderfully named "optical error," doubtless one of those Nietzschean errors about life that are necessary for life. Reading Proust we come to understand our own optical errors, the squalors of our own jealousies, yet also our motives for metaphor, for turning to read yet another novel. A grand comedian of the spirit, Proust now seems to have anticipated our burden of belatedness, of having arrived too late in the story, at the millennium. Proust defined friendship as being "halfway between physical exhaustion and mental boredom," and said of love that it was " a striking example of how little reality means to us." Whereas Nietzsche warned that lying was an exhaustion, Proust exalted "the perfect lie" as our opening upon newness. I referred earlier to the rapid diminishment of serious readers of the novel, and I realize, rereading Proust, that the flight from the novel is a rejection of wisdom literature. For where shall we still find wisdom?

Proust's wisdom is not George Eliot's or Jane Austen's, and yet there seems to be a common sapience of the great novelists. Call it novelistic pragmatism, in which the only true differences are those that make a difference to the masters of prose fiction. Of death, Proust remarks that it cures us of the desire for immortality, which is an irony perhaps too savage for Eliot and Austen, but which legitimately extends their own battle against illusions. More profoundly, Proust finds innumerable ways of telling us that the self and society are irreconcilable, which does not mean that our selves are mere delusions, whether of language or of social contexts. Our personality, as Proust says, is a "composite army," which is a recognition implicit in George Eliot and more emphasized by Proust, as befits his novel-of-novels, which touches true grandeur when it dares to name the lost Albertine as "a mighty goddess of Time." *We* can say that of Eliot's Dorothea Brooke in *Middlemarch* or of Austen's Emma Woodhouse, but their creators could not; Proust teaches us both a retrospective divination by seeing his characters as divinities in time and a retrospective jealousy, and hints that the two sensations are one. His heroes and heroines are like the gods in Homer, who also are consumed by sexual jealousy and strife.

Despite Proust's healing power, I cannot read a novel in quite the way I did half a century ago, when I lost myself in what I read. I first fell in love (if I remember accurately) not with an actual girl but with Marty South in Thomas Hardy's *The Woodlanders*, and I grieved dreadfully when she cut off her beautiful hair in order to sell it. Few other experiences quite touch the reality of falling in love with a heroine, and with her book. One measures oncoming old age by its deepening of Proust, and its deepening by Proust. How to read a novel? Lovingly, if it shows itself capable of accommodating one's love; and jealously, because it can become the image of one's limitations in time and space, and yet can give the Proustian blessing of more life.

Thomas Mann:
The Magic Mountain

When I was a boy, first reading fiercely, some sixty years ago, Thomas Mann's *The Magic Mountain* was widely received as a work of modern fiction almost comparable to Joyce's *Ulysses* and Proust's *In Search of Lost Time*. I have just reread *The Magic Mountain* (1924) for the first time in fifteen years, and am happy to discover again its undiminished pleasure and power. Anything but a period piece, it is as fresh and sharp a reading experience as ever it has been, though subtly altered by time.

Mann has unfortunately been somewhat eclipsed during the last third of this century, being anything but a novelist of the counterculture. *The Magic Mountain* cannot be read sandwiched in between *On the Road* and some chunk of cyberpunk. It represents the high culture that is now in some jeopardy, since the book demands considerable education and reflection. Its protagonist, Hans Castorp, a young German engineer, arrives to visit his cousin at a tuberculosis sanatorium in the Swiss Alps, intending only a brief visit. Castorp, once he himself is diagnosed with the disease, stays seven years on the Magic Mountain, to be cured, and also to continue his *Bildung* or cultural education and development.

Mann initially describes Hans Castorp as a "perfectly ordinary" young man, but this is an irony. Castorp is no Everyman, nor is he essentially a spiritual quester, at least to begin with. But he is hardly ordinary. Endlessly teachable, immensely susceptible to profound conversation and to study, Castorp undergoes a remarkable, advanced education on the Magic Mountain, primarily through speaking and listening to antithetical teachers: Settembrini, Italian liberal humanist and disciple of the poet and free-thinker Carducci, who comes first and asserts his priority, and then, halfway through the novel, Naphta. Naphta is a radical reactionary, a Jewish Jesuit nihilist-Marxist who opposes democracy, looks back to the medieval religious synthesis, and who laments the European falling away from faith. The debates between Settembrini, standing for the Renaissance and the Enlightenment, and Naphta, apostle of the Counter-Reformation, are always merciless, reaching an early crux when Naphta cries out a prophecy of what was to triumph in Germany a decade after publication of *The Magic Mountain*:

> "No!" Naphta continued. "The mystery and precept of our age is not liberation and the development of the ego. What our age needs, what it demands, what it will create for itself, is—terror."
>
> (Translated by John E. Woods)

Both Naphta and Settembrini engage the reader's attention, but only Settembrini, despite Mann's endless ironies, causes us to grow fond of him. Irony is at once Mann's most formidable resource, and perhaps his ultimate weakness (as he knew). His protest, in 1953, against his critics remains useful:

I always feel a bit bored when critics assign my own work so definitely and completely to the realm of irony and consider me an ironist through and through, without also taking account of the concept of humor.

Irony has many meanings in literature, and the irony of one age is rarely the irony of another. My experience of imaginative writing is that it always possesses some degree of irony, which is what Oscar Wilde meant when he warned that all bad poetry is sincere. But irony is not the condition of literary language itself, and meaning is not always a wandering exile. Irony broadly means saying one thing and meaning another, sometimes even the opposite of what is being said. Mann's irony is frequently a subtle kind of parody, but the reader open to *The Magic Mountain* will find it a novel of gentle high seriousness, and ultimately a work of great passion, intellectual and emotional.

Mann's wonderful story now primarily offers not irony nor parody, but a loving vision of reality now vanished, of a European high culture now forever gone, the culture of Goethe and of Freud. In 2000, a reader must experience *The Magic Mountain* as a historical novel, the monument of a lost humanism. Published in 1924, the novel portrays the Europe that was to begin to break apart in World War I, the catastrophe that Hans Castorp descends his Magic Mountain in order to join. Much of humanistic culture survived the great war, but Mann prophetically senses the Nazi horror that was to take power a short decade after his novel's appearance. Where Mann may have intended a loving parody of European culture, the counterironies of change, time, and destruction make *The Magic Mountain,* in the year 2000, an immensely poignant study of the nostalgias.

Hans Castorp himself now seems to me both a subtler and a more likable character than he did when I first read the novel, more than fifty years ago. Though Mann is willing to see Castorp as a seeker, I do not find that any quest is central to the novel's protagonist. Castorp is not eager to pursue a grail or an ideal. A figure of the most admirable detachment, he will listen with equal contentment to the enlightened Settembrini, the terroristic Naphta, or the weirdly vitalistic Mynheer Peeperkorn, who arrives late at the Mountain in the erotic company of the Slavic beauty Clavdia Chauchat, with whom the infatuated Castorp has enjoyed only a single night of fulfillment. Hans Castorp's erotic detachment seems quite extraordinary; after seven months of being in love with Clavdia, he has the single moment of high passion, and then subsides for the remainder of his seven-year sojourn on the Mountain, nor does he feel much jealousy because of Peeperkorn, in whose company Clavdia returns. Castorp has been an orphan since the age of seven, and had experienced an adolescent homoerotic attachment of great intensity to his Slavic schoolmate Przibislaw Hippe, Clavdia's forerunner. His love for Clavdia renews his repressed passion for Hippe, and rather mystically the fused infatuation produces the symptoms of tuberculosis in him and keeps him on the Mountain for a seven-year education in the spirit of a dying humanism.

That falling in love should be a disease like consumption is a persuasive fantasy on Mann's part, and doubtless reflected his own barely repressed homoeroticism, the grand monument of which remains the novella *Death in Venice*. The reader stays on the Magic Mountain because Castorp falls in love with Clavdia at first sight. Whatever the clinical reality of Castorp's illness, the reader is charmed into the novel's progress, since the common experience of changing plans or location or psychic condition when one falls in love is shrewdly integrated with the reader's own induction into the world of the Magic Mountain. I don't know that the reader (of either gender) necessarily conceives a passion for the sinuous and enigmatic Clavdia, but identification with Castorp, in his endless goodwill and sexual detachment, is difficult to resist, so skilled is Mann's art. We do not always see, feel, and think as Hans does, but we are always close to him. Except for Joyce's Poldy, my namesake in *Ulysses,* there is no more sympathetic character in modern fiction than Castorp. Joyce's attempts at detachment did not succeed, and Leopold Bloom reflects many of Joyce's most attractive personal qualities. The ironic parodist Thomas Mann, for all his contrary efforts, cannot keep himself apart from Castorp.

Since critical fashion nowadays denies the reality both of authors and of literary characters (like all fashion, this will pass away), I urge the reader not to refuse the pleasures of identification with favorite characters, any more than authors have been able to resist such pleasures. There are limits to my urging: Cervantes is not Don Quixote, Tolstoy (who loved her) is not Anna Karenina, and Philip Roth is not "Philip Roth" (either of them!) in *Operation Shylock.* Yet generally novelists, however ironic, find themselves again within their protagonists; so do dramatists. Kierkegaard, the Danish religious philosopher who wrote *The Concept of Irony,* remarked that Shakespeare was the master ironist, which is indisputable. Yet even that ironist of ironists found himself more truly and more strange in the character of Hamlet, as I intimate elsewhere in this book. Why read? Because you can know, intimately, only a very few people, and perhaps you never know them at all. After reading *The Magic Mountain* you know Hans Castorp thoroughly, and he is greatly worth knowing.

Rereading *The Magic Mountain,* I conclude now that Mann's greatest irony (perhaps unintended) was to begin the book by saying of Hans Castorp that "the reader will come to know him as a perfectly ordinary, if engaging young man." I have been a university teacher these forty-five years, and am compelled to say of Castorp: he is that ideal student the universities used to proclaim (before their current self-degradation) yet never found. Castorp is intensely interested in everything, in all possible knowledge, but knowledge as a good in itself. Knowledge is in no way power for Castorp, whether over others or himself; it is in no way Faustian. Hans Castorp is enormously valuable for readers in the year 2000 (and beyond) because he incarnates a now archaic but always relevant ideal: the cultivation of self-development until the individual can realize all of her or his potential. Eagerness to confront ideas and personalities combines in Hans with remarkable spiritual stamina; never merely skeptical, he is also never overwhelmed (except at the height of his sexual passion for the somewhat dubious Clavdia). The humanistic eloquence of Settembrini, the terroristic exhortings of Naphta, and the Dionysian stammerings of Peeperkorn all break over Castorp, yet never wash him away.

Though Mann keeps insisting upon Castorp's colorlessness, that becomes something of a joke, since the young naval engineer has an affinity for mystical and even occult experiences. He had arrived at the Magic Mountain carrying the book *Ocean Steamships,* but he becomes an endless reader of works on the life sciences, psychology and physiology in particular, and goes on from them to incessant "culture-traveling." Any lingering sense that we may have retained (and only from Mann's ironies) of Hans Castorp's "ordinariness" dissolves in the wonderful chapter "Snow," just before the end of the sixth of the novel's seven sections. Trapped by a snowstorm while out on a solitary skiing expedition, Hans barely survives, and then is granted a series of visions. When these subside, he grants that "death is a great power," but affirms, *"for the sake of goodness and love, man shall grant death no dominion over his thoughts."*

After that, *The Magic Mountain* goes into its own dance of death, as the outbreak of World War I approaches. Naphta challenges Settembrini to a duel with pistols; Settembrini fires into the air, and the furious Naphta kills himself with a single shot to the head. Poor Settembrini is thereafter shattered, and his humanistic pedagogy ceases. The Dionysian Peeperkorn, affirmer of personality and of the religion of sex, confronts his own aging impotence, and he also kills himself. Hans Castorp patriotically goes off to fight for Germany, and Mann tells us that, while the young man's chances of survival are not good, the question must be left open.

The reader, almost despite Thomas Mann, can rate Castorp's

chances as being rather better, because there is something magical or enchanted about him, altogether timeless. He may *seem* to be an apotheosis of the average, but clearly is demonic, and really does not require the endless cultural instruction he receives (though he is the better for it). Hans Castorp bears the Blessing, as Mann's Joseph will in the later tetralogy *Joseph and His Brothers*. Saying farewell to his protagonist, Mann tells us that Castorp mattered because of his "dream of love." Hans Castorp matters now, in 2000 and beyond, because the reader, seeking to understand him, will come to ask herself or himself, what is my dream of love, or my erotic illusion, and how does that dream or illusion affect my own possibilities of development or unfolding?

SUMMARY OBSERVATIONS

It seems clear that reading a novel in 2000 is a very changed act from what it was back in 1944, when I first started, after several earlier years of reading nothing but poetry and Scripture. Major novelists such as Philip Roth tell me that the readership is not renewing itself, and evidently an art not fully developed until the eighteenth century may expire after the second millennium that rushes upon us. Perhaps cyberpunk fiction, the latest form of romance, is a presage of a cyclic revenge of romance upon its ungrateful child, the novel. The more or less realistic novel has dominated Western literature for most of these last three centuries; its great monuments extend from Samuel Richardson's *Clarissa* through Marcel Proust's *In Search of Lost Time*. How shall we read a novel when we fear that the form will vanish from us all too soon? Shall we not find ourselves feeling a poignance quite apart from the pathos of the novel's own protagonists?

One potentially valuable lesson in how to read a great novel is to ask the question: Do the principal characters change and, if they do, what causes them to change? In Marcel Proust's magnificent *In Search of Lost Time,* the Shakespearean pattern of change through self-overhearing dominates, whereas in Thomas Mann's *The Magic Mountain,* the likable hero, Hans Castorp, follows the Cervantine design, with the liberal philosopher Settembrini playing the role of an intellectualized Sancho to Castorp's Quixote.

Change, in Shakespeare, is that playwright's greatest invention, following the medieval English poet Chaucer rather than the Roman poet Ovid, who nevertheless, with Chaucer and Christopher Marlowe, was one of the three authentic influences upon Shakespeare. When characters like Hamlet, King Lear, Antony, and Cleopatra change, more often than not it is because they overhear themselves, almost as if someone else had spoken. Antony, after he hears himself remark to his armor-bearer, Eros: "Eros, thou yet beholdst me?" is so struck by his own observation that he doubts his own identity:

> Here I am Antony
> Yet cannot hold this visible shape, my knave.

The reader might reflect how often she herself is conscious of the will to change, after she has the surprise of overhearing herself. I suspect that, in English- or German-speaking countries, where Shakespeare has influenced us most intimately, we change more frequently in that mode than the Cervantine, where close converse with a good companion leads more readily to self-reflection, and consequent psychic alteration. Stendhal, Jane Austen, Dostoevsky, Henry James, and Proust follow the Shakespearean paradigm, while Dickens and Mann are more in Cervantes's mode, as are Maupassant and Calvino among short-story writers. The other masters of the short narrative that I have discussed in this book—Turgenev, Chekhov, Hemingway, and Borges in particular—seem to me more indebted to Shakespeare. Much the same is true of the American novelists I discuss in my final chapter, with the exception of the superbly outrageous Thomas Pynchon.

Does good reading help us to learn how to listen to one another as on the Cervantine model? I venture that it is impossible to listen to other people the way we listen to a very good book. Lyric poetry, at its strongest, teaches us how to talk to ourselves, rather than to others. The solitary reader may be a vanishing breed, but more than the enjoyment of solitude then will vanish also. The ultimate answer to the question "Why read?" is that only deep, constant reading fully establishes and augments an autonomous self. Until you become yourself, what benefit can you be to others? I remember always the admonition of the sage Hillel, most humane of ancient rabbis: "If I am not for me, then who will be for me? And if I am for myself only, then what am I? And if not now, when?"

How do we read a novel in which the author, like Shakespeare, or perhaps Jane Austen, seems to have obliterated himself or herself? Cervantes is at the opposite pole, as are Stendhal and Thomas Mann, though neither match Charlotte Brontë in her marvelous *Jane Eyre,* where frequently she bashes the reader even as she advises him. With George Eliot, I value the novelist's overt moral reflections as much as I do the power of her narration or the subtle qualities with which she endows her protagonists. The meddling novelist is more than welcome, if we are given the wisdom of Cervantes or of George Eliot. Novelists like Flaubert in *Madame Bovary* or James Joyce in *Ulysses* seem to be in enigmatic reserve behind their characters, but oddly they may identify with their creations more profoundly than Cervantes does, when he overtly commends himself for having created Sancho and the Don. Flaubert notoriously confessed: "I am Madame Bovary," and Joyce, despite the high art of his withdrawal from Leopold Bloom, is finally at one with the indomitable and humane Poldy.

A good biography of a novelist, such as George Painter's *Proust,* can be a considerable aid to reading, provided that the reader avoid the error that good biographers avoid, which is to read the life too closely into the work. What is more vital is the work in the writer, the effect of Proust's ambitious project upon the author's own life.

These days, many novels are overpraised for social purposes, and what should be regarded as supermarket fiction is canonized by the universities. Jane Austen's formidable social and moral irony is a defense against such vulgarization of taste and judgment, as I have tried to indicate. A great novelist, even when as sophisticated as Austen or Henry James, shares with Dickens the power to make us read as if we could be children again. A child in love with reading, first encountering *David Copperfield* or *Great Expectations,* will read for the story and the characters and not to expiate social guilt or to reform bad institutions.

Major novels do, however, tend to address crucial enigmas, or brood upon central questions. One mark of good reading is to allow such enigmas or concerns to reveal and uncover themselves, rather than hunt them out too strenuously. If it is vital that you locate the puzzle as to why Isabel Archer chose the truly dreadful Osmond, or why Raskolnikov finds it so difficult to repent, then Henry James and Dostoevsky have the responsibility for alerting and guiding you, and you can trust them to do so. Novels on the grandest scale, such as *Don Quixote* and *In Search of Lost Time,* invest their exuberance more prodigally, so that the enigma becomes the work itself. The world at play in *Don Quixote* touches a limit when the Don becomes "sane," and dies soon afterwards. The past recaptured in Proust's visionary epic is the novelist's triumph, and the prelude to his demise.

How should one read a marvelous long novel? Going back to it, day after day, we may still have trouble holding on to the plot. Dr. Samuel Johnson, who greatly admired (as I do) Samuel Richardson's *Clarissa,* a novel as long as Proust's, observed that if you read *Clarissa* for the plot, you would hang yourself. You do not read *Don Quixote* or *In Search of Lost Time* for the plot, but for the progressive development of the characters and for the gradual unfolding, indeed the revelation, of the author's vision. Sancho Panza and Don Quixote, Swann and Albertine, become presences as intimate and yet ultimately as enigmatic as your dearest friends.

With regard both to Stendhal and to Dickens, I have espoused the idea of rereading, which seems to me even more essential with Jane Austen and with Cervantes (as it is with Shakespeare). There is a pure pleasure in the first reading of a great novel, and yet I think it is a different and better experience when you reread *Great Expectations* or *The Charterhouse of Parma*. You are liberated into perspectives not previously available to you, and the pleasures of rereading can be more various and enlightening than your first experience of the novel. You know what is going to happen, but how and why it happens can be increasingly a new realization. Perhaps, to some degree, you become what you behold, the second time around.

When we are young, and read most passionately and repeatedly, we are likely to identify, perhaps somewhat naively, with favorite characters in a novel. As I observed in regard to Mann's *The Magic Mountain,* such pleasure of identification is a legitimate part of the reading experience, at any age, even if such pleasure passes, in middle age and later, from naïve to sentimental. Novels, like our lives, can scarcely exist without encounters with love, however ironically Mann and other novelists tend to represent eros and its discontents. Characters meet other characters as we meet new persons, open to the disorders of discovery, and we need to be open to what we read, in a parallel way.

When you meet a new person, you are ill-advised to begin the acquaintance either with condescension or with fear. When you read even the most formidable literary work for a first time—be it Dante's *Divine Comedy* or Henry James's *The Wings of the Dove*—condescension or fear would destroy your understanding and your pleasure. Perhaps we all need initially to relax our will-to-power when we open a book. Such a will may return after we have immersed ourselves, and have given the writer every chance to usurp our attention. There are many different ways to read well, but all involve a receptivity in our attention. I have little understanding of Buddhism (my temperament being an impatient one), so Wordsworth's "wise passivity" seems my best synonym for the kind of attention that good reading requires.

IV

Plays

Introduction

I have chosen three plays to discuss in this book: Shakespeare's tragedy, *Hamlet;* Henrik Ibsen's tragicomedy, *Hedda Gabler;* Oscar Wilde's comedy, *The Importance of Being Earnest.* My choices, while necessarily arbitrary, nevertheless illuminate the nature and history of Western drama down to the threshold of the century now ended.

No introduction to how to read a play could omit William Shakespeare, the supreme dramatist of all time. Of Shakespeare's earlier tragedies, *Titus Andronicus* is a bloody farce, possibly even a parody. *Romeo and Juliet* is a lyrical triumph, yet the tragedy is more familial than individual. *Julius Caesar* is a model of the well-made play, but Dr. Samuel Johnson found it cold, and so do I. *Hamlet* is the first great tragedy after the Oedipus cycle of Sophocles, the Agamemnon trilogy of Aeschylus, and the humane pathos that Euripides brought to the Athenian stage.

Hamlet is Shakespeare's largest play, and one of his most difficult. It has been more than popular, and is now so familiar, even to those who have never read it or attended a performance (or seen a film version), that reading it well is akin to removing the varnish that disfigures an old painting. I attempt to take off some of the varnish here.

I have chosen *Hedda Gabler* as the second play because Ibsen is (together with Molière, seventeenth-century French master of comedy) the principal European dramatist since Shakespeare. Molière, a profound psychologist, nevertheless held fast to comedy, except in his *Don Juan*. Though we too often think of Ibsen as a social realist, father of Arthur Miller, that is an error. Shakespeare pervades Ibsen, whether in the tragedy of *Brand,* the heroic comedy of *Peer Gynt,* or the visionary romance of *When We Dead Awaken.* Hedda Gabler is a remarkable blend of Shakespeare's Cleopatra with his Iago, and her tragicomedy fitly concludes the nineteenth century, which dies uneasily to her self-mocking laughter, thus ending the Aesthetic adventure of critics like Walter Pater, poets like Algernon Swinburne, and even of the great novelist Henry James. For the Aesthetes, life and literature alike were affairs of perception, sensation, and consciousness. All of these have turned venomous in Hedda Gabler, whose hysterical temperament prophesies the exacerbated sensibilities of women and men alike throughout the post-Ibsenite drama of the twentieth century.

Oscar Wilde's delightful *The Importance of Being Earnest* is a true antidote to *Hedda Gabler.* In what may be the best English stage comedy since William Congreve, if not since William Shakespeare, Wilde transports us through Lewis Carroll's looking glass, and we are in the lovely world of cucumber sandwiches and Lady Bracknell, who merges the flamboyant bluster of Sir John Falstaff with the rolling periods of Dr. Samuel Johnson. Wilde, too good-natured to be a satirist, parodies the upper social world so that its inhabitants become children at play. Wit, charm, pleasure, warmth, and the gorgeous nonsense of Carroll's Alice books blend with the controlled absurdities of Gilbert and Sullivan to give us a drama of pure entertainment, with subtle overtones of Wilde's own impending tragedy.

William Shakespeare:
Hamlet

1

There are magnificent writers who have the highest spiritual ambitions: Dante, Milton, Blake. Shakespeare, like Chaucer and Cervantes, had other interests: primarily, in the representation of the human. Though Shakespeare perhaps ought not to have become a secular scripture for us, he does seem to me the only possible rival to the Bible, in literary power. Nothing, when you stand back from it, seems odder or more wonderful than that our most successful entertainer should provide an alternative vision (however unintentionally) to the accounts of human nature and destiny in the Hebrew Bible, the New Testament, and the Koran. Yahweh, Jesus, Allah, speak with authority, and in another sense so do Hamlet, Iago, Lear, and Cleopatra. Persuasiveness is larger in Shakespeare because he is richer; his rhetorical and imaginative resources transcend those of Yahweh, Jesus, and Allah, which sounds rather more blasphemous than I think it is. Hamlet's consciousness, and his language for extending that consciousness, is wider and more agile than divinity has manifested, as yet.

Hamlet has many enigmas; they will go on being uncovered, just as the theologians and mystics will continue to expound the mysteries of God. There is always less urgency in our meditations upon Hamlet than upon God, and yet I am tempted to remark of Hamlet what the ancient Gnostics affirmed about Jesus: *first* he resurrected, and *then* he died. The Hamlet of act 5 has risen from the dead self of the earlier Hamlet. It is the resurrected Hamlet who says "Let it be," rather than "To be or not to be." There are less subtle resurrections in the late romances; I know of nothing subtler in all literature than the transformation and apparent apotheosis of Hamlet.

Hamlet speaks about fifteen hundred lines, an outrageously long part, representing not quite 40 percent of the play's uncut text. Since Hamlet is a bookish intellectual and a man who haunts theaters (the Globe in particular), his natural mode is an extreme ambivalence. If someone, or something, is to be esteemed, then your own estimate must create the esteem. Horatio to us seems a faithful straight man; to Hamlet he is the best of all human beings. It is hard not to doubt the validity of Hamlet's praise of Horatio, and yet we sense that somehow Hamlet intends the compliment to us as audience, so we are reluctant to refuse it:

> Nay, do not think I flatter,
> For what advancement may I hope from thee,
> That no revenue hast but thy good spirits
> To feed and clothe thee? Why should the poor be
>   flatter'd?
> No, let the candied tongue lick absurd pomp,
> And crook the pregnant hinges of the knee
> Where thrift may follow fawning. Dost thou hear?
> Since my dear soul was mistress of her choice,
> And could of men distinguish her election,
> S'hath seal'd thee for herself; for thou hast been
> As one, in suff'ring all, that suffers nothing,
> A man that Fortune's buffets and rewards
> Hast ta'en with equal thanks; and blest are those
> Whose blood and judgment are so well commeddled
> That they are not a pipe for Fortune's finger
> To sound what stop she please. Give me that man
> That is not passion's slave, and I will wear him
> In my heart's core, ay, in my heart of heart,
> As I do thee.
>
> (Act 3, scene 2, 57–74)

Certainly Hamlet, for once, intends no irony; normally he is as mocking as Falstaff. His instant popularity, like Falstaff's, had something to do with the appeal of dramatic irony. Both ironists, Hamlet and Falstaff, think much too well for their own good, yet their audience benefits. Hamlet's is a tragic irony, and Falstaff's is comic, except that Hamlet's ferocious ironies can be hilarious and Falstaff's hilarity is at last tragic. But Hamlet is being totally sincere in his praise of Horatio, who is the one person at the court of Elsinore who cannot be manipulated by Claudius. When Hamlet says that Horatio has been "As one, in suff'ring all, that suffers nothing," he clearly intimates that Horatio has become a surrogate for the audience. As Shakespeare's audience, we indeed suffer all that Shakespeare offers us, yet since we know this is a play, we also suffer nothing. In praising Horatio as a man "That is not passion's slave," Shakespeare desires his audience also to become more stoic and wise.

I have been chided by reviewers for suggesting that Shakespeare "invented the human," as we now know it. Dr. Johnson said that the essence of poetry was invention, and it should be no surprise that the world's strongest dramatic poetry should have so revised the human as pragmatically to have reinvented it. Shakespearean detachment, whether in the Sonnets or in Prince Hamlet, is a rather original mode. Like so many Shakespearean inventions, it has Chaucerian origins, but tends to outrun Chaucerian ironies. G. K. Chesterton, still one of my critical heroes, points out that Chaucer's humor is sly, but lacks the "wild fantasticality" of Hamlet. Chaucer's slyness, Chesterton remarks, is a kind of prudence, quite unlike Shakespearean wildness. I find that useful; Hamlet's wild detachment is another of the prince's quests for freedom: from Elsinore, and from the world. Even Chaucer's Wife of Bath, fierce and idiosyncratic, does not quest for Hamlet's wild freedom.

Hamlet speaks seven soliloquies; they have two audiences, ourselves and Hamlet, and we gradually learn to emulate him by overhearing rather than just hearing. We overhear, whether or not we are Hamlet, contrary to the speaker's awareness, perhaps even against the speaker's intention. Overhearing Yahweh or Jesus or Allah is not impossible, but is rather difficult, since you cannot become God. You overhear Hamlet by becoming Hamlet; that is Shakespeare's art in this most original of all his plays. Refusing identity with Hamlet is by now almost unnatural, particularly if you tend to be an intellectual. A number of actresses have played Hamlet. I wish that more would attempt the role. As a representation, Hamlet transcends maleness. He is the ultimate overhearer, and that attribute is beyond gender.

We tend to define "genius" as extraordinary intellectual power. Sometimes we add the metaphor of "creative" power to the definition. Of all fictive personages, Hamlet stands foremost in genius. Shakespeare gives copious evidence of the prince's intellectual strength. For the power of creation, we are given mostly equivocal signs, except for the Player-King's great speech, and the mad little songs Hamlet intones in the graveyard.

I suggest that the play *Hamlet* is a study in its protagonist's balked creativity, the prince's unfulfilled renown as a poet. My suggestion scarcely is original; it is implicit in William Hazlitt, and is central to Harold Goddard's interpretation of the drama. But I want to be as clear as I am capable of being; I do not mean that Hamlet was a failed poet, that being the French Hamlet of T. S. Eliot. The Hamlet of the first four acts is balked by his father's ghost, that is to say, by the prince's partial and troubled internalization of his father's spirit. In act 5, the Ghost has been exorcised, by a great creative effort that Shakespeare leaves largely implicit. The exorcism takes place at sea, in the interval between acts 4 and 5. Shakespeare, who generally seems the most open of all writers, can also be the most elliptical. He loves to be excessive at putting things in, while he slyly also educates us by leaving things out. *Hamlet* is a huge play, and yet it is also a giant torso, with much, on purpose, omitted. How to read *Hamlet* is a challenge that touches a height in the transition between act 4 and act 5. Why read *Hamlet?* Because, by now, this play makes us an offer we cannot refuse. It has become our tradition, and the word *our* there is enormously inclusive. Prince Hamlet is the intellectual's intellectual: the nobility, and the disaster, of Western consciousness. Now Hamlet has also become the representation of intelligence itself, and that is neither Western nor Eastern, male nor female, black nor white, but merely the human at its best, because Shakespeare is the first truly multicultural writer.

One learns from Shakespeare that self-overhearing is the prime function of soliloquy. Hamlet, in his seven soliloquies, teaches us what imaginative literature *can* teach, which is how to talk to oneself, and not how to talk to others. Hamlet is not interested in listening to anyone, except perhaps the Ghost. Shakespeare, through Hamlet, shows us that poetry has no *social* function whatsoever, beyond entertainment. But it has a crucial function for the self; Hamlet very nearly heals himself, but then touches a limit beyond which even the most intelligent of literary characters cannot progress.

It cannot be overstated that Hamlet has no creed, whether social or religious, and I suspect that Shakespeare himself was equally skeptical, or even just evasive. What Hamlet does have is an enormous sense of his own ever-burgeoning inner self, which he suspects may be an abyss. That suspicion seems to me the true subject of all seven of the soliloquies, not one of which is spoken in act 5. The reader is likelier than the playgoer to puzzle out that *Hamlet* is almost two separate plays, acts 1–4 and act 5, because the prince of act 5 seems at least a decade older than the truant student of the first four acts.

It is difficult to compare *Hamlet* to any other literary work, whether to other dramas by Shakespeare or simply to literature of its eminence: by Dante and Chaucer, Cervantes and Molière, Goethe and Tolstoy, Chekhov and Ibsen, Joyce and Proust. *Hamlet* is not at one with itself, and Prince Hamlet, even at the end, says that he knows more than he has time to tell us. Montaigne, whom the prince seems to have absorbed, is the only useful analogue. Compared to Montaigne, Prince Hamlet is savage, both to himself and to others. We cannot say that the Montaigne even of the great essay "Of Experience" is wiser than the prince of act 5, but he is more generous with his wisdom than Hamlet is inclined to be. In act 5 one feels that the Blessing has abandoned Hamlet, however charismatic he remains.

By the Blessing, in the biblical sense, I mean: "More life, into a time without boundaries." Something in Hamlet dies when he is at sea; he returns to Denmark free of his father's ghost, but in some sense already a dead man. Throughout act 5, his perspective seems spookily posthumous, which may account for his dying obsession that he not bear, for posterity, "a wounded name." The reader of *Hamlet,* or the playgoer, may feel a certain puzzlement when the prince restrains his grieving follower, Horatio, from suicide, solely to tell Hamlet's story, in order to cure the prince's wounded name. In fact, there are stains enough upon Hamlet, even if we accept the momentary reality of his highly equivocal madness. He has been sadistically brutal to Ophelia, helping to drive her to madness and suicide. He has murdered Polonius, thrusting his sword through a curtain in total unawareness of whom he may kill, and manifests only glee afterwards. Rosenkrantz and Guildenstern are timeservers and false friends, but they do not deserve Hamlet's gratuitous sending of them to their deaths, which the prince subsequently shrugs off. Sigmund Freud was convinced that Gertrude was Jocasta to Hamlet's Oedipus; I am not at all persuaded, particularly when Hamlet's final salutation to his dead mother is the perfunctory "Wretched Queen, adieu!" Hamlet is bad news, and I suppose might be called one of Shakespeare's hero-villains, like Iago, Edmund, and Macbeth, but to so name him would be a mistake. He deserves a wounded name, but he doesn't have one, and not just because the survivor Horatio will go on repeating the story from the perspective of the person who loved Hamlet best.

2

We can surmise that Hamlet, were he not a tragic protagonist, might well have become a poet-playwright, more given to composing comedies than tragedies. That is not a fashionable surmise these days, but current fashions will fade away, in a generation, at most, and Hamlet's genius will abide. Like Shakespeare himself, Prince Hamlet is adept at character analysis; everyone he speaks to in the play (except the Ghost) is clarified for us by Hamlet's questionings, even if he or she cannot accept self-clarification. Why read *Hamlet*? Because it will clarify the reader, if the reader can make that acceptance.

Imagine that you are one of these "attendant lords" with whom T. S. Eliot's J. Alfred Prufrock identifies: "one that will do / To swell a progress, start a scene or two." What would it be like to be confronted by Hamlet? Iago, who can so easily manipulate everyone in *his* play, would be unmasked by Hamlet in ten lines or less, and the Edmund of *King Lear* would do no better. Claudius is rendered furious or incoherent each time Hamlet tests him, and the badly outclassed Rosenkrantz and Guildenstern have great trouble even at keeping up with what the Prince of Denmark is saying to them.

> *Hamlet.* What news?
> *Rosenkrantz.* None, my lord, but that the world's grown honest.
> *Hamlet.* Then is doomsday near. But your news is not true. Let me question more in particular. What have you, my good friends, deserved at the hands of Fortune, that she sends you to prison hither?
> *Guildenstern.* Prison, my lord?
> *Hamlet.* Denmark's a prison.
> *Rosenkrantz.* Then is the world one.

Hamlet. A goodly one, in which there are many confines, wards, and dungeons, Denmark being one of the worst.
Rosenkrantz. We think not so, my lord.
Hamlet. Why then 'tis none to you, for there is nothing either good or bad, but thinking makes it so. To me it is a prison.
Rosenkrantz. Why then your ambition makes it one. 'Tis too narrow for your mind.
Hamlet. O God, I could be bounded in a nutshell and count myself a king of infinite space—were it not that I have bad dreams.

(Act 2, scene 2, 236–56)

By the time this first encounter between Hamlet and his old friends is over, Rosenkrantz and Guildenstern are already dead men. We need to feel how appalling Hamlet's cruelly witty game is; it is as though a contemporary crown prince, say of Jordan, confronted in Amman his two closest friends at Yale, where all three are still undergraduates. The king is dead, the prince wants to go back to Yale but is detained at court, and suddenly his two New Haven cronies pop up in Amman, where he has *not* succeeded to the throne. Horatio, a hanger-on of this set at Yale, will replace them as Hamlet's closest friend. Hamlet has realized immediately that they are suborned by the King and Queen, while Horatio is not, and cannot be. Wisest of all fools, Hamlet is an extremely dangerous prince, as he warns Laertes, a Harvard undergraduate but old acquaintance at court, where after all he was Hamlet's brother-in-law-elect, for a time:

Hamlet. [*Coming forward.*] What is he whose grief
Bears such an emphasis, whose phrase of sorrow
Conjures the wand'ring stars, and makes them stand
Like wonder-wounded hearers? This is I,
Hamlet the Dane.

[*Laertes climbs out of the grave.*]
Laertes. The devil take thy soul! [*Grappling with him.*]
       Hamlet. Thou pray'st not well.
I prithee take thy fingers from my throat,
For though I am not splenetic and rash,
Yet have I in me something dangerous,
Which let thy wiseness fear. Hold off thy hand.

(Act 5, scene 1, 253–63)

"Wonder-wounded hearers" has become a permanent phrase to describe Shakespeare's audience, and we thrill to the prideful aggressivity of "This is I, / Hamlet the Dane." Yet the controlled menace, not wholly ironic, that follows tells us again that this is the man who, in his letter to Horatio, announcing his return from the sea, dryly remarks: "Rosenkrantz and Guildenstern hold their course for England." He has sent them to their deaths, quite gratuitously. Horatio responds with some shock: "So Guildenstern and Rosenkrantz go to 't." We are to remember that they were, after all, his Yale college companions, when we hear Hamlet's shrug: "Why man, they did make love to this employment." No, we are not Prince Hamlet, nor were meant to be.

Like Iago, after him, Hamlet has a certain genius for writing with the lives of the other characters. Why do we fear this in Iago, and yet remain charmed by Hamlet? One of the many mysteries of this most intellectually complex of all fictive persons is his charismatic sway over us. Unless you are an ideologue or a puritanical moralist, you are likely to fall in love with Hamlet, a universal malady for the last two centuries or so. Hamlet does not love you or need you, until the very end, when he expresses anguish that he leaves behind him "a wounded name." He says this on a stage strewn with corpses: his mother, Claudius's, and Laertes', while he himself is dying. Since he has already murdered Polonius, brutally driven Ophelia into madness and suicide, and casually obliterated poor Rosenkrantz and poor Guildenstern, his name ought to be somewhat wounded! But I do not think that he laments any of these eight deaths, his own included. It is "Hamlet the Dane," the son and not the father, whose name, he fears, will not wound us with wonder. Where is his achievement? In proportion to his amazing gifts, no other fictive character seems to have been quite so adept at throwing it all away.

3

It is best to dismiss the notion that the prince procrastinates his revenge, or rather, his father's revenge. For how does an ironist take revenge by hacking someone down with a sword? I rather enjoyed the film *Shakespeare in Love,* but was startled by seeing its Shakespeare battling with a sword. My sense of Shakespeare is that he sensibly went the other way, fast, whenever violence approached. He wrote no Revenge Plays after *Hamlet,* and he probably disliked the subgenre. *Hamlet* is a play about theatricality, and not about revenge; I cannot think of any Western play, before *Hamlet,* so obsessed with theatricality. The audience at the Globe found itself watching four plays in one. There is act 1 through act 2, scene 1, which is Revenge Tragedy, of a sort. Amazing interludes upon theatricality follow, from act 2, scene 2, when the players arrive, through act 3, scene 2, when Claudius bolts away from *The Mousetrap,* "frighted with false fire." A third play goes on through act 4, and this is nearly impossible to characterize, it being a kaleidoscope that has something for everyone. Finally, in act 5, Hamlet is suddenly a decade or so older, after a lapse of a few weeks, and the Ghost is not even a memory, and fatherhood seems only a distant memory. Let us say then that *Hamlet* began as Revenge Tragedy, abruptly broke into a wild meditation upon plays and players, and entered the whirlpool of Shakespeare's creative mind, to emerge into a transcendental tragedy in which a new kind of great man dies, afflicted with an absolute self-knowledge that death both mocks and is mocked by. That is the strongest of the plays, and remains perhaps the most perplexing, particularly because few among us can let it alone.

I have argued elsewhere (in a large book, *Shakespeare: The Invention of the Human*) that the earlier *Hamlet* revised by Shakespeare's play was initially Shakespeare's own botched effort. But that cannot be proved or disproved, and I think *Hamlet* as we know it would have exploded theatrical illusion even if the ghost of a prior play did not haunt it. I need to be precise by what I mean about destroying theatrical illusion. The audience at the Globe, and the audience at any uncut *Hamlet* now, behold not just a play within a play, but have to contend with a flood of theatrical gossip, banter about acting technique, and actually two plays within a play, since the outrageous, nameless tragedy of Priam's slaughter precedes the equally outrageous *The Murder of Gonzago,* with both of them trumped in outrage by Hamlet's revision, *The Mousetrap.* That is piling it on, as if Shakespeare desired the audience to drown in theatricality. As we go from act 2, scene 2, through act 3, scene 2, we cannot maintain the illusion that we are watching the tragedy of *Hamlet, Prince of Denmark.* What we experience is quite otherwise; Shakespeare, having played the Ghost, stays off center, but for nearly a thousand lines Richard Burbage, who first played the Prince of Denmark, slides in and out of Hamlet's role, and in certain swatches is playing Will Shakespeare.

That ought to blow up the entire play, but nothing could destroy *Hamlet,* and the phrase "entire play" doesn't apply, as I have tried to show. After four centuries, *Hamlet* remains the most experimental drama ever staged, even in the Age of Beckett, Pirandello, and all the Absurdists. It isn't at all clear to me that we should think of *Hamlet* as a tragedy; certainly not in any of the senses that *Othello, King Lear,* and *Macbeth* are tragedies. As for tragic flaws, or tragic virtues, why, Hamlet the Dane has every one you could think of, and a great many more. Emerson defined freedom as wildness, and *Hamlet* is the wildest and freest of plays.

Shakespeare could have transferred the subtitle of *Twelfth Night* to it: *Hamlet, or What You Will.*

Does anything happen in *Hamlet?* The question ought to be ridiculous, as there are eight deaths, including the climactic death of the hero, and yet it all depends upon your perspective. From the Ghost's point of view, nothing happens until the very end, and then even his thirst for revenge upon the living must be sated. But the Ghost's perspective isn't ours, and it is another of Shakespeare's ironies that he acted the part. All that matters in the play is the scandalous ever-expanding circumference of Hamlet's consciousness. If a solitary consciousness is infinite in its range, how much can events matter? Self-revision never stops for Hamlet; he changes each time he speaks. Can *that* be fully represented upon a stage? The mind of Hamlet is itself a theater, and therefore the play has two plots, external and internal. The external plot, in all its complexity, is necessary if we are to believe that Hamlet is a man, rather than a god or a monster. But Shakespeare either could not or would not chasten the internal plot, in which a poet fails to be consistently a poet.

Why does Hamlet return from the sea? He could have made his way to Wittenberg or Paris or London. If you are Hamlet the Dane, doubtless you feel that it is necessary to be as the Danes in Denmark, even if Denmark is a prison. My question is in one way merely fantastic, because Hamlet cannot be a student at Wittenberg again; the prince of act 5 has nothing more to learn.

4

And yet, as readers, we are never at all certain how to read his play. Every reader seems to confront a different play each time she rereads. Claudius, Hamlet's "mighty opposite," is anything but that; he is a master of "shuffling," no more. When he prays, ineffectually, he says of heaven, "there is no shuffling there," but this does not deter him from prodding Laertes, "with a little shuffling," to exchange rapiers with Hamlet, so as to give the prince a poisoned wound. Hamlet yearns to "shuffle off this mortal coil"; the word-play upon *shuffling* is Shakespeare's hint at how utterly incommensurate Hamlet and Claudius are.

The other characters also offer no true foils to Hamlet. Laertes—empty-headed, conventional, manipulable—could be any avenger, while Fortinbras is one more military head-basher, ironically given the last word ("shoot") as he appropriates the dead Hamlet for a military funeral. Ophelia's role has pathos, but she is only a victim, pushed back and forth between her father and her not very loving lover. Polonius is a fool, Rosenkrantz and Guildenstern are minor-league opportunists, and the admirable Horatio lacks all personality, being Hamlet's straight man. Queen Gertrude is a sexual magnet but little more. Only the gravedigger-clown is able to offer Hamlet some companionship in wit. The play is endlessly different because Hamlet is so extraordinarily mutable, and there is no other possible center of interest upon the stage with him, except (quite briefly) the equivocal Ghost of the warrior-lover-unfather, King Hamlet.

Shakespeare, ironical beyond our comprehension, has given us a play that is all-Hamlet: subtle, volatile, supremely intelligent. If you read well and deeply, then you have no choice: you will become Hamlet, sometimes to your bewilderment. What matters most about Hamlet is not his predicament, but his endowment: he will expand your mind and spirit, because there is no other way of apprehending him. But nothing is got for nothing, and he will also draw you into the abyss of his consciousness, which has in it elements of nihilism surpassing Iago's, or Edmund's in *King Lear,* or Leontes' in *The Winter's Tale.*

Shakespeare is, by definition, more comprehensive and varied than Hamlet can be, but if we can personify the nihilist poet in Shakespeare by any single figure, it must be Hamlet, since Iago "writes" with other characters and their lives, while Hamlet writes fresh passages for the players and improvises uncanny little songs.

Yet Hamlet is a nihilist poet in a double sense: subject and stance. In a play that talks about plays, in language that discourses upon itself, Hamlet believes in nothing, including language and the self. Christian critics ought to be uneasier with Hamlet than generally they are; Hamlet is still ahead of much of his audience in post-Christianity. Not that we can credit even Hamlet with mere skepticism; how, in this play, can we know when he is an actor and when he is the prince? Hamlet has, at moments, the unsettling detachment that Shakespeare himself manifests in the Sonnets. Both speak only what is already dead in their hearts, though only Hamlet expresses a kind of contempt for the act of speaking. And yet he sincerely professes an admiration for good playing, for actors who will speak precisely what Shakespeare wrote. And he is himself the best of actors. He requires an audience, and captures his audience forever. But is he more an actor or more a poet?

Shakespeare, we gather, was what we now call a "character actor," particularly good at playing older men and English kings. Heroes, villains, and clowns were not roles for him. It startles me (though it shouldn't) to think of him onstage as the Ghost addressing his son Hamlet. Poor Shakespeare was in armor, and even stage armor is heavy stuff. We don't want to see Hamlet in armor and we don't. The prince is theatrical enough without it, and as an ironist or nihilist poet he would deride it. We would wince at hearing Hamlet cry out: "Once more into the breach, dear friends, once more; / Or close the wall up with our Danish dead." Prince Hal, particularly in *Henry IV, Part I,* has a touch of Prince Hamlet, but after he becomes Henry V he is more like Fortinbras, though an unlikely Fortinbras who has been educated by Sir John Falstaff, the Socrates of Eastcheap.

Shakespeare, brilliantly but sadly, this being after all tragedy, does make Hamlet more actor than poet. Or rather, the reader, though dazzled by Hamlet's poetry, is necessarily even more engaged in trying to work out when Hamlet is acting, and when he is not. When reading *Hamlet* one must always keep an eye upon both the actor and the poet in him. And so I turn to the soliloquy of soliloquies.

We are in act 3, scene 1, approaching the close of that long gap Shakespeare cuts into whatever dramatic illusion a drama centering upon Hamlet could possess. Ahead of us are Hamlet's instructions to the players, and his production of *The Mousetrap*. There can be no central passage in *Hamlet;* the play is too various for that, and its protagonist too volatile. Yet for more than two centuries, the "To be, or not to be" speech has been so popular that it now appears staled with repetition. I greatly admire the Romantic critic Charles Lamb, who was my precursor in exalting the reading of Shakespeare over attending wretched stage performances, but I don't want readers to yield to Lamb's despair as to the possibility of freshly confronting this gorgeous soliloquy:

> I confess myself utterly unable to appreciate that celebrated speech . . . or to tell whether it be good, bad, or indifferent; it has been so handled and pawed about by declamatory boys and men, and torn so inhumanly from its living place and principle of continuity in the play, till it has become to me a perfect dead member.

The soliloquy, third of seven in the play, explores the negative relation between knowledge and action, and so is the seedbed of the great poem that Hamlet will write for the Player-King, with its climactic lines:

> But orderly to end where I begun,
> Our wills and fates do so contrary run,
> That our devices still are overthrown;
> Our thoughts are ours, their ends none of our own.
>
> (Act 3, scene 2, 192–95)

The great soliloquy opens so familiarly (to the reader, now) that it is of some importance to listen very minutely to what Hamlet is saying, to himself and so to us:

To be, or not to be, that is the question:
Whether 'tis nobler in the mind to suffer
The slings and arrows of outrageous fortune,
Or to take arms against a sea of troubles,
And by opposing end them.

Even here, Hamlet is ironic, if you pay attention to the metaphor of fighting with the sea, which all your soldierly prowess cannot hope to end. The sea will end your troubles, and you, as Hamlet implies. The reader should be wary of assuming that the question of being or not-being altogether refers to suicide; Hamlet does not truly contemplate self-slaughter. His high irony, like Shakespeare's in the Sonnets, always intimates a measure of detachment that is a little beyond us. Hamlet primarily is brooding upon the will, as Shakespeare so frequently does in the Sonnets. Does one have a will to act, or does one only sicken unto action, and what are the limits of the will? How can a consciousness even so vast as Hamlet's ever be aware enough of all relevant contingencies to will any end, when it cannot know what the ends of its own thought will turn out to be?

Hamlet's malaise, as Nietzsche recognized, is not that he thinks too much but that he thinks much too well. He will perish of the truth, unless he turns to art, but he is royal as well as noble, and a nostalgia for action haunts him, though his intellect is profoundly skeptical of action:

Thus conscience does make cowards of us all,
And thus the native hue of resolution
Is sicklied o'er with the pale cast of thought,
And enterprises of great pitch and moment
With this regard their currents turn awry
And lose the name of action.

(Act 3, scene 1, 83–88)

Let us read these lines closely. The metaphor of the sea of troubles still reverberates in "their currents," which assimilates the enterprise of revenge to the baffled reality of "troubles" and ironizes the "great pitch and moment" so that we hear the sea's motion mimicked in the language. Hamlet, like Shakespeare's disciples Milton and the Romantics, wishes to assert the power of mind over a universe of death or sea of troubles, but cannot do so, because he thinks too lucidly. The prince prophesies our limits four centuries later, when any of us comes to realize that even enormous knowledge of our own consciousness is of little help in knowing what is not conscious, the mystery that baffles the will.

5

Before the slaughter that ends the play, Hamlet says to Horatio: "I shall win at the odds. But thou wouldst not think how ill all's here about my heart." That is foreboding, yet relates also to the fear of leaving behind one a wounded name. Hamlet, at the close, desires our good opinion, and little else:

> If it be now, 'tis not to come; if it be not to come, it will be now; if
> it be not now, yet it will come. The readiness is all.

His spirit is ready (willing) and his flesh is not weak. He dies extraordinarily, to the music of his own: "Let it be." No death in secular literature haunts the reader more. Why? Hamlet's final words—"the rest is silence"—are spiritually ambiguous, yet I read them as anticipating annihilation rather than resurrection. Therein may be the best answer to the question "Why read *Hamlet*?" He does not die as a vicarious atonement for us, but rather with the single anxiety of bearing a wounded name. Whether we ourselves expect annihilation or resurrection, we are likely to end caring about our name. Hamlet, the most charismatic and intelligent of all fictive characters, prefigures our hopes for courage at our common end.

Henrik Ibsen:
Hedda Gabler

There must be troll in what I write.
—Ibsen

I must disclaim the honor of having consciously worked for women's rights. I am not even quite sure what women's rights really are.
—Ibsen

If Ibsen was a feminist, then I am a Bishop.
—James Joyce

Hedda Gabler (1890) is a great tragicomedy, and the masterpiece of the Aesthetic Age. I place it here between *Hamlet* (1600) and *The Importance of Being Earnest* (1895), partly because it occupies a middle position between the ironic tragedy of Hamlet and the sublimely nonsensical comedy of Lady Bracknell and Wilde's other zanies. But since *Hedda Gabler* is, subtly and profoundly, a Shakespearean play, I choose it also to show something of the extent to which even Ibsen, a superb original, had to be post-Shakespearean, in all of his modes. How to read *Hedda Gabler* is also a training in how to read most post-Ibsenite drama.

Oscar Wilde, after attending *Hedda Gabler,* wrote: "I felt pity and terror, as though the play had been Greek." Wilde, in 1891, did not add that the pity and terror were also for himself, as he was too astute not to recognize in Hedda's self-destructiveness something of his own doom-eagerness. But Wilde was no Iago; he did not destroy others. Hedda Gabler is a marvelous blend of Iago and Shakespeare's Cleopatra, at once a genius revising the lives of others and a heroically fatal woman.

Partly because of Ibsen's overwhelming influence upon Arthur Miller, too many readers and playgoers think of the poet of *Brand* and *Peer Gynt* as being a purely social dramatist. Ibsen had some social concerns, but they were peripheral in comparison to his demonic obsessions with character and personality, to what I would have to call his trollishness. A borderline troll, like his own Peer Gynt, Ibsen essentially portrayed himself in the great troll (or more precisely *huldre*) Hedda Gabler. In Norwegian mythology, a *huldre* is a daughter of Lilith, Adam's first wife, who abandoned him, according to the Kabbalah, after a dispute over the proper position for sexual intercourse. Trolls incarnate fiercer versions of our erotic and also our destructive drives, and though they are demons or fairy folk, they can masquerade as human.

Norwegian folklore is replete with stories of men who marry *huldres,* the most deceptive and enticing of female trolls. Cold beauties, their trollish nature takes the external form of a cow's tail, which drops off outside the church where they marry their human husbands. Hedda, the daughter of the late General Gabler, is of course not literally a *huldre,* but that is certainly a part of her symbolic identity in the play. Just as Cleopatra is Antony's "serpent of old Nile," so there is something serpentine about Hedda. But Cleopatra is one of Shakespeare's most magnificent creatures, and the superb Hedda shares Cleopatra's wit and allure, as well as Iago's manipulative splendor.

What Hedda does not share with Cleopatra is either the Egyptian queen's social audacity or her joyous sexuality. Like Ibsen himself, who was unfulfilled by his marriage, Hedda desires sexual love yet dreads it, and again like Ibsen, Hedda has a horror of losing her societal respectability. That horror is related to the fear of being exposed as a *huldre,* or in Ibsen's case revealing his lustful trollishness to his public.

Hedda, twenty-nine years old, has married down, is pregnant with an unwanted child, and is hideously bored by her husband, George Tesman, a fairly typical good-natured but foolish academic researcher. But even a more fascinating husband, like her former admirer the Dionysiac poet Eilert Loevborg (a satire upon Strindberg), would not rescue Hedda from her malaise. Nor would a military career like her father's, General Gabler's, save her from herself, not that this is available to her in the Norway of 1890. It would be pointless to lament that Hedda is "trapped in a woman's body," or in an absurd marriage, or that she cannot head up the Norwegian armaments industry. Her first entrance establishes the state of her soul; the maid has left the French windows open, and the room is flooded with sun: "This light's blinding me."

William Hazlitt remarked of Iago that he "plots the ruin of his friends as an exercise for his understanding and stabs men in the dark to prevent *ennui*." Ibsen took the hint from Iago, except that Hedda plots the ruin of Loevborg by burning his manuscript, and then coolly gives him one of her father's dueling pistols, urging him to "Do it beautifully." He is to shoot himself in high style, thus gratifying Hedda's authentic aestheticism (in which Iago again is her forerunner). In notes towards the composition of the play, Ibsen remarked that "Hedda represents *ennui*" and added: "Life for Hedda is a farce which isn't worth seeing through to the end." She hastens that end, by writing her own farce, with Loevborg as initial victim, but herself as the final self-destroyer.

Yet, if she is a female Iago, with much of his brilliance, she is also a Cleopatra, with more than we might expect of Cleopatra's fatal attractiveness, though she does not share an "infinite variety." If her inner self is Ibsen's, we can understand the dramatist's palpable relish in her annihilation of the drunken poet Loevborg, a sly portrait of the playwright Strindberg, who hated Ibsen with fierce envy, and whose hatred Ibsen joyously returned. As of yet, we are only on the outside of this extraordinary play, and it is time to read our way deep within Ibsen's savage masterwork.

Though she has flirted fiercely with Loevborg, before her marriage, he was for Hedda an experience in vicarious sensation, since she served as confidante for his Dionysian exploits. Her actual desire, as is intimated throughout the play, was a repressedly lesbian sadism towards her younger schoolmate, the beautiful Thea Elvsted. It is perfectly plain that, at the least, Hedda wishes to pull out Thea's splendid head of hair, then make a bonfire of it. This is an ambition that goes back to their schoolgirl days. Hedda's pyromania again stems from Iago's; both would burn all humankind away.

There are only seven characters in *Hedda Gabler*, and two are inconsequential, Tesman's aunt and Hedda's maid. Besides Hedda and her husband, Tesman, and Loevborg and his "inspirer," Thea, there is also the play's villain, Judge Brack, who lusts after Hedda, and who will prompt her suicide, at the close. It is vital that the reader recognize that Hedda is a heroine-villain, as it were, Cleopatra as well as Iago. We never lose *dramatic* sympathy with Hedda (or with Cleopatra, or Iago), even as we fight her *huldre* fascination, which is incessant. Hedda's greatest fear, besides public scandal, is that she will be bored to death, yet she herself is so sublimely perverse that she could never bore anyone else. But Judge Brack is merely manipulative; we quickly loathe him, and we understand why Hedda chooses suicide when she falls into his power. He discovers that Hedda has instigated Loevborg's accidental suicide, with the gift of one of her father's pistols, and he gives her the choice either of public exposure or of becoming his mistress, each totally unacceptable to her.

Brack is a power-monger; even his desire for Hedda seems more an assertion of the will than of the loins. What does Hedda Gabler want? Cleopatra wished to rule over all the world, in company with her Antony, while Iago longed to disintegrate Othello, and brilliantly achieved this ruin. Restless, vibrant yet life-denying, equivocal in every respect, Hedda desires a *huldre's* revenge upon human reality. Even her barely repressed passion for Thea is frighteningly destructive; any sexual embrace of Thea would be followed by an attempt to burn Thea alive. Since Thea has "rescued" Loevborg from dissipation, and inspired him to write a supposedly great manuscript on the future of civilization, it becomes necessary for Hedda to burn the only copy of what would have been Thea's book by Loevborg, that is to say, their child:

> *Hedda. She throws one of the pages into the stove and whispers to herself.*
> I'm burning your child, Thea! You with your beautiful wavy hair!
> *She throws a few more pages into the stove.*
> The child Eilert Loevborg gave you.
> *Throws the rest of the manuscript in.*
> I'm burning it! I'm burning your child!
>
> (Translated by Michael Meyer)

This remarkable deed and utterance closes the third of the four acts. The reader is to remember that Hedda herself is pregnant; there is some question whether the manuscript is not only a surrogate for Thea's hair, but also for Hedda's own child, who will never be born. Splendidly lurid as is the scene, its hysterical malevolence contains a strong element of what Henry James, attending its London performance in 1891, called "an ironical pleasantry." Ibsen's ironic humor crests in Hedda's dismay that Loevborg has not committed a Dionysian self-immolation with "beautiful" style, but rather has died accidentally in a high-toned bordello:

> *Hedda.* So they found him there?
> *Brack.* Yes, there. With a discharged pistol in his breast pocket. The shot had wounded him mortally.
> *Hedda.* Yes. In the breast.
> *Brack.* No. In the—hm—stomach. The—lower part—
> *Hedda. Looks at him with an expression of repulsion.* That too!

Oh, why does everything I touch become mean and ludicrous? It's like a curse!

(Translated by Michael Meyer)

With a great actress, such as Peggy Ashcroft or Maggie Smith, playing Hedda, this was both horrible and delicious. No one truly loves anyone in this play; they are all solipsists, Hedda the most sublime of all. Thea and Tesman get happily to work assembling the notes from which they may reconstruct Loevborg's masterpiece on the future of civilization, which of course is as likely to be ludicrous as was poor Loevborg's end, since he evidently (in a bordello scuffle) shot himself in his private parts. One sees why Strindberg was so enraged, though the trollish Ibsen must have been laughing with a terrible laughter. Flaubert confessed: "I am Madame Bovary"; no confession from Ibsen was necessary. More than the scamp Peer Gynt, Hedda is Ibsen, and even he may have flinched a little at the end he composed for her:

Hedda, from the rear room. I can hear what you are saying, Tesman. But how shall I spend the evenings out here?

Tesman, looking through the papers. Oh, I'm sure Judge Brack'll be kind enough to come over and keep you company.

Brack, in the armchair, calling gaily. I'll be delighted, Mrs. Tesman. I'll be here every evening. We'll have great fun together, you and I.

Hedda, loud and clear. Yes, that'll suit you, won't it, Judge? The only cock on the dunghill—!

A shot is heard from the rear room.

(Translated by Michael Meyer)

We can be certain that Hedda Gabler has done it beautifully, if hardly as elegantly as Cleopatra, in her apotheosis of a suicide. Not exactly a feminist martyr, and restricted to a narrower stage than Cleopatra's world-theater, Hedda has nevertheless done the best she could manage in the stifling middle-class morality of Ibsen's Norway. If she does not dazzle us quite as Iago does, we must grant her that Loevborg is no Othello. With scabrous irony, Ibsen has surrounded the *huldre* Hedda exclusively with second-raters, who scarcely provide her with provocations to anything like the full potential of her beautiful wickedness.

Yet I wonder sometimes if I am as fond of any character in the drama of the last hundred-odd years, as I am of Hedda? There is Lady Bracknell in Wilde's *The Importance of Being Earnest*, but she comes out of the world of nonsense: Lewis Carroll, W. S. Gilbert, Edward Lear. Chekhov's heroines are lovable, and I enjoy them greatly, but from a distance. The disturbed and disturbing Hedda Gabler is up close. Ibsen kept a scorpion under glass on his writing desk, and delighted in feeding it chunks of melon. Hedda Gabler, deadly and fascinating, is the child of that sensibility.

Oscar Wilde:
The Importance of Being Earnest

1

After Shakespeare, most of the best stage comedies in English were written by Anglo-Irishmen. William Congreve's *The Way of the World*, Oliver Goldsmith's *She Stoops to Conquer*, Richard Brinsley Sheridan's *The School for Scandal*, were joined in later times by Oscar Wilde's *The Importance of Being Earnest*, George Bernard Shaw's *Pygmalion*, John Millington Synge's *The Playboy of the Western World*, and Samuel Beckett's *Waiting for Godot*. Wilde's delightful play, *Earnest* as I shall call it, for short, may also be the best British comedy since Shakespeare's *Twelfth Night*, surpassing the rival works that I have listed. *Earnest* is a miracle of a play, perpetually fresh and thus refreshing, and it is Wilde's masterpiece, wonderful as two of his critical essays are: "The Soul of Man under Socialism" and the dialogue "The Decay of Lying."

The true affinities of *Earnest* are with Lewis Carroll and with Gilbert and Sullivan; Wilde did not compose light comedy in *An Ideal Husband, Lady Windemere's Fan,* and *A Woman of No Importance.* These still stage very well, but could not in genre be compared to *Patience, Iolanthe,* and *Through the Looking-Glass,* and even to the *Nonsense Books* of Edward Lear. *Earnest* is part of the cosmos of Nonsense literature; one could add the short stories of Saki (H. H. Munro) and the novels of Ronald Firbank. Nonsense literature, at its finest, frees us of ordinary nonsense, by taking us into a realm at once weirdly light and ultimately unsettling. The masterpieces of Nonsense in English are Carroll's Alice books, but *Earnest* is worthy of dwelling close by.

In the original, four-act version of *Earnest* (greatly improved by condensation into three), Wilde's surrogate, Algernon, states Wilde's Law:

> My experience of life is that whenever one tells a lie one is corroborated on every side. When one tells the truth one is left in a very lonely and painful position, and no one believes a word one says.

In "The Decay of Lying" Wilde's spokesman, Vivian, casts aside the weak lies of politicians:

> They never rise beyond the level of misrepresentation, and actually condescend to prove, to discuss, to argue. How different from the temper of the true liar, with his frank, fearless statements, his superb irresponsibility, his healthy, natural disdain of proof of any kind! After all, what is a fine lie? Simply that which is its own evidence. If a man is sufficiently unimaginative to produce evidence in support of a lie, he might just as well speak the truth at once.

For Wilde, to originate or to set in motion is to lie. When Alice, in *Through the Looking-Glass,* gives her name in answer to

Humpty-Dumpty's gruff demand, he interrupts her to ask: "What does it mean?" "*Must* a name mean something," Alice asks doubtfully, and Humpty-Dumpty replies: "Of course it must . . . *my* name means the shape I am." The importance of being Earnest (the name that both Gwendolen and Cecily desire for a husband), as Wilde knows but does *not* tell us, is that *earnest* (or Ernest) goes back to the Indo-European root *er,* which means to originate. To be earnest is to be original, a Nonsense formulation that Wilde slyly enjoys because originality usually is alien to his own genius. No character in *Earnest* is at all original; each is sublimely outrageous, but always in a traditional mode, and yet the play is marked by a vivacious originality.

The grand personage in *Earnest* is Lady Bracknell, perhaps the most outrageous comic character since Sir John Falstaff, the star turn in Shakespeare's *Henry IV* plays, and Shakespeare's only creation who competes with Hamlet in popularity, from Shakespeare's days until our own. Here is Lady Bracknell, imperiously concluding her interview with Jack, after he has proposed to Gwendolen. On being informed by Jack that he had lost both his parents, Lady Bracknell had observed: "To lose one parent, Mr. Worthing, may be regarded as a misfortune; to lose both looks like carelessness." There, as in the interview's conclusion, one hears the style of Dr. Samuel Johnson, which melds with Falstaff's mockeries of pomposity to produce Lady Bracknell's rolling periods:

> *Lady Bracknell.* In what locality did this Mr. James, or Thomas, Cardew come across this ordinary hand-bag?
> *Jack.* In the cloak-room at Victoria Station. It was given to him in mistake for his own.
> *Lady Bracknell.* The cloak-room at Victoria Station?
> *Jack.* Yes. The Brighton line.
> *Lady Bracknell.* The line is immaterial. Mr. Worthing, I confess I feel somewhat bewildered by what you have just told me. To be born, or at any rate bred, in a hand-bag, whether

it had handles or not, seems to me to display a contempt for the ordinary decencies of family life that reminds one of the worst excesses of the French Revolution. And I presume you know what that unfortunate movement led to? As for the particular locality in which the hand-bag was found, a cloak-room at a railway station might serve to conceal a social indiscretion—has probably, indeed, been used for that purpose before now—but it could hardly be regarded as an assured basis for a recognized position in good society.

Jack. May I ask you then what you would advise me to do? I need hardly say I would do anything in the world to ensure Gwendolen's happiness.

Lady Bracknell. I would strongly advise you, Mr. Worthing, to try and acquire some relations as soon as possible, and to make a definite effort to produce at any rate one parent, of either sex, before the season is quite over.

Jack. Well, I don't see how I could possibly manage to do that. I can produce the hand-bag at any moment. It is in my dressing-room at home. I really think that should satisfy you, Lady Bracknell.

Lady Bracknell. Me, sir! What has it to do with me? You can hardly imagine that I and Lord Bracknell would dream of allowing our only daughter—a girl brought up with the utmost care—to marry into a cloak-room, and form an alliance with a parcel. Good morning, Mr. Worthing!

(Lady Bracknell sweeps out in majestic indignation.)

Lady Bracknell's gratuitous asides are Wildean triumphs, poised upon the verge of Nonsense: "The line is immaterial," "whether it had handles or not," "of either sex," "a girl brought up with the utmost care," "an alliance with a parcel." How are we to read Lady Bracknell's grand pronouncements? That, I take it, is much the same question as "Why does Lady Bracknell delight us so much?"

In part, Lady Bracknell is so funny because she is so humorless, in stark juxtaposition to Falstaff. But since Wilde is composing a farce on the border of Nonsense, Lady Bracknell is in no way a representation of an actual person. Shakespearean comedy is not Wilde's prime model. In 1881, Wilde had been satirized as Bunthorne, the "aesthetic sham" of Gilbert and Sullivan's *Patience*. After that, Gilbert hovered in Wilde's creative mind, though without real effect until *Earnest,* which owes rather more to *Iolanthe* and *The Pirates of Penzance* than to *Patience*. Algernon, Jack, Gwendolen, Cecily, Miss Prism, and Canon Chasuble are none of them as fantastic and imposing as Lady Bracknell, but they are no more attached to the Reality Principle than she is. Wilde's aesthete-dandies, and his grotesques, always return us to Wilde himself, a master of language, fantasy, and of the paradoxes of art. W. S. Gilbert was rather less than that, but Wilde (like Shakespeare) cheerfully appropriated from everyone, and *Earnest* subsumes Gilbert and Sullivan, but in the interest of an aesthetic vision alien to them.

In a subtle sense, *Earnest* is more akin to Falstaff's ethos and to Sancho Panza's than to anything else in literature. Wilde's "A Trivial Comedy for Serious People" (its misleading subtitle) takes us into the realm of childlike playing, a world where the presence or absence of cucumber sandwiches is as momentous a crisis as any other could be. Indeed, when I think of *Earnest,* I remember first Lady Bracknell, and next the cucumber sandwiches, an item of cuisine that now permanently suggests the sublime Oscar. Part of how to read *Earnest* is to munch the occasional cucumber sandwich as one proceeds, accompanied either by tea or champagne, both in the play's spirit. Having devoured *all* the cucumber sandwiches, while denying them to Jack, Algernon then engages his servant, Lane, in a wonderful exchange:

> *Lady Bracknell.* And now I'll have a cup of tea, and one of those nice cucumber sandwiches you promised me.

Algernon. Certainly, Aunt Augusta. *(Goes over to tea-table.)*
Lady Bracknell. Won't you come and sit here, Gwendolen?
Gwendolen. Thanks, mamma, I'm quite comfortable where
  I am.
Algernon. (Picking up empty plate in horror.) Good heavens!
  Lane! Why are there no cucumber sandwiches? I ordered
  them specially.
Lane. (Gravely.) There were no cucumbers in the market this
  morning, sir. I went down twice.
Algernon. No cucumbers!
Lane. No, sir. Not even for ready money.
Algernon. That will do, Lane, thank you.
Lane. Thank you, sir. *(Goes out.)*
Algernon. I am greatly distressed, Aunt Augusta, about there
  being no cucumbers, not even for ready money.

Algernon's incessant interest in eating is an obsession of this
young dandy, and goes on throughout the play. It must seem odd
to compare Algernon to Falstaff, who has only a negative relationship to the world of elegance, but Wilde (who loved Falstaff)
seems to have divided Falstaff between Lady Bracknell (language)
and Algernon (appetite). "Everything matters in art except the
subject," Wilde remarked, another of those aphorisms particularly valuable in our ideological era.

2

Wilde might have titled his best play: *The Importance of Being
Insouciant,* except that, as we have seen, the secret meaning of
earnest for Wilde was to originate. To be original was to lie, but to
lie insouciantly, in the interest of art. The play's philosophy, Oscar
told a friend was "that we should treat all trivial things very seri-
ously, and all the serious things in life with sincere and studied

triviality." One thinks again of Algernon's interest in food: "I hate people who are not serious about meals. It is so shallow of them."

Are we to read *Earnest* as farce, as nonsense, or as Wilde's great morality play? As all three, I would urge the reader, since Wilde manifests his beautiful genius so definitively here, and perhaps here alone. Everyone in the play is admirably selfish, that being a prime virtue in its absurd realm. Wilde's characters, as Gwendolen proudly remarks, never change, except in their affections, and they are always serious liars. Presiding over them is Lady Bracknell, who like a High Romantic poet imposes her vision upon reality, though her vision is a parody of mere selfishness.

There is neither sin nor guilt in the understructure of *Earnest,* where the paradox of serious lying is that everyone in the play tells the truth, whether as an afterthought, or through outrageousness and hyperbole. That is because aesthetic lying is visionary, and opposes not truth nor reality but time, and time's vassal, nature. Lady Bracknell is a grand figure because she is a triumph over time, the goddess of "sincere and studied triviality."

Jorge Luis Borges observed that Oscar was always right, or almost always. As a playwright, Wilde is a superb critic, "always original in his quotations," as Arthur Symons remarked, and he is also a civilized autobiographer, since that, for Oscar, was the essence of criticism. Wilde warns the critic against falling into "careless habits of accuracy," since the higher criticism ought to see the object "as in itself it really is not." This means that *Earnest* rejects both nature and society, and disdains imitating them. The "passionate celibacy" to which Lady Bracknell (momentarily) condemns Gwendolen and Jack, Cecily and Algernon, is a wise joke, and not the refined perversion we might be tempted to envision, since Wilde's characters are not human beings. They are paradoxes-at-play in the field of Wilde's most joyous vision. Like Wilde's satire, always gentle in *Earnest,* the drama's essential gaudiness is kept under careful control.

I spoke of Lady Bracknell's triumph over time. In truth, the play ends as Lady Bracknell's triumph; her selfish virtues dominate the wonderful conclusion, where everyone is on the verge of marriage, all with her firm blessing. Should we not read the drama with the realization that Lady Bracknell, and not Jack or Algernon, is Wilde's true surrogate? If Ibsen was Hedda Gabler, then Oscar was Lady Bracknell, since her outrageousness transcends that of everyone else in the play:

> Lady Bracknell. (Pulls out her watch.) Come, dear. (Gwendolen rises.) We have already missed five, if not six, trains. To miss any more might expose us to comment on the platform.

I once wanted to use this as the epigraph to my book *The Western Canon* (it has no epigraph), but was voted down by my editors. It seems to me a touchstone for the reader in the year 2000, and for all truly canonical imaginative literature. How to read *The Importance of Being Earnest*? We should begin by recognizing what Lady Bracknell sublimely cannot: no one, on the platform, seeing Gwendolen and her formidable mother, could possibly know that they have missed any trains, let alone five, or six! So egomaniacal is Lady Bracknell that all the world is not only her audience, but indeed her schedule keeper. Yet that is her zany greatness, and the play's, and that is why we need to go on reading *The Importance of Being Earnest*.

SUMMARY OBSERVATIONS

Shakespeare, whose art is so rich, is also the master of ellipsis, the art of leaving things out. In *Antony and Cleopatra* we do not see the imperial lovers alone together; we have to imagine how they are to one another when their onstage audience of followers and retainers are not present. *King Lear* is a play in which the prime villain, Edmund, and Lear never speak to one another. Shakespeare wants us to surmise why it would be unfeasible for them to communicate. In *Hamlet,* as I've indicated, there is an extraordinary difference between the Prince in acts 1–4, where he is perhaps seventeen or eighteen, and the mature figure of act 5, who is at least thirty, though the lapsed time depicted in the play seems no more than three or four months.

Reading Shakespeare's plays, you learn to meditate upon what is left out. That is one of the many advantages that a reader has over a theatergoer in regard to Shakespeare. Ideally, one should read a Shakespearean play, watch a good performance of it, and then read it again. Shakespeare himself, directing his play at the Globe, must have experienced discomfort at how much a performance had to neglect, though we have no evidence of this. However instructed by Shakespeare, it is difficult to imagine the actor Richard Burbage catching and conveying all of Hamlet's ironies, or the clown Will Kemp encompassing the full range of Falstaff's wit in the Henry IV plays.

Even the most aware of readers probably cannot absorb all the theatricality in Hamlet and his play, which is a "poem unlimited," never to be exhausted. That is the glory of *Hamlet,* and helps account for its centrality in literary experience. Ibsen, subtly and covertly influenced by Shakespeare, blends Cleopatra and Iago, as we have seen, in the madly attractive Hedda Gabler, an authentically fatal woman. Theatricality in Hedda is not as infinite as in Hamlet, but still is strongly present. Both Shakespeare and Ibsen enhance theatricality, the play's consciousness that it is a play, partly to suggest a context of nihilism that in Dostoevsky is represented by the yellow atmosphere of Petersburg. Since in drama we learn what we must learn in soliloquy or in dialogue, the informing voice of the novelist is substituted for by theatricality itself. Shakespeare's immense influence upon most of the novels considered in this book testifies to how extraordinarily successful *Hamlet* was and is in expanding the horizons of literary art.

I have argued that Ibsen be read as we read Shakespeare, and not as we read (or attend) Arthur Miller. Oscar Wilde's great comedy clearly requires a different kind of reading, one more appropriate to the literature of Nonsense, the art of Lewis Carroll, Edward Lear, and Gilbert and Sullivan. Nonsense is a variant of literary fantasy, and addresses itself to the adult implicit in the child, and the child hidden in the adult. Though Lady Bracknell has Falstaffian elements, as I have remarked, she would be more illuminated if she had to contend with Humpty-Dumpty. *The Importance of Being Earnest* is best read in close conjunction with the Alice books. Sometimes it is good to fantasize Shakespeare surviving into later times, partly so that he could sample literature centuries after his own triumph. If there is an afterlife, and people go on reading in it (surely more appropriate than their watching celestial television), I would want to hear Shakespeare reading aloud from *Through the Looking-Glass.*

V

NOVELS, PART II

Herman Melville:
Moby-Dick

Herman Melville's *Moby-Dick* is the indisputable ancestor of the six modern American novels I shall consider in this chapter, in two sequences. The first is constituted by William Faulkner's *As I Lay Dying,* Nathanael West's *Miss Lonelyhearts,* Thomas Pynchon's *The Crying of Lot 49,* and Cormac McCarthy's *Blood Meridian.* The second comprises just two novels, Ralph Waldo Ellison's *Invisible Man* and Toni Morrison's *Song of Solomon.* But since the binding force, ultimately, for both sequences is *Moby-Dick,* I want to begin by glancing briefly at that most negative of all American visions, at least before McCarthy's *Blood Meridian.*

How to read *Moby-Dick* is a vast enterprise, as befits one of the few authentic contenders for our national epic. But since Captain Ahab is the protagonist of the novel, I will confine myself to glancing at some of the problems in reading that Ahab presents. Clearly a Shakespearean figure, with affinities both to King Lear and Macbeth, Ahab is (like Macbeth) technically a hero-villain. After more than sixty years of rereading *Moby-Dick,* I have not swerved from my reading experience as a nine-year-old; Ahab, to me, is primarily a hero, as the persona "Walt Whitman" and Huckleberry Finn are rival American heroes. Yes, Ahab is responsible for the death of his entire crew, himself included, with the single exception of the Jobean survivor, the narrator who asks us to call him Ishmael. Yet, Ahab has rallied his entire crew to him, even his reluctant first mate, Starbuck, when he appeals to them to join his revenge quest to hunt down and kill the evidently unkillable Moby-Dick, the snow-white leviathan sperm whale. Whatever his culpability (their choice was free, though only refusal as a group could have deterred Ahab), it seems best to think of the *Pequod*'s captain as a tragic protagonist, closely akin to Macbeth and to Milton's Satan. In his visionary obsessiveness, Ahab has a touch of the Quixotic in him, though his harshness has nothing in common with the Don's spirit of play.

William Faulkner remarked that *Moby-Dick* was the book he wished he had written; his closest version of it was *Absalom, Absalom!* where the obsessed protagonist, Thomas Sutpen, may be considered Faulkner's Ahab. In his highest rhetoric, Faulkner observed that Ahab's end was "a sort of Golgotha of the heart become immutable in the sonority of its plunging ruin." "Ruin" there is hardly dispraise, since Faulkner added: "There's a death for a man, now."

Moby-Dick is the fictional paradigm for American sublimity, for an achievement on the heights or in the depths, profound either way. Despite Melville's considerable debts to Shakespeare, *Moby-Dick* is an extraordinarily original work, at once our national Book of Jonah and Book of Job. Both biblical texts are cited explicitly by Melville; Father Mapple preaches his marvelous sermon, using Jonah as text, while Ishmael's "Epilogue" takes as epigraph the formula used by all four messengers who report to Job the destruction of his family and worldly goods: "And I only am escaped alone to tell thee."

Radical originality marks Faulkner's *As I Lay Dying*, which I judge to be his masterpiece, surpassing even *Light in August, Sanctuary, The Sound and the Fury,* and *Absalom, Absalom!* The same originality attends Nathanael West's short novel *Miss Lonelyhearts,* and Thomas Pynchon's *The Crying of Lot 49*. A frightening originality is the mark of Cormac McCarthy's *Blood Meridian*, which seems to me, as we enter the twenty-first century, the strongest imaginative work by any living American writer. True originality, always difficult to achieve after Shakespeare and Cervantes, is particularly hard for American literature of the nineteenth and twentieth centuries. Concerning the twenty-first, I make no prophecies, but since the United States is already the Evening Land of Western high culture, a sense of belatedness will be hard to evade.

Starbuck tells Ahab that the hunt for Moby-Dick is against God's purpose, but just who is Melville's God, or the God of those who came after him: Faulkner, West, Pynchon, Cormac McCarthy? Like Prometheus, in ancient and in Romantic literature, and like Milton's Satan, Ahab opposes himself to the sky god, even if you want to call that god Yahweh or Jehovah. Ahab appears to have converted from Quaker Christianity to a Parsee version of Manichaeism, in which the cosmos is in contention between two rival deities. The demonic captain of the *Pequod* has smuggled on board a crew of Parsees (Persian Zoroastrians from India) to man his personal whaleboat, with Fedallah as harpooner. Fedallah is Ahab's shadowy double; at the end of the great chapter 132, "The Symphony," Ahab stares at the ocean and observes "two reflected, fixed eyes in the water there." They are Fedallah's eyes, yet also Ahab's own.

Melville was not a Christian, and tended to identify with the ancient Gnostic heresy, in which the creator God of this world is a bungler and impostor, while the true God, called the Stranger or Alien God, is exiled somewhere in the outer regions of the cosmos. Early, major Faulkner is a kind of unknowing Gnostic; West, Pynchon, and McCarthy in their different ways are very knowing indeed. My subject is how to read their best fiction, and why, and not how to instruct my own readers in ancient heterodoxies (at least not here!), but the first sequence of four novels that I have chosen, in the wake of Melville, achieve their negative splendors in modes parallel to Gnostic visions, as we will see.

In the Book of Job, Yahweh boasts to the wretched Job of the power over humankind of Leviathan, whom Melville names the White Whale, Moby-Dick. Maimed by Moby-Dick, Ahab asserts his own pride and will-to-vengeance, his own spark or flame, invoked by him in chapter 119, "The Candles":

> Oh! thou clear spirit of clear fire, whom on these seas I as Persian once did worship, till in the sacramental act so burned by thee, that to this hour I bear the scar; I now know thee, thou clear spirit, and I now know that thy right worship is defiance. To neither love nor reverence wilt thou be kind; and e'en for hate thou canst but kill; and all are killed. No fearless fool now fronts thee. I own thy speechless, placeless power; but to the last gasp of my earthquake life will dispute its unconditional, unintegral mastery in me . . . Come in thy lowest form of love, and I will kneel and kiss thee; but at thy highest, come as mere supernal power; and though thou launchest navies of full-freighted worlds, there's that in here that still remains indifferent. Oh, thou clear spirit, of thy fire thou madest me, and like a true child of fire, I breathe it back to thee.

You rightly worship fire, according to Ahab, by asserting your own sacred selfhood against it. "I'd strike the sun if it insulted me!" the Promethean Ahab cries out, establishing a standard of defiance that no one in his wake has matched.

I have confined my reading of *Moby-Dick* to a brief analysis of Captain Ahab, since he is the forerunner of all the American questers I will consider in this chapter. But I cannot abandon Melville's epic, a book I have venerated since childhood, without praising its extraordinary zest as a narrative. We are captured by Ahab, even as we recoil from his monomania. He is American through and through, fierce in his desire to avenge himself, but always strangely free, probably because no American truly feels free unless he or she is inwardly alone.

William Faulkner:
As I Lay Dying

The finest opening section of any twentieth-century American novel belongs to William Faulkner's masterpiece, *As I Lay Dying* (1930). The book consists of fifty-nine interior monologues, fifty-three of them spoken by members of the Bundren family, a proud clan of poor whites, who struggle heroically through flood and fire to carry the coffin containing the corpse of their mother, Addie, back to the graveyard in Jefferson, Mississippi, where she wished to be buried next to her father. Nineteen of the sections, including the first, are spoken by the remarkable Darl Bundren, a visionary who finally crosses the border into madness. We hear Darl speaking the novel's opening, as he follows his enemy brother, Jewel, up to the house where Addie is dying:

> Jewel and I come up from the field, following the path in single file. Although I am fifteen feet ahead of him, anyone watching us from the cottonhouse can see Jewel's frayed and broken straw hat a full head above my own.

As Darl and Jewel mount the path, Darl hears the saw of his carpenter brother, Cash, who is making the coffin for their mother, and we listen to Darl's dispassionate observation:

> A good carpenter. Addie Bundren could not want a better one, a better box to lie in. It will give her confidence and comfort.

Unloved by Addie, the dissociated Darl insists he has no mother, and his extraordinary consciousness reflects his conviction. Stark, simple, dignified, suggestive—the opening of *As I Lay Dying* intimates the superb originality of Faulkner's most surprising novel. Faulkner's principal rivals have nothing comparable; F. Scott

Fitzgerald's *The Great Gatsby* begins with Nick Carraway's father telling him: "Just remember that all the people in this world haven't had the advantages that you've had," which is a healthy admonition not to criticize others, but a long way from the Faulknerian sublimity. Hemingway's *The Sun Also Rises* begins with the ironical observation that "Robert Cohn was once middleweight boxing champion of Princeton." Again, Faulkner is rather beyond that. The only possible rival for an opening in Faulkner's class seems to me the start of Cormac McCarthy's astonishing *Blood Meridian* (1985), where the narrator introduces us to the Kid, the tragic protagonist who will finally be destroyed by the uncanny and Iago-like Judge Holden:

> See the child. He is pale and thin, he wears a thin and ragged linen shirt. He stokes the scullery fire. Outside lie dark turned fields with rags of snow and darker woods beyond that harbor yet a few last wolves. His folk are known for hewers of wood and drawers of water but in truth his father has been a schoolmaster. He lies in drink, he quotes from poets whose names are now lost. The boy crouches by the fire and watches him.

The accents of Herman Melville and of Faulkner fuse in this great prose. But *Blood Meridian* comes at the end of my sequence, so I return us to *As I Lay Dying*. A deliberate tour de force, the book refers in its title to Addie Bundren, who dies soon after it begins, but Faulkner quoted from memory the bitter speech of the ghost of Agamemnon to Odysseus (*Odyssey*, Book XI, "The Descent to the Dead"):

> As I lay dying the woman with the dog's eyes would not close my eyes for me as I descended into Hades.

Murdered by his wife and her lover, Agamemnon, and his fate, have little to do with Faulkner's novel. Faulkner wanted the phrase, rather than its context, and took it, though he may also have wished to suggest that the lack of love between Addie Bundren and her son Darl has elements in it akin to the Clytemnestra relationship with Orestes and Electra. Clytemnestra is "the woman with the dog's eyes" who sends Agamemnon open-eyed into Hades, and Addie is, if anything, more unpleasant than Clytemnestra.

Though Faulkner does not number the sections or fifty-nine interior monologues that make up his book, I suggest that the reader do so in her paperback copy of *As I Lay Dying*, for convenience of cross-reference (the best edition is the current Vintage reprint, which has the Library of America corrected text). Addie speaks only one section, the fortieth (pp. 169–76), but it is more than sufficient to alienate every reader:

> I could just remember how my father used to say that the reason for living was to get ready to stay dead a long time. And when I would have to look at them day after day, each with his and her secret and selfish thought, and blood strange to each other blood and strange to mine, and think that this seemed to be the only way I could get ready to stay dead, I would hate my father for having ever planted me. I would look forward to the times when they faulted, so I could whip them. When the switch fell I could feel it upon my flesh; when it welted and ridged it was my blood that ran, and I would think with each blow of the switch: Now you are aware of me! Now I am something in your secret and selfish life, who have marked your blood with my own for ever and ever.

One sees why this sadistically disturbed woman wishes to be buried next to her father. Addie, dead, is even more of a curse than when alive, as we are told the grotesque, heroic, sometimes hilarious, always outrageous saga of how her five children and husband go through flood and fire to carry her corpse back to her desired resting place. Faulkner's *As I Lay Dying* is tragic farce, yet it has enormous aesthetic dignity, and is a sustained nightmare of what Freud grimly called "family romances." Some pious critics have tried to interpret *As I Lay Dying* as an affirmation of Christian family values, but the reader will be baffled by such a judgment. As elsewhere in Faulkner's great decade as a novelist (1929–39), the novelist's vision founds itself upon a horror of families and of community, and offers the one value of stoic endurance, which does not suffice to save the gifted Darl Bundren from the madhouse.

So ironical are the tonalities of Faulkner's interior monologues, particularly of Darl's nineteen soliloquies, that the reader may feel at first that Faulkner does too little to guide our responses. There is no genre we can turn to in aiding our understanding of this epic narrative of Mississippi poor whites fulfilling the dying request of their quite dreadful mother. Family honor is almost the only principle holding the Bundrens together, since the father, Anse, is in his own way as destructive as Addie. Anse is given three monologues—numbers 9, 26, 28 (if you have numbered them)—and they establish him as wily, shiftless, a trickster and manipulator, as selfish as his wife, Addie, was.

Dewey Dell, the one Bundren daughter, has her own dignity, but cannot find strength to mourn her mother's death, because as an unmarried, pregnant, poor white young woman, she is compelled to seek vainly for a secret abortion. The child Vardaman simply denies Addie's death; he bores holes in her coffin so that she can breathe, and finally identifies her with a large fish he caught as she lay dying: "My mother is a fish." Faulkner centers the novel on the consciousness of Darl Bundren, and on the heroic actions of the other sons, Cash the carpenter and Jewel the horseman (Addie's natural son through an adulterous relationship with the Reverend Mr. Whitfield).

Jewel is fierce, fearless, and capable of expressing himself only through intense action. His one monologue (number 4), in protest against Cash's coffin-making, concludes with a possessing vision of guarding his dying mother against the family and all the world:

> . . . it would not be happening with every bastard in the county coming in to stare at her because if there is a God what the hell is

He for. It would just be me and her on a high hill and me rolling the rocks down the hill at their faces, picking them up and throwing them down the hill faces and teeth and all by God until she was quiet . . .

Jewel and Darl hate one another with mutual passion, and there is a dark, implicitly incestuous hostility between Darl and Dewey Dell. Cash, who is on warm terms with all his siblings, is simple, direct, and heroically enduring, and like Jewel a man of unreflective, physical courage. But Darl is the heart, and the greatness, of *As I Lay Dying*, and clearly Faulkner's surrogate narrator.

Darl ends in what looks like what we call schizophrenia, but his uncanniness and visionary power cannot be reduced to madness. All of his nineteen interior monologues are remarkable, as here in the conclusion to number 17:

> . . . And since sleep is is-not and rain and wind are *was*, it is not. Yet the wagon *is*, because when the wagon is *was*, Addie Bundren will not be. And Jewel *is*, so Addie Bundren must be. And then I must be, or I could not empty myself for sleep in a strange room. And so if I am not emptied yet, I am *is*.
>
> How often have I lain beneath rain on a strange roof, thinking of home.

Doubting his own identity, Darl has a Shakespearean awareness of nothingness, which is a version of Faulkner's own nihilism (again, in his great phase, 1929–39), and of Faulkner's wartime experience, of training for the British Royal Air Force, but never taking off in a plane. Darl too has been away at World War I, but it has left little mark upon his consciousness. Hating the terrible wagon odyssey of bringing Addie's corpse back to its birthplace, Darl nearly sabotages the effort with a barn-burning, but this only inspires Jewel to fresh heroics.

Darl is a *knower*, as Faulkner continuously emphasizes. He knows that his sister is pregnant, that Jewel is not Anse's son, that his mother is in no true sense *his* mother, and that the human predicament is a kind of aboriginal disaster. And he knows that even the landscape is an emptiness, a falling-away from a prior reality, as here in section number 34:

> . . . Above the ceaseless surface they stand—trees, cane, vines—rootless, severed from the earth, spectral above a scene of immense yet circumscribed desolation filled with the voice of the waste and mournful water.

An intuitive poet and metaphysician, Darl is dangerously close to a verge over which he must fall. His psychic wounds are the legacy in him of Addie's coldness and Anse's selfishness; he is fated for alienation. No escape is possible for Darl; his only sexual desires are for his own sister, and his family is his doom.

In Darl's final monologue (number 57), he is so dissociated from himself that all his perceptions, uncannier than ever, observe him in the third person. Two guards escort him to the state asylum on the train, and we hear his voice at its most shattering:

> . . . One of them sat beside him, the other sat on the seat facing him, riding backward. One of them had to ride backward because the state's money has a face to each backside and a backside to each face, and they are riding on the state's money which is incest. A nickel has a woman on one side and a buffalo on the other; two faces and no back.

Darl, split in half, holds conversations with himself, yet remains a seer: "the state's money which is incest." The passage is haunted by Iago's Rabelaisian jest of heterosexual love being a beast with two backs, yet there is a deeper Shakespeareanism in seeing the state's money as being incest; *Measure for Measure* is close by.

The reader must find *As I Lay Dying* difficult: it *is* difficult, yet legitimately so. Faulkner, who acutely felt the need to be his own father, infuriates some feminists by his obsessive, implicit identification of death and female sexuality. Darl's sanity dies with his mother, but in some sense his derangement makes explicit what is muted in his siblings. Nature, in *As I Lay Dying*, is itself a wound. André Gide oddly observed that Faulkner's characters lacked souls; what Gide meant to say is that the Bundrens, like the Compsons in *The Sound and the Fury*, had no hope, could not believe that their doom would ever lift. God will not make any covenant with the Bundrens or the Compsons, perhaps because they come out of an abyss and must go into it again. That may be why Dewey Dell cries out so desperately that she believes in God. *As I Lay Dying* portrays the human condition as being catastrophic, with the nuclear family the most terrible of the catastrophes.

Nathanael West:
Miss Lonelyhearts

Flannery O'Connor associated *As I Lay Dying*, in spirit, with Nathanael West's *Miss Lonelyhearts*, and called them her two favorite modern novels. Her insight was worthy of her: not on the surface, but in their depths, there is an affinity between these two apocalyptic books. Like *As I Lay Dying*, *Miss Lonelyhearts* is tragic farce and not satire. West, a parodist with rancid genius, achieved his masterwork in *Miss Lonelyhearts*. Published when West was just thirty, *Miss Lonelyhearts* might in time have been surpassed by its author, who died in a car crash at thirty-seven. And yet the book is so sublime in its negativity, so perfect in its farcical despair, that one would not wish it different or better.

The reader, encountering *Miss Lonelyhearts* for a first time, will be startled, but it is not a difficult book, such as *As I Lay Dying*. West, born Nathan Weinstein, is certainly the major American Jewish writer before the recent phase of Philip Roth that has produced *Sabbath's Theater* and *American Pastoral*. Something of a Jewish anti-Semite, with no interest in or knowledge of Jewish esoteric tradition (Kabbalah), West ironically became a significant literary figure in the history of Jewish Gnosticism. A reader desiring to find appropriate context for *Miss Lonelyhearts* ought to read the great essay "Redemption Through Sin" in Gershom Scholem's *The Messianic Idea in Judaism.*

West risks two unsympathetic protagonists in his superb short novel: Miss Lonelyhearts, who writes the agony column in the New York *Post-Dispatch* daily newspaper, and his editor, Shrike. We are never given any other name for Miss Lonelyhearts, a humanly inadequate would-be Christ, but Shrike's name could not be bettered. Shrikes are small-to-medium-sized birds with remarkably hooked bills, and rather nasty face masks. Their name in Latin, *Lanius,* means "butcher," and shrikes are commonly called butcher birds, since their practice is to impale insects on the thorns of bushes, and then devour their prey. That suggests crucifixion, and Shrike is a kind of American Satan who torments Miss Lonelyhearts, and would crucify him, if he could.

There is a desperate tonality throughout the novel, a savagery almost hysterical in its intensity. This style suits Miss Lonelyhearts's nature and predicament; he is a fallen American Adam, a would-be Walt Whitman, proclaiming universal love but cold to his core. Shrike, as much as Miss Lonelyhearts, is consumed by religious hysteria, by a despair that emanates from a nostalgia for God, a longing for Christ.

West foregrounds the novel by letting the reader understand that, well before the book opens, Shrike's endless (and eloquent) impaling language has already destroyed Miss Lonelyhearts. Crossing a little park, Miss Lonelyhearts "walked into the shadow of a lamp-post that lay on the path like a spear. It pierced him like a spear." West regarded his book as a "lyric novel"; nearly every sentence counts, in a spectacular verbal economy. The reader may be haunted, as I am, by certain letters received by Miss Lonelyhearts for his agony column, particularly by one from a sixteen-year-old girl who was born without a nose:

I sit and look at myself all day and cry. I have a big hole in the middle of my face that scares people even myself so I can't blame the boys for not wanting to take me out. My mother loves me, but she cries terrible when she looks at me.

What did I do to deserve such a terrible bad fate?

We laugh at this, but defensively, as we tend to laugh uneasily at all the grotesque violence in which West abounds, and which will literally destroy Miss Lonelyhearts in the novel's final sentence. The fifteen tableaux, each with its title, seethe with violence, repressed or overt. Even a reflection on a late spring prompts: "It had taken all the brutality of July to torture a few green spikes through the exhausted dirt."

Shrike and Miss Lonelyhearts are inverted doubles, both representing West himself, split between the satanic intelligence of Shrike and the inability to believe of Miss Lonelyhearts. So convinced is the latter that the whole world is dead that "he wondered if hysteria were really too steep a price to pay for bringing it to life." Shrike's demonic greatness achieves its negative epiphany in the eight section "Miss Lonelyhearts in the Dismal Swamp," where the reader is offered a superb parody of all "the ways out" she might choose to take. One hears West himself in Shrike's savage send-ups, starting with D. H. Lawrence's sexual vitalism:

. . . you sow and weep and chivy your kine, not kin or kind, between the poignant rows of corn and taters. Your step becomes the heavy sexual step of a dance-drunk Indian and you tread the seed down into the female earth.

The parody of Herman Melville's early primitivism, in *Typee* and *Omoo,* seems to me even funnier:

Your body is golden brown like hers, and tourists have need of the indignant finger of the missionary to point you out. . . . And so you dream away the days, fishing, hunting, dancing, swimming, kissing, and picking flowers to twine in your hair . . .

One can almost be fond of Shrike for the lovely narcissism of picking flowers to twine, not in the beloved's hair, but in one's own. The wonderful parodies go on, the very best of them being the last word on Aestheticism, the faith of the sublime Walter Pater and the divine Oscar Wilde:

> Tell them that you know that your shoes are broken and that there are pimples on your face, yes, and that you have buck teeth and a club foot, but that you don't care, for tomorrow they are playing Beethoven's last quartets in Carnegie Hall and at home you have Shakespeare's plays in one volume.

The placement of that "yes" is wonderful, and the aesthetic is dismissed as another tiresome evasion, akin to drugs, alcohol, and suicide. Mounting to the satanic summit of his eloquence, Shrike cries out: "All is desolation and a vexation of the spirit. I feel like hell . . ." He *is* hell, nor is Miss Lonelyhearts out of it: the second half of the novel depicts the descent of the American failed Christ into the abyss of Fay Doyle, ungratified wife of Peter Doyle (the name of Walt Whitman's beloved). In the heartless final section, grimly entitled "Miss Lonelyhearts Has a Religious Experience," the crippled Doyle arrives with a gun. Miss Lonelyhearts, become Christ, greets him ecstatically:

> The gun inside the package exploded and Miss Lonelyhearts fell, dragging the cripple with him. They both rolled part of the way down the stairs.

Those are the final words of *Miss Lonelyhearts,* and are an epitome of Nathanael West's vision. How to read *Miss Lonelyhearts*? With nervous attention, appropriate to a "lyric novel," that is at once a parody of American religiosity and a major instance of its prevalent power. No nation, as West prophesied, is now as religious or as implicitly violent as we are. A mere handful of Americans do not believe in God, and only another handful of those who do fail to believe that God loves each one of them on a personal and individual basis. Baruch Spinoza, the great Dutch-Jewish philosopher of ethics, famously remarked that it was essential that we learn to love God without ever expecting that he would love us in return. I do not know of a more un-American statement. Why read *Miss Lonelyhearts*? To understand better our obsession with guns and violence, our fanatic need to be loved by God, our Gnostic roots (which we deny overtly) that teach us redemption through sin, but most of all to experience the pleasures provided by our greatest of parodists since Mark Twain himself.

We will have no more Nathanael Wests; literary parody expired with him, though it had a brief afterglow in his brother-in-law, S. J. Perelman. Flare-ups of the mode in the late Terry Southern and in the metamorphic Gore Vidal have subsided. There were Hemingway's self-parodies, in his later years, and Norman Mailer's still later parodies, both of Hemingway and of himself. All these formidable talents have been subsumed by American media realities; who can match television news and talking heads, and even the daily *New York Times,* in self-parody? Reality in America is more grotesque and hilarious than any parodist could hope to trump. There is something curiously wistful now about *Miss Lonelyhearts,* a judgment upon my part that would have infuriated Nathanael West. Still, he was not a satirist, secretly hoping to improve us, but a demonic parodist, providing some music to celebrate our march down into hell. Read him for his prophecy, and for the unsettling laughter he will bring you, as you too approach the abyss prepared for the American soul by the American religion.

Thomas Pynchon:
The Crying of Lot 49

Oedipa Maas, the heroine of *The Crying of Lot 49,* in one way resembles the ideal reader of *How to Read and Why.* Oedipa's quest is to discover how and why to read the story in which she finds herself. Pynchon's Oedipa is not always a good reader, but she deserves her first name: like Sophocles' Oedipus she unceasingly seeks the truth. We never learn whether she is on its track, or whether she is the victim of a paranoid joke played by her deceased former lover Inverarity, a name whose relation to truth is ambiguous. *The Crying of Lot 49* never stops teaching you how to read it, but since the teaching is ambivalent, the reader is left in doubt about the "how." What is clearer is why one should read this short novel; it carries on compellingly from *As I Lay Dying* and *Miss Lonelyhearts,* and is the next step in achieving an apocalyptic understanding of the United States.

The best advice for a reader of *The Crying of Lot 49* is to ignore clues that are too obvious, such as the Pentecostal references that flicker throughout the book. Pynchon plies you with redundant information, and much of it is white noise. He is a playful Kabbalist, of the tarot pack variety, so that anything in the novel can mean everything or nothing. The initial pleasures of *The Crying of Lot 49* may be the best clues to its meaning: it is wildly funny, but not with the cruel humor of *Miss Lonelyhearts.* Pynchon too is a parodist, but not a savage one, and the reader (unless jaundiced) ought to become very fond of Oedipa Maas, who always means well, even when she does not know what it all means. Oedipa's all but universal goodwill is a piquant contrast to the paranoid conspiracy of the Tristero that she either uncovers or else partly invents. Even paranoids have enemies, but Oedipa has none, unless the deceased Inverarity is playing that role from beyond the grave. Oedipa, in the Tristero universe, can never know all the facts, because they proliferate endlessly on every side.

The book's best critic, Sir Frank Kermode, points out that Oedipa loses all her friends—whether to death, madness, or infatuation—until her isolation is complete at the close. In this again, she stands for the reader, no matter how many commentaries or companions *The Crying of Lot 49* accumulates. And yet Oedipa is not insane, nor are most of the readers, and so, being myself a Kabbalist, I vote for the reality of Tristero, thus transgressing Pynchon's apparent intentions. And yet one can wonder as to those intentions—not so much as to their existence, as to their pragmatic importance, since Pynchon, partly in the mode of Kafka, has made himself uninterpretable except by the reader's personal and perhaps arbitrary choice. Thus, as a passionate admirer of Cormac McCarthy's *Blood Meridian* (1985), published not two decades after *The Crying of Lot 49*, I wonder if Pynchon's 49 does not have some reference to the California gold rush of 1849. Pynchon intimates that the Tristero reached the United States in 1849–50, which is when most of the slaughter in McCarthy's novel is enacted. One motive for the expedition of the Glanton–Judge Holden paramilitary force is to take the scalps of as many Southwestern Native Americans as possible, so as to clear the way to the gold fields. Glanton's raiders become their own anarchic government, and even their own communications system. McCarthy, a Faulknerian and not a Pynchonite, is thus linked to the Tristero in my own reader's paranoia.

The Tristero is at once Pynchon's most surprising invention (in this novel) and perhaps also a historical reality, insofar as it began as the enemy of a European private postal system owned and operated by the noble house of Thurn and Taxis in early modern times. In nineteenth-century America, the Tristero assaults both the Pony Express and Wells, Fargo. Also spelled Trystero, this shadow organization is anarchist in its apparent ideology, rather like the London underground movement of Joseph Conrad's *The Secret Agent* and Henry James's *The Princess Casamassima,* and in a more comic register, G. K. Chesterton's *The Man Who Was Thursday.* There is also a Borgesian touch to the Tristero; it has some of the stigmata of those conspiracies that reorganize reality, such as Borges's Tlön. How ought the reader to regard the Tristero? Clearly it is a good or a bad thing, depending upon your perspective.

My own experience as a reader is that Faulkner's *As I Lay Dying* captured me the first time around, though only with rereading could I put it together. West's *Miss Lonelyhearts* also won me over immediately, its gorgeous rancidity being irresistible, though again rereadings added understanding to my admiration. But my first reading of *The Crying of Lot 49* was mostly an exasperation; at second reading the book suddenly took me over, and has held me ever since. I therefore urge readers who may not know the book to *begin* by reading it twice through. What perhaps irritates at first becomes a dazzlement, and one of the centers of that enchantment is the Tristero, an ambiguous but sublime mythmaking. At once a tryst or erotic encounter and a melancholy, the name *Tristero* pretty much means what the reader wants it to mean. Is there "terror" in it? Or a sacred terror? Perhaps, like so many underground societies, the Tristero is, at the least, morally ambiguous. Pynchon, in *Gravity's Rainbow,* could be judged to advocate what he calls "sado-anarchism," and that may be the most accurate ideology to associate with the Tristero. Yet all this is, at times, hilariously funny, as in the grand send-up of a Jacobean revenge play, *The Courier's Tragedy* by Richard Wharfinger, a fit companion for Cyril Tourneur, John Ford, and John Webster. The pages giving a plot summary, with outrageous excerpts, of *The Courier's Tragedy* (pp. 65–75 of the Harper Perennial Library paperback) provoke simultaneous laughter and horror, though more of the former.

The Crying of Lot 49, though it might seem to be an open-ended allegory, in the sense that allegory always means something other than what is said, can never quite be an allegory of any kind, because Pynchon has no definite doctrine to propose, whether religious, political, philosophical, or psychological. Sado-anarchism is hardly a politics, and paranoia, however structured, cannot become, in itself, an ideology. What will sustain the reader of *The Crying of Lot 49,* and keep her eagerly going, is the local life of the novel, the human surprises that belong neither to the Tristero nor to American paranoia (assuming, as I do, that we can keep that duo apart). When I think about *The Crying of Lot 49,* I always first recall Oedipa's vivid descent into the night world of San Francisco, with its repeated appearances of the image of a muted post horn, symbol of the Tristero, which appears to be indeed the underground organization of those whom Dostoevsky had called "the insulted and injured." Oedipa goes into the San Francisco night so as to cure her Tristero obsession: "She had only to drift tonight, at random, and watch nothing happen, to be convinced it was purely nervous, a little something for her shrink to fix." Swept by tumultuous tourists into a gay bar, she instantly spots a pin on a sport coat in the shape of the Tristero emblem. It turns up again in a Chinatown herbalist's window, and chalked on a sidewalk, in rhymes chanted at a jump-rope game, until she reencounters Jesús Arrabal, a Mexican anarchist who defines a miracle as "another world's intrusion into this one." This has its affinities to the Tristero's code name, W.A.S.T.E.: We Await Silent Tristero's Empire. Again and again, too numerous to count, the enigmatic signs of the sado-anarchist conspiracy confront Oedipa and the reader. By morning, Oedipa is convinced that the dispossessed have withdrawn wholly from the United States government and its postal system. What follows that self-persuasion is a moment of astonishing poignance, though I suppose nothing in Pynchon should ever astonish his reader.

Oedipa encounters a huddled old man, shaking with grief, but with the post horn tattooed on the back of his left hand. Hardly knowing what she does, she comforts him, holding him to her breast while she rocks him, as though he were her baby (she is childless). After mailing a letter for the old man, via Tristero, she attempts to trace the underground postal system, but fails. That, and all her subsequent adventures, and all previous, may count for less than her cradling of the destitute old man in her arms. Like West's Shrike and Miss Lonelyhearts, Oedipa has been more a deliberate cartoon than a Faulknerian or Shakespearean character, *until now.* I think she gets away from Pynchon here, as no one else in his work does until the great change in his art in *Mason &*

Dixon, where both personages in the title are fully humanized figures. How are we to read Oedipa's sudden emergence into so superb a compassion? Other moments of reality break through the fantasy structures of *The Crying of Lot 49,* but this is the grandest. In the pages of nearly any other writer, it might seem sentimental, but not when it manifests in Pynchon.

In the book's closing scene, Oedipa attends the auction of Inverarity's invaluable stamp collection, including the Tristero "forgeries," which are to be sold, as lot 49. The final moment comes, as the auctioneer clears his throat, and Oedipa settles back, "to await the crying of lot 49." We have come full circle to the title again, and have more clues to what might happen than any reader will be inclined to interpret. It *may* be forty-nine days since Easter Sunday, and then again it may not. I think not. We are not about to hear Oedipa break out into a Pentecostal speaking with tongues, nor is it likely that either an angel or a dove will descend. Nor do I think that Oedipa herself will bid for lot 49. Presumably a representative of the Tristero will bid for it successfully, but if Oedipa follows him out, he will speed away, and she will be left in limbo, which is where Pynchon has placed her, and with her the readers. There are worse places to be.

Cormac McCarthy:
Blood Meridian

Blood Meridian (1985) seems to me the authentic American apocalyptic novel, more relevant even in 2000 than it was fifteen years ago. The fulfilled renown of *Moby-Dick* and of *As I Lay Dying* is augmented by *Blood Meridian,* since Cormac McCarthy is the worthy disciple both of Melville and of Faulkner. I venture that no other living American novelist, not even Pynchon, has given us a book as strong and memorable as *Blood Meridian,* much as I appreciate Don DeLillo's *Underworld,* Philip Roth's *Zuckerman Bound, Sabbath's Theater,* and *American Pastoral,* and Pynchon's *Gravity's Rainbow* and *Mason & Dixon.* McCarthy himself, in his recent Border trilogy, commencing with the superb *All the Pretty Horses,* has not matched *Blood Meridian,* but it is the ultimate Western, not to be surpassed.

My concern being the reader, I will begin by confessing that my first two attempts to read through *Blood Meridian* failed, because I flinched from the overwhelming carnage that McCarthy portrays. The violence begins on the novel's second page, when the fifteen-year-old Kid is shot in the back and just below the heart, and continues almost with no respite until the end, thirty years later, when Judge Holden, the most frightening figure in all of American literature, murders the Kid in an outhouse. So appalling are the continuous massacres and mutilations of *Blood Meridian* that one could be reading a United Nations report on the horrors of Kosovo in 1999.

Nevertheless, I urge the reader to persevere, because *Blood Meridian* is a canonical imaginative achievement, both an American and a universal tragedy of blood. Judge Holden is a villain worthy of Shakespeare, Iago-like and demoniac, a theoretician of war everlasting. And the book's magnificence—its language, landscape, persons, conceptions—at last transcends the violence, and convert goriness into terrifying art, an art comparable to Melville's and to Faulkner's. When I teach the book, many of my students resist it initially (as I did, and as some of my friends continue to do). Television saturates us with actual as well as imagined violence, and I turn away, either in shock or in disgust. But I cannot turn away from *Blood Meridian,* now that I know how to read it, and why it has to be read. None of its carnage is gratuitous or redundant; it belonged to the Mexico-Texas borderlands in 1849–50, which is where and when most of the novel is set. I suppose one could call *Blood Meridian* a "historical novel," since it chronicles the actual expedition of the Glanton gang, a murderous paramilitary force sent out both by Mexican and Texan authorities to murder and scalp as many Indians as possible. Yet it does not have the aura of historical fiction, since what it depicts seethes on, in the United States, and nearly everywhere else, as we enter the third millennium. Judge Holden, the prophet of war, is unlikely to be without honor in our years to come.

Even as you learn to endure the slaughter McCarthy describes, you become accustomed to the book's high style, again as overtly Shakespearean as it is Faulknerian. There are passages of Melvillean-Faulknerian baroque richness and intensity in *The Crying of Lot 49*, and elsewhere in Pynchon, but we can never be sure that they are not parodistic. The prose of *Blood Meridian* soars, yet with its own economy, and its dialogue is always persuasive, particularly when the uncanny Judge Holden speaks (chapter 14, p. 199):

> The judge placed his hands on the ground. He looked at his inquisitor. This is my claim, he said. And yet everywhere upon it are pockets of autonomous life. Autonomous. In order for it to be mine nothing must be permitted to occur upon it save by my dispensation.
>
> Toadvine sat with his boots crossed before the fire. No man can acquaint himself with everything on this earth, he said.
>
> The judge tilted his great head. The man who believes that the secrets of this world are forever hidden lives in mystery and fear. Superstition will drag him down. The rain will erode the deeds of his life. But that man who sets himself the task of singling out the thread of order from the tapestry will by the decision alone have taken charge of the world and it is only by such taking charge that he will effect a way to dictate the terms of his own fate.

Judge Holden is the spiritual leader of Glanton's filibusters, and McCarthy persuasively gives the self-styled judge a mythic status, appropriate for a deep Machiavelli whose "thread of order" recalls Iago's magic web, in which Othello, Desdemona, and Cassio are caught. Though all of the more colorful and murderous raiders are vividly characterized for us, the killing-machine Glanton with the others, the novel turns always upon its two central figures, Judge Holden and the Kid. We first meet the Judge on page 6: an enormous man, bald as a stone, no trace of a beard, and eyes without either brows or lashes. A seven-foot-tall albino almost seems to have come from some other world, and we learn to wonder about the Judge, who never sleeps, dances and fiddles with extraordinary art and energy, rapes and murders little children of both sexes, and who says that he will never die. By the book's close, I have come to believe that the Judge is immortal. And yet the Judge, while both more and less than human, is as individuated as Iago or Macbeth, and is quite at home in the Texan-Mexican borderlands where we watch him operate in 1849–50, and then find him again in 1878, not a day older after twenty-eight years, though the Kid, a sixteen-year-old at the start of Glanton's foray, is forty-five when murdered by the Judge at the end.

McCarthy subtly shows us the long, slow development of the Kid from another mindless scalper of Indians to the courageous confronter of the Judge in their final debate in a saloon. But though the Kid's moral maturation is heartening, his personality remains largely a cipher, as anonymous as his lack of a name. The three glories of the book are the Judge, the landscape, and (dreadful to say this) the slaughters, which are aesthetically distanced by McCarthy in a number of complex ways.

What is the reader to make of the Judge? He is immortal as principle, as War Everlasting, but is he a person, or something other? McCarthy will not tell us, which is all the better, since the ambiguity is most stimulating. Melville's Captain Ahab, though a Promethean demigod, is necessarily mortal, and perishes with the *Pequod* and all its crew, except for Ishmael. After he has killed the Kid, *Blood Meridian*'s Ishmael, Judge Holden is the last survivor of Glanton's scalping crusade. Destroying the Native American nations of the Southwest is hardly analogous to the hunt to slay Moby-

Dick, and yet McCarthy gives us some curious parallels between the two quests. The most striking is between Melville's chapter 19, where a ragged prophet, who calls himself Elijah, warns Ishmael and Queequeg against sailing on the *Pequod,* and McCarthy's chapter 4, where "an old disordered Mennonite" warns the Kid and his comrades not to join Captain Worth's filibuster, a disaster that preludes the greater catastrophe of Glanton's campaign.

McCarthy's invocation of *Moby-Dick,* while impressive and suggestive, in itself does not do much to illuminate Judge Holden for us. Ahab has his preternatural aspects, including his harpooner Fedellah and Parsee whaleboat crew, and the captain's conversion to their Zoroastrian faith. Elijah tells Ishmael touches of other Ahabian mysteries: a three-day trance off Cape Horn, slaying a Spaniard in front of a presumably Catholic altar in Santa, and a wholly enigmatic spitting into a "silver calabash." Yet all these are transparencies compared to the enigmas of Judge Holden, who seems to judge the entire earth, and whose name suggests a holding, presumably of sway over all he encounters. And yet, the Judge, unlike Ahab, is not wholly fictive; like Glanton, he is a historic filibuster or freebooter. McCarthy tells us most in the Kid's dream visions of Judge Holden, towards the close of the novel (chapter 22, pp. 309–10):

> In that sleep and in sleep to follow the judge did visit. Who would come other? A great shambling mutant, silent and serene. Whatever his antecedents, he was something wholly other than their sum, nor was there system by which to divide him back into his origins for he would not go. Whoever would seek out his history through what unraveling of loins and ledgerbooks must stand at last darkened and dumb at the shore of a void without terminus or origin and whatever science he might bring to bear upon the dusty primal matter blowing down out of the millennia will discover no trace of ultimate atavistic egg by which to reckon his commencing.

I think that McCarthy is warning his reader that the Judge is Moby-Dick rather than Ahab. As another white enigma, the albino Judge, like the albino whale, cannot be slain. Melville, a professed Gnostic, who believed that some "anarch hand or cosmic blunder" had divided us into two fallen sexes, gives us a Manichean quester in Ahab. McCarthy gives Judge Holden the powers and purposes of the bad angels or demiurges that the Gnostics called archons, but he tells us not to make such an identification (as the critic Leo Daugherty eloquently has). Any "system," including the Gnostic one, will not divide the Judge back into his origins. The "ultimate atavistic egg" will not be found. What can the reader do with the haunting and terrifying Judge?

Let us begin by saying that Judge Holden, though his gladsome prophecy of eternal war is authentically universal, is first and foremost a Western American, no matter how cosmopolitan his background (he speaks all languages, knows all arts and sciences, and can perform magical, shamanistic metamorphoses). The Texan-Mexican border is a superb place for a war-god like the Judge to be. He carries a rifle, mounted in silver, with its name inscribed under the checkpiece: *Et In Arcadia Ego*. In the American Arcadia, death is also always there, incarnated in the Judge's weapon, which never misses. If the American pastoral tradition essentially is the Western film, then the Judge incarnates that tradition, though he would require a director light-years beyond the late Sam Peckinpah, whose *The Wild Bunch* portrays mildness itself when compared to Glanton's paramilitaries. I resort though, as before, to Iago, for only he is worthy to consort with Judge Holden. Iago, who transfers war from the camp and the field to every other locale, is a pyromaniac setting everything and everyone ablaze with the flame of battle. The Judge might be Iago before *Othello* begins, when the war god Othello was still worshiped by his "honest" color officer, his ancient or ensign. The Judge speaks with an authority that chills me even as Iago leaves me terrified:

This is the nature of war, whose stake is at once the game and the authority and the justification. Seen so, war is the truest form of divination. It is the testing of one's will and the will of another within that larger will which because it binds them is therefore forced to select. War is the ultimate game because war is at last a forcing of the unity of existence.

If McCarthy does not want us to regard the Judge as a Gnostic archon or supernatural being, the reader may still feel that it hardly seems sufficient to designate Holden as a nineteenth-century Western American Iago. Since *Blood Meridian,* like the much longer *Moby-Dick,* is more prose epic than novel, the Glanton foray can seem a post-Homeric quest, where the various heroes (or thugs) have a disguised god among them, which appears to be the Judge's Herculean role. The Glanton gang passes into a sinister aesthetic glory at the close of chapter 13, when they progress from murdering and scalping Indians to butchering the Mexicans who have hired them:

> They entered the city haggard and filthy and reeking with the blood of the citizenry for whose protection they had contracted. The scalps of the slain villagers were strung from the windows of the governor's house and the partisans were paid out of the all but exhausted coffers and the Sociedad was disbanded and the bounty rescinded. Within a week of their quitting the city there would be a price of eight thousand pesos posted for Glanton's head.

I break into this passage, partly to observe that from this point on the filibusters pursue the way down and out to an apocalyptic conclusion, but also to urge the reader to hear, and to admire, the sublime sentence that follows directly, because we are at the visionary center of *Blood Meridian.*

> They rode out on the north road as would parties bound for El Paso but before they were even quite out of sight of the city they had turned their tragic mounts to the west and they rode infatuate

and half fond toward the red demise of that day, toward the evening lands and the distant pandemonium of the sun.

Since Cormac McCarthy's language, like Melville's and Faulkner's, frequently is deliberately archaic, the *meridian* of the title probably means the zenith or noon position of the sun in the sky. Glanton, the Judge, the Kid, and their fellows are not described as "tragic"—their long-suffering horses are—and they are "infatuate" and half-mad ("fond") because they have broken away from any semblance of order. McCarthy knows, as does the reader, that an "order" urging the destruction of the entire Native American population of the Southwest is an obscene idea of order, but he wants the reader to know also that the Glanton gang is now aware that they are unsponsored and free to run totally amok. The sentence I have just quoted has a morally ambiguous greatness to it, but that *is* the greatness of *Blood Meridian,* and indeed of Homer and of Shakespeare. McCarthy so contextualizes the sentence that the amazing contrast between its high gestures and the murderous thugs who evoke the splendor is not ironic but tragic. The tragedy is ours, as readers, and not the Glanton gang's, since we are not going to mourn their demise, except for the Kid's, and even there our reaction will be equivocal.

My passion for *Blood Meridian* is so fierce that I want to go on expounding it, but the courageous reader should now be (I hope) pretty well into the main movement of the book. I will confine myself here to the final encounter between the preternatural Judge Holden and the Kid, who had broken with the insane crusade twenty-eight years before, and now at middle age must confront the ageless Judge. Their dialogue is the finest achievement in this book of augmenting wonders, and may move the reader as nothing else in *Blood Meridian* does. I reread it perpetually and cannot persuade myself that I have come to the end of it.

The Judge and the Kid drink together, after the avenging Judge tells the Kid that this night his soul will be demanded of him.

Knowing he is no match for the Judge, the Kid nevertheless defies Holden, with laconic replies playing against the Judge's rolling grandiloquence. After demanding to know where their slain comrades are, the Judge asks: "And where is the fiddler and where the dance?"

> I guess you can tell me.
>
> I tell you this. As war becomes dishonored and its nobility called into question those honorable men who recognize the sanctity of blood will become excluded from the dance, which is the warrior's right, and thereby will the dance become a false dance and the dancers false dancers. And yet there will be one there always who is a true dancer and can you guess who that might be?
>
> You aint nothin.

To have known Judge Holden, to have seen him in full operation, and to tell him that he is nothing, is heroic. "You speak truer than you know," the Judge replies, and two pages later murders the Kid, most horribly. *Blood Meridian,* except for a one-paragraph epilogue, ends with the Judge triumphantly dancing and fiddling at once, and proclaiming that he never sleeps and he will never die. But McCarthy does not let Judge Holden have the last word.

The strangest passage in *Blood Meridian,* the epilogue is set at dawn, where a nameless man progresses over a plain by means of holes that he makes in the rocky ground. Employing a two-handled implement, the man strikes "the fire out of the rock which God has put there." Around the man are wanderers searching for bones, and he continues to strike fire in the holes, and then they move on. And that is all.

The subtitle of *Blood Meridian* is *The Evening Redness in the West,* which belongs to the Judge, last survivor of the Glanton gang. Perhaps all that the reader can surmise with some certainty is that the man striking fire in the rock at dawn is an opposing figure in regard to the evening redness in the West. The Judge never sleeps, and perhaps will never die, but a new Prometheus may be rising to go up against him.

Ralph Ellison:
Invisible Man

It seems reasonable to judge that the greatest aesthetic achievement by African-Americans is the work of the major masters of jazz: Louis Armstrong, Charlie Parker, Bud Powell, and others. But then jazz is the only indigenous American art. African-American writers, despite critical confusions among some of their politicized academic cheerleaders, were in no position to found an original literary art. *Invisible Man* (1952), by the late Ralph Ellison, remains much the strongest novel by an American black, and its palpable (and, by Ellison, acknowledged) debts are to Melville, Mark Twain, Faulkner, Dostoevsky, and to the poetic language of T. S. Eliot. Toni Morrison, though she passionately argues otherwise, is also a child of Faulkner, as well as of Virginia Woolf. Ellison was a writer of immense and mordant sensibility, and his pride at having composed *Invisible Man* was the largest single factor in his refusal to publish a second novel during his lifetime. I urge the reader towards *Invisible Man,* and not to *Juneteenth,* edited from Ellison's manuscripts. I do not believe he would have sanctioned its publication: more than once, he had asked me if any American novelist, except for Henry James, had really composed a second masterwork?

Presumably he was thinking of Melville, Twain, Hemingway, Fitzgerald—among others—and I would have been tactless to suggest candidates, and so did not. Yet he was well aware of Faulkner, who in his grand early phase had created *The Sound and the Fury, As I Lay Dying, Light in August,* and *Absalom, Absalom!* Faulkner, a Southern white, faced many cultural pressures, but nothing like those that bothered Ellison in the last quarter century of his life. Feminist critics, Marxists, and African-American nationalists complained of Ellison's insistence at setting art above ideology. Refusing polemic, the novelist partly withdrew into his massive dignity. There are essays galore (he commented upon some of them, to me, with ironical dismissal) that chide Ellison, and his narrator-protagonist, Invisible Man, for not embracing the true "political" faith. Though Ellison, as the reader will see for herself, ends with an ambiguity tinged with hope, the typical condemnation is that Invisible Man will never come up from underground, because he lacks the black mother, black Muse, or Marxist wiliness that could propel him back to society. Ellison wrote his own novel, and we do best to learn how to read it, and why. Another age will come, with other cultural politics, while *Invisible Man* will retain the American, and universal, imaginative vitality with which Ralph Waldo Ellison endowed it.

At *Invisible Man*'s conclusion, the narrator again invokes Louis Armstrong, who throughout has been his chosen precursor, indeed his spiritual guide, Virgil to his Dante:

> And there's still a conflict within me: With Louis Armstrong one half of me says, "Open the window and let the foul air out," while the other says, "It was good, green corn before the harvest."

In the prologue, Invisible Man listens to Armstrong playing and singing "What Did I Do to Be So Black and Blue," and reflects: "Perhaps I like Louis Armstrong because he's made poetry of being invisible." Ellison, a deep student of Armstrong's work, understood that jazz changed from a music of the folk to a high art of innovation because of Armstrong. In some sense, Ellison transformed Charles Chestnutt and Richard Wright rather as Armstrong transcended his precursors in jazz, a movement from folklore to High Modernism.

Invisible Man is a historical novel, because most of it takes place in the 1920s and 1930s, when the United States was hardly less racist a society than it had been in the 1870s and 1880s. Though we need not congratulate ourselves that much of what goes on in Ellison's novel could not happen now (it can and does), public attitudes have altered (to some degree), and the law at least is different. The book's Brotherhood (the Communist Party) scarcely exists, and the remarkable Ras the Exhorter has been replaced by the more mundane Reverend Al Sharpton. The even more remarkable Rinehart, reverend and drug-runner, has a host of contemporary equivalents, but here nature falls short of Ellison's art, and the exuberant Rinehart remains larger than life.

Invisible Man, Melvillean-Faulknerian like *Miss Lonelyhearts, The Crying of Lot 49,* and *Blood Meridian,* shares the negative sublimity of all the novels I have been reading in this chapter, and shares also in their greatness. Kenneth Burke, most admirable of twentieth-century American critics, several times in conversation urged me to meditate upon Ellison as the American master of the novel of education, the genre of the German *Bildungsroman,* of Thomas Mann's *The Magic Mountain* and Goethe's *Wilhelm Meister.* Mann's novel, as we have seen, is a lovingly ironic parody of the genre but Ellison's seems to me a demonic or tragic parody. His Invisible Man in some respects is closer to Dostoevsky's Underground Man than to a developmental hero of the Goethean-Mannian sort.

Ellison himself cited Malraux, T. S. Eliot, Hemingway, Faulkner, and Dostoevsky as his literary "ancestors." Interestingly, he excluded *Moby-Dick,* which lends *Invisible Man* its crucial Jonah component. I suspect that Melville, like Faulkner, was a touch too close, while Dostoevsky was safely distant, in place and in time. The hero of Dostoevsky's *Notes from Underground* suffers humiliations, and narrates his subsequent rejection of the world, withdrawing to a hovel. This symbolic withdrawal is to some extent a rejection of Western values and ideas, though the Underground Man is well aware that European rationalism has an inescapable position in his own consciousness. But he rebels against it, profoundly believing that it violates his integrity. Ellison's

Invisible Man is considerably more gifted than Dostoevsky's angry protagonist, and as an African-American he has a more complex predicament. Dostoevsky wanted to reject Europe; Ellison passionately refuses to give up on America, though his Invisible Man will not accept it upon its hypocritical terms.

Moby-Dick is haunted by the Book of Jonah, and so is *Invisible Man.* I don't know whether Melville knew that the Book of Jonah is read aloud to the congregation on the Jewish Day of Atonement, but Ellison certainly did. The Book of Jonah is not apocalyptic but survivalist; Jonah, the evasive prophet, is resurrected from the belly of the whale, after he has repented fleeing from Yahweh out of pique. Humor clearly dominates the Hebrew text, since Jonah's vexation against Yahweh is that the prophecy proved successful and the people of Nineveh turned away from evil, thus averting the city's destruction.

The Invisible Man, like Jonah, is always in repression, to which Freud assigned the metaphor of fleeing. False fathers—Bledsoe, Lucas Brockway, Jack of the Brotherhood—continually betray him, even as Jonah feels betrayed by God the Father, who declined to obliterate Nineveh. Chased by whites into a manhole, Invisible Man becomes Jonah in the whale's belly, thus beginning his underground existence, from which (as I read it) he is about to emerge as the novel concludes. The book's prologue, with its lyrical power, sweeps the reader downwards to a Dantesque vision, as Invisible Man, listening to Armstrong play and sing "What Did I Do to Be So Black and Blue," descends the levels of an African-American Inferno. In his phantasmagoria, he hears a preacher, taking as text the "Blackness of Blackness," which touches its nadir in the Jonah-motif of the whale's belly: ". . . *It'll put you, glory, glory, Oh my Lawd, in the* WHALE'S BELLY."

Covertly, Ellison alludes to Father Mapple's great sermon on Jonah in *Moby-Dick,* where each of us is adjured to be "only a patriot to Heaven." And yet Ellison enforces the African-American difference. Blackness puts you in the whale's belly, and blackness alone is insufficient to resurrect you (though nothing American society offers is going to resurrect you either). Self-reliance (even if you are named for Emerson) will not send you out of the whale's belly, and yet it can change the nature of your sojourn. *Invisible Man* is as intricate and rich in texture as *Moby-Dick* and *As I Lay Dying*, and the reader is best advised to take the book slowly and steadily, reading aloud to herself (and others) whenever the prose is richest. The rewards are immense. This is a novel that transcends politics and ideology, while never for a moment evading the Invisible Man's obligation to prophesy the destruction of the new Nineveh, the United States of America, unless it turns now, away from the hatefulness of the final consequences of African-American slavery.

Since his symbolic function is so dominant, the reader may slight the Invisible Man's personality and character, which would be a loss. Ellison, perhaps with an eye upon James Joyce's *Ulysses*, magnificently fuses naturalism and symbolism in his novel, rather as Faulkner (also influenced by Joyce) did in *As I Lay Dying*. Though necessarily nameless, Invisible Man's personality renders any name redundant. We hear his voice incessantly: ironic, eloquent, jazz-influenced, sometimes furious with outrage, yet always open to a vision that others yet might match his own humane sensibility. Perhaps he is the black Ulysses, on the implicit model of Joyce's Poldy, who abhors all violence and hatred. Far more of an outsider even than Poldy, the Invisible Man, to survive, answers violence with violence and hatred with fierce irony. A surrogate for Ellison, Invisible Man's cultural aesthetic is jazz. Ellison, with profound insight into jazz, defined it as a perpetual contest, a "cutting" in which each innovator transcends his forerunners while ironically incorporating them. That is the secret of the Invisible Man's language, and is the basis of the continuous stylistic splendor of Ellison's novel. Its narrative techniques and evolving styles have set a standard for what should be called novelistic jazz that no one else has been able to attain.

The fusion of a jazz aesthetic with an essentially Faulknerian style made *Invisible Man* a book that remains unique, though Toni Morrison has come closest to Ellison's synthesis. There is a subtle polyphony that goes on throughout *Invisible Man:* the narrative line is clear, but something else frequently plays against it, as in the great epiphany of Rinehart—holy man, pimp, drug racketeer—who appears in a cardinal's robe in front of his congregation, under the gold rubric LET THERE BE LIGHT! Backing away from Rinehart's apotheosis, the Invisible Man, who has weathered nearly anything you can imagine, is shocked into the realization that Rinehart and truth are one:

> It was too much for me. I removed my glasses and tucked the white hat carefully beneath my arm and walked away. Can it be, I thought, can it actually be? And I knew that it was. I had heard of it before but I'd never come close. Still, could he be all of them: Rine the runner and Rine the gambler and Rine the briber and Rine the lover and Rinehart the Reverend? Could he himself be both rind and heart? What is real anyway? But how could I doubt it? He was a broad man, a man of parts who got around. Rinehart the rounder. It was true as I was true. His world was possibility and he knew it. He was years ahead of me and I was a fool. I must have been crazy and blind. The world in which we lived was without boundaries. A vast seething, hot world of fluidity, and Rine the rascal was at home. Perhaps *only* Rine the rascal was at home in it. It was unbelievable, but perhaps only the unbelievable could be believed. Perhaps the truth was always a lie.

This is a paradigm for Ellison's achievement of an intricate verbal jazz. Playing just off the beat are the variations on a refrain, "Could he himself be both rind and heart?" and "Rinehart the rounder" and "Rine the rascal," triumphantly repeated. Ras the Exhorter, vividly and sympathetically portrayed by Ellison, is not a temptation for the Invisible Man, but the metamorphic Rinehart heartbreakingly (and hilariously) is. Though Ellison's picaresque hero finally identifies Rinehart's freedom with chaos, rather than imagination, again we may trust the tale and not the teller. Ras the Destroyer is a figure of sinister pathos, but still we are moved because, in the background, we can hear the jazz of Ras the Exhorter. What do we hear in Rinehart's great music?

It would be difficult to disengage Rinehart from the contexts in which jazz originated. One might go further and mention Rinehart's literary comrades: Villon, Marlowe, Rimbaud—major poets who were cut-throats, thieves, spies, runners. The Invisible Man accepts Rinehart as context, but not as forerunner. There he chooses Louis Armstrong, who broke through context. Ellison, not quite willing to assert as much for himself, famously ends the novel by implicating the reader in the imagination of invisibility: "Who knows but that, on the lower frequencies, I speak for you?"

Toni Morrison:
Song of Solomon

Toni Morrison, born in 1931, is best known for her lyrical fantasy novel *Beloved* (1987), but I continue to prefer *Song of Solomon* (1977) as her most permanent achievement, to date. Though she has not yet surpassed it, she is very much at work, and so I will venture no prophecy as to her final eminence. Here I desire only to give a brief account of *Song of Solomon*, both for its own sake and because it shrewdly hints at a subtle critique of the tradition of Melville, Faulkner, and Ellison, which it joins, though warily and under protest, as befits the work of a self-proclaimed African-American Marxist and feminist. And yet, literary tradition chooses an authentic writer, more than the other way around. Something also of Virginia Woolf's asetheticism lingers on in Morrison's style and vision, altogether (I think) to Morrison's benefit.

Milkman Dead, the protagonist of *Song of Solomon*, quests for visibility, in a clear reversal of Ellison's hero, and with the mingled gain and loss of coming a quarter century after *Invisible Man*. Morrison, commendably, is an immensely ambitious novelist, who takes large artistic risks. Milkman, her near-surrogate, is extraordinarily audacious, and becomes so incessant in his quest for his family's truth that pragmatically he must be judged doom-eager.

It cannot be accidental that only two out of six protagonists discussed in this chapter, up to now, have proper or authentic family names, Darl Bundren and Oedipa Maas, and both of those are close to ideograms—the visionary Darl's family name is very much a burden to him, and the female Oedipus seeks truth wherever the Tristero leads her. Call me Ishmael, or Miss Lonelyhearts or the Kid or Invisible Man. Dead is not Milkman's true name; it turns out to be Shalimar, pronounced *Shalleemone* or Solomon. Morrison, with her own visionary irony, uniquely gives us a hero who recovers his true name, at the cost of no less than everything, his life included. As parable, this is powerful; how can you be yourself until you void others' misnaming of you? Born Chloe Anthony Wofford, the novelist changed her name to Toni, modifying Anthony, while still an undergraduate. Milkman's best friend, or "enemy brother," is called Guitar, and the book ends with them engaged in a death struggle. Yet Milkman, unlike Guitar, is spiritually redeemed. He has recovered family history, personal truth, and a heroic myth, that of his ancestor Solomon/Shalimar, who flew back to Africa (without benefit of airplane) to escape bondage.

Morrison has an uncanny gift for fantasy; I find it becomes extravagant in *Beloved*, but aesthetically it is kept within limits in *Song of Solomon*. The reader (and this is Morrison's skill) never quite knows where reality and fantasy come into conflict in Milkman's story, which begins with a black insurance man's suicidal attempt at flight the day before the birth of baby Milkman (nursed at his mother's breast until he was four). Also at four, the child learned that unaided flight was impossible, and "he lost all interest in himself." Weaned into an exasperated dullness, Milkman suffers his impossible parents: Macon Dead, a slum landlord, and Ruth, who is deranged.

It is fair to say of the young man Milkman Dead that he combines his father's rapacity and his mother's solipsism. He emulates Hamlet by goading his Ophelia, Hagar, to madness, coldly rejecting her, and since Hagar cannot bring herself to kill Milkman, she dies instead. After a vain drive to go beyond his father in financial greed, Milkman starts out upon another quest, which is the primary strength of *Song of Solomon*. He goes South to the ancestral Shalimar, where an astonishingly aged crone, Circe, narrates his family's true history to him.

The return to Shalimar brings about a Circean metamorphosis in reverse, as Milkman painfully and slowly achieves his true inner form. Here Morrison brilliantly parodies Faulkner's famous saga "The Bear," where Ike McCaslin is initiated into the hunt. Milkman undergoes the same ritual with a black difference, taking on the living heart of a slain bobcat. Transformed, Morrison's hero recovers his true, Solomonic name, and leaps courageously to his final death-duel with Guitar.

It is remarkable that Morrison is able to sustain her symbolic parable with such a wealth of social realism that the fantastic seems only another version of the everyday. Refusing to continue as an Invisible Man, the refound Solomon learns to make a surrender to the air, and so to ride upon it as his ancestor did. What makes Milkman's apotheosis persuasive is Morrison's sheer brio, and her sure grasp of all her traditions.

Commenting upon *Song of Solomon* with the polemical fervor of her fused ideologies, Morrison insists that her reader must ask the questions of a community, and not of an individual:

> The reader as narrator asks the questions the community asks, and both reader and "voice" stand among the crowd, within it, with privileged intimacy and contact, but without more privi-

leged information than the crowd has. The egalitarianism which places us all (reader, the novel's population, the narrator's voice) on the same footing reflected for me the force of flight and mercy, and the precious, imaginative yet realistic gaze of black people who (at one time, anyway) did not mythologize what or whom it mythologized. The "song" itself contains this unblinking evaluation of the miraculous flight of the legendary Solomon . . .

Morrison is certainly telling us why *Song of Solomon* should be read, but how can the solitary reader be true to herself if she does not ask her own questions, rather than the community's? You can argue (if you wish) that we ought to read to socialize ourselves, but who then will decide whether what or whom is mythologized ought to have been? Morrison seems to argue that a black folk gaze could once mythologize and not mythologize simultaneously. I hear a totalizing ideology in that more-than-rational assertion, and I return to my opening contention in this book: to read in the service of any ideology is not to read at all. Fortunately, the earlier Morrison had not yet incarnated the Spirit of the Age, and *Song of Solomon* remains a spur to the quest of how to read and why.

SUMMARY OBSERVATIONS

The seven American novels discussed in this section I've termed the school of Melville, since *Moby-Dick* is their authentic starting point. As D. H. Lawrence observed, *Moby-Dick* is an American apocalypse, a catastrophic vision of the American nation and its destiny. Faulkner, West, Pynchon, McCarthy, Ellison, and Morrison all are Melville's children, though Pynchon evades his inheritance, and Morrison argues that a hidden strand in *Moby-Dick* concerns not just the whiteness of the whale, but the insane whiteness that excludes African-Americans from Melville's overt vision.

A reader might ask, what are the pleasures, and self-enhancements, to be gained from reading *As I Lay Dying* or *Blood Meridian,* and indeed all of these post-Melvillean apocalypses? When novels become this difficult, and this negative in their visions, do they still persuade us that there is a substance in us that prevails? The question holds for the best of current American fiction, aside from Pynchon and Morrison. Do the disasters of Philip Roth's brilliant *Sabbath's Theater* and poignant *American Pastoral,* or the sublime maelstrom of Don DeLillo's *Underworld,* somehow teach us how to live, what to do? What is the reader's use of apocalyptic fictions?

Negativity cleanses, though at the high price of nihilism. At the close of *Moby-Dick* we are left with "the great shroud of the sea," and the floating Ishmael, "only another orphan." I do not think that there is a higher aesthetic achievement by a twentieth-century American writer than *As I Lay Dying,* a work of shattering originality, but "shattering" is the most precise adjective for the effect of this novel upon me. Darl Bundren is Faulkner's surrogate, and the figure with whom the sensitive reader must identify, but Darl, an intuitive genius, follows the downward path not to wisdom, but to madness, the victim of an outrageously selfish father and a totally unloving mother. The Bundrens' quest to bury their mother as she desired may be heroic, but it becomes a Mississippi apocalypse, a nightmare of fire and flood.

Miss Lonelyhearts is a parody that must be acclaimed as great writing, yet its nihilistic rancidity is unparalleled since Shakespeare's *Measure for Measure* and *Troilus and Cressida.* Very little of America survives *The Crying of Lot 49;* we are given a choice between cultivating paranoia or practicing sado-anarchism. Ellison's Invisible Man, survivor of white hypocrisy and black apocalypticism, implies that he will return to ordinary life, but is still an Underground Man when last we see him. And Milkman Dead, Toni Morrison's most persuasive quester, ends locked in a death duel with his "enemy brother," the terrorist Guitar. What kind of a self can be helped or augmented by living through these awesome negations of what ought still to be Walt Whitman's America?

Deliberately, I have passed over the apocalypse of apocalypses, *Blood Meridian,* whose incessant frenzy of violence accurately depicts our past, frequently represents our gun-crazy present, and doubtless prophesies our bloody future. The United States, for two centuries now, has been obsessed with God and with guns, and neither fascination is likely to wane. We see around us the lineal descendants of the Glanton freebooters: heavily armed Aryan posses, shooters who break into children's centers and schools, exploders of federal buildings. The relevance of Cormac McCarthy is absolute; he is the Homer of our tragic epic of slaughter and religiosity. Judge Holden, as he promised, will never die, and right now the Judge is dancing and fiddling somewhere out there in the Western night.

It is not the function of reading to cheer us up, or to console us prematurely. But I conclude by affirming that all of these American visions of the End of our Time offer us more, much more, than their cleansing negativity. Reread what is most worthy of rereading, and you will remember what strengthens your spirit. When I recall *Moby-Dick,* I think first of the fraternal love between Ishmael and Queequeg, and then I respond again to the courageous defiance of Ahab's American Prometheanism. The final effect of the six Melvillean novels that follow is not nihilistic but ambiguous, and in those ambiguities are embedded superb rewards for the reader's self. Ahab, Addie Bundren, Shrike, the anonymous agents of the Tristero, the malevolent Judge Holden, Ras the Exhorter/Destroyer, Rinehart the Runner and Reverend, and Guitar constitute a nightmare panoply, but they do not eclipse, for the reader, the quests (however baffled) of Ishmael, Darl Bundren, Miss Lonelyhearts, Oedipa Maas, the Kid, Invisible Man, and Milkman Dead. There are survivors among these: Ishmael, Oedipa, Invisible Man. Why read? Because you will be haunted by great visions: of Ishmael, escaped alone to tell us; of

Oedipa Maas, cradling the old derelict in her arms; of Invisible Man, preparing to come up again, like Jonah, out of the whale's belly. All of them, on some of the higher frequencies, speak to and for you.

COMPLETING THE WORK

Rabbi Tarphon said:

The day is short and the work is great, and the laborers are sluggish, and the wages are abundant, and the master of the house is demanding.

Rabbi Tarphon also used to say:

It is not necessary for you to complete the work, but neither are you free to desist from it.

I first read *The Sayings of the Fathers (Pirke Abot)* when I was a boy, and while I was struck by certain aphorisms of Hillel and Akiba, it was the apothegms of the less celebrated Tarphon that gave me the most lasting wounds. *The Sayings of the Fathers* constitute an epilogue added on to "tame" the Mishnah, the great code of oral law edited by Rabbi Judah the Patriarch around the year 200 of the Common Era. About fifty years later, the tractate of the Fathers' Wisdom sayings was attached to the Mishnah, and from then to now it has been the one popular part of the great code of Rabbinic law.

The Sayings of the Fathers deliberately begins with a magnificent but historically dubious drumroll affirming normative Judaism as a continuous tradition, thus legitimating the Oral Law:

Moses received Torah from Sinai and delivered it to Joshua, and Joshua to the Elders, and the Elders to the Prophets, and the Prophets to the men of the Great Synagogue. These said three things: Be deliberate in judging, and raise up many disciples, and build a fence about the Torah.

"Sinai" there is a stand-in for Yahweh himself; we do not know where Mount Sinai was, and evidently the Rabbis did not either. This simply does not matter. As for the Great Synagogue, that is mythology also. It appears to mean the followers of Ezra the Scribe, who may himself have been the Great Redactor who gave us the Hebrew Scriptures as essentially we now have them, that is, as they were brought back from the Babylonian Exile. Still, no one should wish to quarrel with the wisdom of "Be deliberate in judging," though "raise up many disciples" is more problematical, and building a fence about the Torah seems to me quite a bad idea. Yet the sweeping grandeur of the opening of *The Sayings of the Fathers* remains poignant, whether persuasive or not.

Rabbinical Judaism, which has now been normative for more than nineteen hundred years, is no more or less belated a religion than Christianity is. Both resulted from the terrible catastrophe of the year seventy of the Common Era, when the Roman legions sacked Jerusalem and destroyed the Second Temple, the temple of Herod the Great. Where Yahweh went, when he was expelled from the Holy of Holies, no one knows, nor do we know the full range of versions of the religion of Judah that were current before the Temple fell. The sages who escaped (with Roman indulgence) to the town Yavneh founded what we still call Judaism. Yavneh itself went up in flames in 132 of the Common Era, when Rabbi Akiba—heroic, old, and perhaps sublimely mad—committed the dreadful mistake of joining the Bar Kochba rebellion against the Romans. Akiba, whose religion can still be considered the definitive expression of normative Judaism, proclaimed Bar Kochba as the Messiah. This disaster engendered a holocaust of the Jews exceeded in magnitude only by the Nazi terror, and concluded with the martyrdom of Akiba himself.

About 120 years after this catastrophe, *The Sayings of the Fathers* quietly ignores it, and indeed dismisses all history as inconsequential when compared to the chain of tradition in which sage comes after sage, and wisdom endures. The Second Temple was gone, the academy of Yavneh was gone, but the genealogy of normative tradition remained serene. What Donald Harman Akenson rightly calls "a great religious invention" had been achieved. Yet we are now something like 1750 years away from *The Sayings of the Fathers*. Does this grand invention retain more than antiquarian interest, particularly here in the United States, where Jews, Protestants, and Catholics begin to blend together in what I have called "the American Religion," an indigenous national faith that I suspect we do not yet begin to understand?

I go back to my interest in Rabbi Tarphon, which has engrossed me for almost all the years of my life. Historically, we know little about Tarphon, particularly when we compare him to his contemporary Akiba. Akiba was so strong and central a personality that we seem to know him, but Tarphon is subsumed by the Rabbinical texts, and we have to listen carefully to his sayings to get some notion of the inner man, who rarely agreed with Akiba on any disputed matter. Since Akiba's disciples invariably are our only source for these arguments, we can reasonably doubt their stories in which Tarphon is always bested. Unlike Akiba, who came out of the common people, Tarphon was a priest, a kind of archaic survival of the earlier time of the Second Temple. One of his prime concerns therefore was with the functions and privileges of priests, which did not interest Akiba at all. Where the two sages collided was on the fascinating question of subjective assumptions as against supposedly objective facts. In a way that reminds me of Sigmund Freud, Tarphon argued for the Reality Principle. The primacy of fact over intention is Tarphon's dominant idea.

Deeds are all that are important, whether we meant to do them or not. Akiba argued rather that what we think and what we want must be taken into account in judging our deeds. *The Sayings of the Fathers* assigns to Akiba this eloquent formulation:

> Silence is a fence for wisdom. All is foreseen, and free will is given, and the world is judged by goodness, and all is according to the amount of work.

One hears a family resemblance here to Tarphon; neither rabbi would have agreed with Jesus that whosoever looks after a woman with lust in his heart has as good as committed adultery with her. But the shadings of difference between Akiba and Tarphon are subtle and important. In Tarphon, the rabbi never quite replaced the priest, but in Akiba the nostalgia for the Temple has yielded to the Mishnah, to the Oral Law. Akiba therefore urges the primacy of the will, and insists that we are what we will to be. Tarphon discounts the will, remembering always the strict discipline of the Second Temple. We are judged by how much goodness we have performed, Akiba says, and adds inventively "and all is according to the amount of work." But, to Tarphon, the day is short and the work endless, and we tend to be sluggish laborers. The Yahweh of the Temple is demanding, since the wages of his Covenant are high: they are the blessing of more life on into a time without boundaries. If Tarphon were always so fierce, I too would prefer Akiba, but Tarphon also used to say:

> It is not necessary for you to complete the work, but neither are you free to desist from it.

Whether one is normative or heretical, Jewish or Christian, secularist or skeptic, Tarphon's wisdom is eternally useful. I go on writing and teaching, as I have these forty-five years, and I keep returning to Tarphon's formulation. If it were necessary for any among us to complete the work, then we might break off in despair, because the work can never be completed. The Temple cannot be redeemed, and reality-testing always must end in the absolute primacy of fact, which is the death of each individual. Why, if the work cannot be completed, are we not free to desist from it?

To answer that is not a simple matter, particularly since the greatest of all writers, Shakespeare, did desist from his marvelous labor of reinventing both the English language and human personality. It fascinates and saddens me that Shakespeare gave up writing, after his collaboration with John Fletcher on *The Two Noble Kinsmen* in 1613. Shakespeare was just forty-nine, and he lived another three years, mostly in retirement at Stratford-on-Avon. Perhaps illness dimmed Shakespeare's final years, but the Shakespearean parts of *The Two Noble Kinsmen* show a new style and a new consciousness, which should have been developed. In the remainder of this epilogue, I want to contrast Shakespeare's abandonment of the work with Tarphon's insistence that we are not free to abandon it.

Shakespeare had been rereading Chaucer's "The Knight's Tale" from *The Tales of Canterbury,* so as to borrow freely from Chaucer for his plot. The Knight sums up Chaucer's ironic ethos in one grim couplet:

> It is ful fair a man to bere hym evene,
> For al day meeteth men at unset stevene

My old friend the late Chaucerian Talbot Donaldson paraphrased this superbly:

> It is a good thing for a man to bear himself with equanimity, for one is constantly keeping appointments one never made.

Chaucer's stoic Knight is a universe of discourse away from Akiba and Tarphon, but he doesn't so much contradict them—instead he offers a secular alternative. Bear yourself with equanimity, for you will go out from here to live a life in which you will constantly find yourself keeping appointments that you never made. Does it matter whether one is required to complete the work or whether one is free to desist from the work if you must meet a final appointment that certainly you did not make? Is bearing yourself with equanimity sufficient? Is stoic composure or uniformity of response enough? Shakespeare, desisting from the work with the final lines of *The Two Noble Kinsmen,* gentles Chaucer yet seems also to see that equanimity has to be enough, unless we can become like children again, or more happily have remained like them:

> O you heavenly charmers,
> What things you make of us! For what we lack
> We laugh; for what we have are sorry; still
> Are children in some kind. Let us be thankful
> For that which is, and with you leave dispute
> That are above our question. Let's go off,
> And bear us like the time.

These enigmatic lines, the last serious poetry that Shakespeare wrote, are a long way off from Tarphon, or from Jesus for that matter. Those "heavenly charmers" are supposed to be the planets Venus and Mars, and moon as Diana, but Shakespeare is being rather more whimsical, even as he abandons the work. Learn to laugh for what you lack, he tells us, and be sorry for what you have, but keep the laughter and the sorrow light, as a child should. Silence may be another fence around Scripture, and being equable may help you keep appointments you never made, but bearing yourself like the time seems to mean: take what time remains pretty much as it comes.

Normative tradition—Judaic, Christian, Islamic, secular—will tell you, as Tarphon does, that Yahweh's work is not to be abandoned, even though you cannot complete it. Shakespeare, who is the secular scripture, tells you to bear yourself like the Time, which means that a Time comes when you desist from the work. At sixty-nine, I do not know whether Tarphon or Shakespeare is right. And yet, though the moral decision cannot be made merely by reading well, the questions of how to read and why are more than ever essential to help us decide whose work to perform.

Harold Bloom is Sterling Professor of the Humanities at Yale University and Berg Professor of English at New York University Graduate School. He was the Charles Eliot Norton Professor of Poetry at Harvard University in 1987–88, and holds honorary degrees from the Universities of Rome and Bologna. In 1999, he received the Gold Medal for Criticism from the American Academy of Arts and Letters, of which he has been a Member since 1990. His other awards include a MacArthur Foundation Prize Fellowship. Among his twenty-four books are three bestsellers: *The Book of J*, *The Western Canon*, and *Shakespeare: The Invention of the Human*.